THE

FOOD

of

PARADISE

THE FOOD

of

PARADISE

Exploring Hawaii's Culinary Heritage

RACHEL LAUDAN

A Kolowalu Book
University of Hawai'i Press
Honolulu

*For the gardener who chatted to me as she picked mangoes, for the market
stall owner who took the time to explain how to use pigweed, for the man in
the mom-and-pop store who answered my questions about cascaron, for the
volunteers in fairs and carnivals who demonstrated andagi and malasadas
and halo-halo, for the students who chatted about their Thanksgiving
dinners, and their mothers' soba noodles, and their fathers' soup of pig's feet,
and for all the other people of Hawaii whose names I never learned but who
gladly talked about their foods to a stranger.*

© 1996 University of Hawai'i Press
Printed in the United States of America

01 00 99 98 97 96   5 4 3 2 1

Library of Congress Cataloging-in-Publication Data
Laudan, Rachel, 1944–
    The food of Paradise : exploring Hawaii's culinary heritage / Rachel Laudan.
      p.   cm.
    "A Kolowalu book."
    Includes bibliographical references and index.
    ISBN 0–8248–1708–7 (cloth : alk. paper). — ISBN 0–8248–1778–8 (paper : alk. paper)
    1. Cookery, Hawaiian. 2. Cookery, Hawaiian—History. I. Title.
TX724.5.H3L38 1996
641.59969—dc20   95-46407
                                                          CIP

Designed by Brian Ellis Martin with assistance from Susan E. Kelly
Produced by Marquand Books Inc., Seattle
Printed and bound in U.S.A.

Photo credits
Front Cover: Plate courtesy of Laguna Art Pottery, Seattle, photo by Rob Vinnedge; Title Page: HSA;
Page viii: HSA; Page 10: author; Part 1: author; Illustration on p. 18 reprinted by permission from *Pupus
to da Max*, © 1986 Peppovision, Inc.; Illustration on p. 67 reprinted by permission from p. 42 of *Hawaii's
SPAM Cookbook* by Ann Kondo Corum © 1989; Part 2: HSA; Part 3: HSA; Part 4: HSA; Back Cover: author.

University of Hawai'i books are printed on acid-free paper and meet the guidelines for
permanence and durability of the Council on Library Resources

CONTENTS

ACKNOWLEDGMENTS

This book could never have been written without the generous assistance of many people. In Hawaii I think of Isabella Abbott, Wanda Adams, David Addison, Ronalene Alboro, Grant Barnes, Sheila Conant, Joan Clarke, Cynthia de la Cruz, Howard Deese, Elizabeth DeMotte, the Haraguchi family, John Heckathorn, Barbara Hoshida, Judy Higa, Judith Hughes, Debbie Ho, Paul Ishii, Alan Iwase, Frank Karpiel, Bob Kato, Toshiko Kobata, Victor Kobayashi, Dan Kwok, Karla McDermid, Mark Merlin, Grace Mokulehua, Nancy Sakamoto, Tiffany Oshiro, Emma Preza, Nanette Napoleon Purnell, Charlene Sato, Teresita Ramos, and Bob Yara. Far from the Islands E. N. Anderson, Elizabeth Andoh, Diana Barkan, Maureen Bartholemew, Dalia Carmel, Alan Davidson, Cara da Silva, De Doring, Doreen Fernandez, Betty Fussell, Johan Mathieson, Jacqueline Newman, Lynn Nyhart, Roger Owen, Raymond Sokolov, Layinka Swinburne, Edward Tenner, Joyce Toomre, and Sam Yamashita answered questions and provided support. I tried out the general themes of the book at a meeting of the Culinary Historians of New York, at the Oxford Food Symposium, at the Big Island Bounty, Ritz-Carlton Mauna Lani, and in the *Radcliffe Culinary Times*, the newsletter of the culinary collection of the Schlesinger Library, Harvard University. Special thanks to my mother, who sent recipes, references, and arrowroot; to Patricia Crosby, Eloise van Niel, and Donald Mizokawa, who read preliminary drafts; to the staff of the University of Hawai‘i Press; and to three anonymous referees whose comments improved the manuscript immeasurably.

Introduction
ENCOUNTERING HAWAII'S FOOD

First Encounters

Hawaii's culinary heritage? When I first arrived in the Islands in the late 1980s, I laughed at the thought. I still wondered whether anyone could possibly eat the sweet-sour glop, pineapple in every dish, that Jim Dole and Trader Vic had persuaded the world was "Hawaiian" or "Polynesian" food. I was relieved to find that they didn't: so-called "Polynesian food" simply did not exist, at least not outside the tourist spots.

But if food in Hawaii did not fit mainland stereotypes, neither was it like any food I had ever experienced. There was the "loco moco"—two scoops of sticky white rice topped by a hamburger and a fried egg, all of it smothered in brown gravy. There were grapefruit-sized balls of a sweet, brown, glutinous substance, which a colleague explained were "just like mochi" as if that settled the matter. There were office birthday parties with the statutory fluffy, white-frosted, pink sponge cake and the (to me) utterly nonstatutory sight of every-one digging in with chopsticks. Soon after I arrived, a local newspaper had a competition for the best grinds (food) in town: the categories were saimin, poke, sushi, Portuguese sausage, laulau, plate lunch, loco moco, kim chee, lumpia, french fries, ice cream, dim sum, manapua, mochi, shave ice, char siu, burgers, hot dogs, crack seed, mango chutney, muffins, and pizza. All my adult life I had traveled widely and devoured cookbooks, but even so only about half those names meant anything to me. It was clear that Hawaii's food was a genre unto itself.

Gradually I figured out that what I had encountered was Local Food, as it is called in Hawaii. Locals (long-term residents of the Islands) eat Local Food—saimin, shave ice, manapua, and plate lunches of rice and teriyaki and macaroni salad. Mainlanders (in Local eyes) eat boring food—meat and potatoes unen-livened by soy sauce—and shudder at the challenge of raw fish. Local Food is Hawaii's food, to be found everywhere: the plate lunch places and saimin stands and crack seed stores and bento boxes in the drug stores; the mangoes and avocados and cookies and cakes that get toted into the office every day; the lavish public bashes that until recently marked the opening of the Legislature with their pupus of poke and sushi and kal bi and sashimi and fried SPAM wonton and lumpia; the paper bags loaded with guava chiffon cake and taro chips and fishcake and azuki bean pie that are carted from island to island as gifts for friends and relatives; the recipes for haupia and butter mochi and musubi that get shared at work; and the smell of teriyaki wafting from a hundred hibachis at big family picnics at the beach parks. All this adds up to a society with one of the richest culinary heritages in the United States.

I arrived in the Islands convinced that I knew a good bit about things culinary. I had grown up on an English farm, where, over three home-cooked meals a day, we discussed what to plant in the garden, how to prepare various puddings, the virtues of game versus poultry, and where to find the best mushrooms. Like many of my generation, my latent interest became an enthusiasm when as an undergraduate I encountered Elizabeth David's work. Later I had the chance to shop and to cook in France and Germany, in Nigeria and Mexico and Australia, and in many different parts of the United States. Did this help in Hawaii? Not at all. I was humbled to find that I was at a complete loss to understand the food in the Islands. Hawaii might be Paradise, as many claimed, apparently without irony, but where the food was concerned, I found myself in a culinary Babel.

A scholar and a bookworm, I turned to cookbooks for help in translating what I saw into terms I could understand. National cookbooks were worse than useless. Most entirely ignored the food of Hawaii, although the Islands have been a territory of the United States since 1900, and a state since 1959. A few books combined bastardized Hawaiian food with the foods of the South Pacific. One author, presumably in desperation, in a book that offered such well-known specialties as cornbread and river catfish for the deep South and baked beans and Indian pudding for New England, even offered up Sri Lankan curry for Hawaii. Admittedly he was in search of good cooks across the country, but of all the multifarious foods that have contributed to Island cooking, the Sri Lankan influence has to be one of the least significant.

Locally published books, most of them community cookbooks, were a little more helpful, but not much. Almost without exception they took for granted long-term familiarity with Island food. Interspersed with items familiar from the mainland—the salad of instant pudding, canned pineapple, marshmallows, and Cool Whip; the ground-beef stroganoff; the pot roast made with canned soup—were instructions for taro soup, pickled ogo, malasadas, bitsu-bitsu, and Japanese fishcake from scratch just like Grandma's. I could read the individual recipes, but they made no larger sense. Why these particular dishes in Hawaii? Who ate which dishes and at which meals? Were the recipes for everyday or for festivals? What were ogo and bitsu-bitsu anyway? For Locals, these messages were obviously completely clear; for me, they were absolutely indecipherable.

Over the next half dozen years, I chatted to my students and friends and market ladies and people in the grocery checkout line, I poked into mom-and-pop stores, I strolled through the People's Open Markets, I gazed over garden fences on my morning walks, I boned up on the history of the Islands, and I hauled home armfuls of cookbooks from the fine collection in the Hawaii State Library. I came to understand that what people in Hawaii eat is a mixture of four distinct kinds of food, introduced at distinct periods, but now all coexisting. The first three reflect the three diasporas that have terminated in Hawaii: the great marine diaspora of the Pacific Islanders that probably reached the Hawaiian Islands sometime in the third century A.D.; the European voyages of discovery that finally came upon the Islands in the late eighteenth century; and the long migration of the Chinese, Japanese, Portuguese, Koreans, Filipinos, and, lately, Southeast Asians, most of whom came to work on the plantations. From these diverse traditions, a fourth, an East-West-Pacific food, is now being created, known in the Islands as Local Food.

A Historical Digression: Exotic Encounters

The Hawaiian Islands are some of the most recent and some of the most isolated lands on earth. Thrown up by volcanos in at most the last ten million years, they lie 2,500 miles from the nearest significant landfall. Before the arrival of the first humans in the third century A.D., they contained essentially nothing edible on land. Very few species had managed to cross those staggering distances; those that did had speciated, providing a fine natural laboratory for evolutionary biologists centuries later. But apart from a few birds and a few ferns, hungry humans found that there was very little to eat on land; most important, there were no edible carbohydrates. If eating was your aim, the Islands were no paradise. Essentially everything that Hawaii eats has been brought in since then, most of it since the nineteenth century. There are few places in the world where the creation of a cuisine is so transparently visible.

When the Polynesians arrived in the Islands, probably from the Marquesas (and later from Tahiti) they brought with them some thirty plants, of which about a dozen were significant sources of food, as well as pigs, dogs, chickens, and, inadvertently, rats. The most important plants were taro and sweet potato. Hawaii's climate and terrain proved particularly suitable for growing wetland taro, and the Hawaiians constructed massive systems of ditches and patches (paddies) for this purpose, quite the most extensive in the Pacific. In dry areas where taro would not grow, sweet potatoes were substituted. Also important were breadfruit, various yams, sugarcane, and coconut. The dietary staple was cooked, pounded taro, called poi (sometimes sweet potato or other starches were used too). Vegetables and fruits were in short supply, being largely confined to the leaves and stems of the taro plant and the banana and mountain apple. Both pigs and dogs were eaten, but, by and large, they were reserved for the nobility. So too were the fish that were cultivated in large, man-made salt- and freshwater ponds. For the bulk of the population, the protein was fish and shellfish from the streams, the shoreline, the reef, and the deep ocean, eaten both raw (often living) and cooked. Fish was preserved by drying and salting against the periods of stormy weather that, particularly in winter, can make fishing impossible for days or weeks. This adequate, if bland, diet was spiced up by the salt that was collected from shorelines around the Islands, by an extensive array of seaweed, and by the roasted and ground nuts of the kukui (candlenut) tree, and it was regulated by an extensive series of taboos.

Voyages to and from the South Pacific stopped, probably around the sixth century A.D., and the Hawaiians and their Islands were isolated until 1778, when Captain James Cook sighted the island of Kauai. Within a matter of years, the Islands, then known as the Sandwich Islands, had become part of world trade. A succession of European and American drifters fetched up on their shores, followed in the 1820s by forceful Congregational missionaries from New England. The old Hawaiian food taboos broke down. Cows, horses, sheep, and goats as well as a bewildering variety of plants were introduced. The Hawaiians added salt meat and salt salmon from the Northeast to their diet, and the newcomers substituted taro for potatoes and bread, and mangoes for apples. By the end of the nineteenth century, the diet was mixed, at times Western, predominantly New England, at times Hawaiian.

Toward the end of the nineteenth century, the third wave of immigrants began arriving, most of them to work on the plantations. These had been established following the breakup of the traditional Hawaiian landholding pattern in the mid-nineteenth century, the subsequent transfer of land into the hands of Americans and Europeans, the search for economically viable products, and the signing of a reciprocity treaty between the Kingdom of Hawaii and the United States in 1876, which allowed the sale of sugar (and later pineapple) to the United States on favorable terms. Because the Hawaiian population (like other indigenous American and Pacific populations) had declined precipitously following Contact, the planters searched elsewhere for labor. Depending on the changing United States immigration laws and on the attitudes of foreign governments, the planters hired contract workers when and where they could. In order, substantial numbers of Chinese, Japanese, Okinawans, Koreans, Puerto Ricans, Portuguese from the Atlantic islands, and Filipinos, as well as smaller numbers of other groups, arrived in the Islands between the 1880s and the 1930s. By the end of that period, the Japanese had become the single largest group in the population, but there were substantial numbers of all the other immigrant groups as well. Each demanded their own food on the plantations, and the plantation stores went quite some way to accommodate them. In addition, flourishing small farms, market gardens, and fishing operations sprang up, as well as enterprises to make sake, tofu, noodles, and other essentials. By the early years of the twentieth century, rice was Hawaii's third largest crop, and the Japanese had largely taken over fishing from the Hawaiians. All these ethnic groups are still to be found in Hawaii and most have their own array of grocery stores, bakeries, restaurants, and community cookbooks—a veritable culinary cacophony.

Local Food began to appear in the 1920s and 1930s, a couple of decades after Hawaii became a territory. It is an East-West-Pacific food created by housewives and lunch wagon cooks, mom-and-pop store proprietors, and entrepreneurs in dozens of small food businesses. In part it came about spontaneously as the newer immigrants encountered the predominant Hawaiian-Caucasian cuisine and as workers from the far ends of the earth shared lunch in the fields. But there were other forces that tended to the same end. One was the arrival in the 1920s of home economists to teach in the newly formed land-grant university, in the electric and gas companies, and in the Extension Services. Another was service in the military following the bombing of Pearl Harbor in World War II, and, for those who stayed in the Islands, the need to accommodate to wartime shortages of traditional foods.

Now, at least in public, most of the population of Hawaii eats Local Food (as well as ethnic food and American food). The centerpiece of Local Food is the plate lunch, large quantities of rice and meat covered with gravy and eaten with chopsticks, available from lunch wagons and from numerous small restaurants and restaurant chains. Poke is the Local fish dish, raw fish cut in small chunks dressed simply with salt and seaweed or more ambitiously with chili peppers, sesame oil, or soy sauce. Teriyaki is the most popular way of treating all meats, including SPAM, which is an Island favorite, and sailor's hardtack (called saloon pilots) remains popular. Soy sauce is the universal condiment. This menu is rounded out by typical snacks (musubi and manapua), soups (saimin), nibbles (crack seed), and sweet things (shave ice and malasadas).

Today with our generous disposable incomes, full bellies, bulging grocery stores, and leisure to experiment, it has become chic to try new foods. Food magazines faithfully chart the latest trend, be it French, Italian, Chinese, Southeast Asian, or Caribbean. For most people, though, including all those successive migrants to Hawaii, experimenting with food was charged with danger. New foods are threatening: they may be unpalatable or indigestible;

they may leave one hungry, sick, or starving. Even if edible, they do not satisfy as the familiar, comfort foods do. Hawaii's peoples were forced, not enticed, into adjusting to this new land. Local Food, whatever the armchair gourmet or the professional nutritionist may think of it, is a record of courage and ingenuity in a strange place.

The Message of Hawaii's Foods

Today, then, Hawaii's foods are a mélange, imperfectly adjusted to the soil and climate of the Islands, imperfectly adjusted among themselves. In this lies their interest. For all the nostalgia for foods rooted in one place, for all the loving stories of peasants around the Mediterranean eating the products of the lands they till, the reality is that what each one of us eats—and indeed relishes eating —is the result of centuries of change. Even the most seemingly stable of culinary traditions—the Chinese—has adapted to numerous new foodstuffs over the past several centuries. After all, there was a time when the Italians did not eat pasta, when white rice was reserved for the privileged few in Japan.

In this changing world of food, islands in general and sugar islands in particular make interesting cases. To the sugar islands were brought laborers from all the ends of the earth and from radically different culinary traditions. In Mauritius, there were the Indians, the Chinese, and the French; in Fiji, the Indians and the Fijians; in the Caribbean, the indigenous peoples, the Africans, the Europeans, and an assortment of other immigrants. The isolation of these sugar islands, their small size, and the incongruous groups of people forced into contact by the plantations produced a series of fusion (creole) foods in the Indian Ocean, the South Pacific, and the Caribbean. Nowhere has this been more pronounced than in Hawaii, the most isolated of all the islands and the most ethnically mixed, a land originally largely barren of edible plants and animals, peopled by three successive waves of migrants struggling to feed themselves and their families and eventually creating a creole food based on imported foodstuffs.

Because the Pacific Islands are so isolated, anthropologists see them as natural laboratories for studying how societies evolve. Because Hawaii has such a range of ethnic groups, no majority, and a 50% intermarriage rate, sociologists turn to it to see how multicultural societies develop. Because Hawaii's peoples, with their diverse tongues, have created "pidgin" (actually a creole technically known as Hawaiian English Dialect) to make communication possible, linguists use the Islands to study how new languages are created. And because nowhere else in the world are Pacific, Asian, and Caucasian food traditions in such close contact; because in few other places can the arrival of the different cuisines be dated with such precision; and because a new fusion cuisine is being created year by year, Hawaii is just as fascinating to anyone interested in foods and their history.

The analogy of food and language in the case of Hawaii appears particularly apt. Hawaii's food is a language. Just as Hawaiian creole has its unique grammar and vocabulary, so too does Local Food. Its grammar is a juxtaposition of Asian staples and Caucasian proteins; its vocabulary, rice, fish, soy sauce, ship's crackers, and canned meat. Eating Local Food welds Hawaii's different ethnic groups as Locals; at the same time, it sets them off from outsiders. Locals mix the language of creole and the language of food explicitly and continually. *Pupus to da Max*[1] (roughly, the ultimate filling snacks)—a book of cartoons combining Local Food and pidgin—is a Local best-seller; mongrels are poi dogs and large, flat feet are luau feet; and the vastly popular Japanese rice ball, the musubi, and the universally used soy sauce, called shoyu in Hawaii, are celebrated in greeting cards declaiming "It musubi your birthday," or "Shoyu care."

But it is more than a matter of jokes and greeting cards. In a society that has little in common except the language "pidgin," where neither religion, nor literature, nor art, nor music, nor social customs, nor a long shared history provide a common ground, Local Food serves as an important, indeed essential, basis that glues the diverse peoples of Hawaii together. Sharing food is so important because this is one way individuals can make contact with their neighbors, so strange in so many other ways. Recognizing this use of food as a common language drives home the point that food sustains more than the body, that it also sustains cultures. What makes people in Hawaii feel they belong is that they share Local Food.

Hawaii Regional Cuisine

This book is devoted to the foods that are eaten every day in Hawaii. But there is another cuisine in the Islands that attracts attention, Hawaii Regional Cuisine. It was so named in 1992, when a group of chefs—Sam Choy, Roger Dikon, Amy Ferguson Ota, Mark Ellman, Beverly Gannon, Jean-Marie Josselin, George Mavrothalassitis, Peter Merriman, Philippe Padovani, Gary Strehl, Alan Wong, and Roy Yamaguchi—incorporated to sponsor a cookbook to be sold for charity. The group has energy: they have taken a tired international upmarket restaurant cuisine, based on imported products, and replaced it with a cuisine based on foods grown in the Islands, combined in unexpected ways. "Boutique farmers" provide beautiful fresh radiccio, sweet onions, ripe, red strawberries, a range of European and Southeast Asian herbs, and the superb Hawaii Vintage Chocolate; fishermen bring in the best of their catch; and hunters supply wild boar and venison from Hawaii's mountains.

Using these ingredients in exciting menus, backed up by an impressive publicity campaign of glossy cookbooks, food extravaganzas in hotels, feature articles in local and national glossy magazines, and television series, in just a few years this group of chefs has made nonsense of the quip that the food in the hotels was one of the best reasons not to vacation in the Islands. Now visitors praise the cuisine and Locals, too, flock to the restaurants, proud of what the Islands have produced.

This is an interesting story, but it is not my story. Food through the ages has been a counterpoint between the food of the chefs, of the court, with its access to whatever ingredients money could command and time for complicated preparations, and the food of the people, put together with whatever the budget could rise to and whatever time was available. Hawaii Regional Cuisine was created by forces quite different from those that drive Local Food. The chefs were catering to well-heeled customers from around the world prepared to spend money on eating out; the Locals were catering to specific Local tastes. The chefs were influenced by international nouvelle cuisine while trying to create their own identity by incorporating ingredients and traditions from Hawaii; Locals were influenced by what could be put together with materials available in the supermarket at reasonable cost. The chefs developed recipes that assumed kitchen help and efficient grills; Locals wanted recipes that could be whipped up in 20 minutes in a tiny high-rise kitchen surrounded by three hungry children. And the chefs had access to locally grown strawberries and chocolate and venison, while Locals had woolly strawberries from California, Hershey Bars, and SPAM. But although the forces creating Hawaii Regional Cuisine and Local Food were different, their current cross-fertilization can be nothing but mutually beneficial, creating a firm regional base for the cuisine of the restaurants and increasing sophistication for the cuisine of the home and the street.

Interpreting the Hawaiian Encounter

This book, then, is the record of my attempts to decipher Hawaii's culinary Babel, to give a sense of the richness and inventiveness of foods in Hawaii, and to enable others to understand what is going on. It is, first and foremost, about Hawaii's food today and thus each essay begins with an encounter with that food, an encounter that puzzled me. To resolve those puzzles, though, inevitably meant coming to terms with the history of the Islands, and so each essay explains how we came to the present. And because it is recipes that give the punch to stories about food and because Hawaii has so many delicious dishes, most essays end with representative recipes. Structuring the book as a series of encounters means that the recipes are sometimes organized by ingredient,

sometimes by ethnicity, and sometimes by their place in the menu. I have tried
to make life easier for readers by listing recipes by ethnicity and category at the
end of the book.

Because this is a book about the present, I begin with contemporary Local
Food, the first food to be encountered if you live in the Islands; from there, I
cast an eye over the ethnic culinary traditions that continue to thrive; then it
is back to the Caucasian foods of the nineteenth century; and, finally, to what
the first Polynesian immigrants brought with them and what they found in
the Islands. In some parts of the world it seems appropriate to look back nos-
talgically to the past, to an authentic food based on local ingredients, but
such a search for past authenticity is moot in Hawaii. My encounters with
Hawaii's food are just one recent echo of the encounters of a long succession
of immigrants who have labored to create foods in these distant Islands, to
turn a wilderness into a Paradise.

NOTES TO THE READER

Four Essential Words

1. **Hawaiian.** In the mainland United States, it would be possible to say "I'm a Californian" to indicate that you reside in California and "Californian food" to indicate food prepared or developed in the state. That is not the case for Hawaii. "I'm a Hawaiian" indicates that you are an ethnic Hawaiian (or at least have some portion of Hawaiian blood); Hawaiian food means food of the native Hawaiians, albeit altered by 200 years of contact. To talk about food eaten in Hawaii, the proper, if awkward, circumlocution is "food of Hawaii" or "Hawaii's food."

2. **Haole.** A haole (pronounced howley) is a white person. The term can be used quite neutrally: "haole parsley" (as opposed to Chinese parsley or cilantro) or "It's a pretty haolified Japanese restaurant." Like many such ethnic epithets, though, haole has a darker side. But given its honorable history, and given the graceless and unfortunate alternative—"Caucasian"—accepted by officialdom, I prefer to use haole.

3. **Kamaaina.** This literally means a child of the land. But as generally used in the Islands, it refers to the long-established, well-to-do haole families with their own clubs and schools and their own closely knit society.

4. **Local.** This usually refers to a nonhaole, often of mixed background, but born and raised in the Islands. Beyond that its meaning becomes fuzzy; whether or not it can be extended to haoles whose families have been in the Islands for several generations (kamaainas) or to nonhaoles who have recently migrated to Hawaii is a matter of some debate.

It is, of course, true that non-Locals can engage in Local activities such as eating Local Food.

Recipes

I wanted to give recipes that represented as faithfully as possibly the foods eaten daily in Hawaii. This presented two problems: Where to find the recipes? And how to describe them for a readership that extends beyond the Islands? I did not grow up in Hawaii and I did not learn the recipes at my mother's knee. Indeed even had I learned them there, given the diversity of Hawaii, the odds are that my mother would have known only a portion of the dishes. Nor does Hawaii have a long tradition of cookbooks: the earliest come from the end of the nineteenth century, and until after World War II such books as there are are overwhelmingly kamaaina. As late as the 1980s, most households in Hawaii did not possess cookbooks. Hence going back to early "authentic" written recipes was out of the question. For Hawaii's recipes, in a cuisine that is changing year by year, the chief sources are the self-published cookbooks, most produced since World War II, some single author, some community, primarily spiral bound, and often produced for fund-raising purposes. A selection of them is listed and described in the bibliography. For each recipe I have tried to find several sources and produce a composite that most closely corresponds to the food I have eaten on the street and in restaurants.

Turning to the second problem, that of presenting the recipes, the chief difficulty has been that Hawaii has an enormous range of ingredients (and to some extent, cooking techniques) not widely known outside the Islands. I have chosen not to suggest substitutes for these ingredients and not to restrict myself to recipes that can be cooked at any culinary distance whatever from the Islands. Partly that is because to do so would be to omit much of what makes Hawaii's food so interesting, partly it is because the range of foods available in most places is rapidly expanding, and partly it is because people in Hawaii (newcomers, of course, but also some long-established residents) may find recipes using Local ingredients worthwhile. To ameliorate the problem, I give an extensive glossary at the back of the book. I also use the common American words for ingredients when there are such words; hence soy sauce (mainland) not *shoyu* (Hawaii), and taro (mainland and South Pacific) not *kalo* (Hawaiian). Ceding to current tastes, I have not specified monosodium glutamate (Locally known as aji) though it is freely used in the Islands. Although the overwhelming majority of the recipes are in common use in Hawaii, in the spirit of culinary change that this book celebrates, I have felt free to add a few that I think would enhance use of Local ingredients. I have not included menus, in part because the structure of meals is described in the essays, in part because at many gatherings, foods are eclectic.

As one might expect of dishes cooked in the home and for lunch wagons and homely eateries, the recipes collected here are unaffected and simple to prepare. The lack of glitz should not deceive. Carefully cooked, with a care for good ingredients, timing, and presentation, they make flavorful eating.

The reader should be aware, though, that there is one way in which the recipes misrepresent the cooking that goes on in Hawaii: they are weighted to the ethnic and the Local, and familiar American recipes are given short shrift. In fact, many families do eat American standards: chicken cacciatore, Swiss steak, tuna casserole, lasagna. This is particularly true of desserts, for most of the ethnic groups in Hawaii have adopted American desserts.

Orthography

Full Hawaiian orthography has a rich array of diacriticals, as does Japanese. The romanization of Chinese, Japanese, and Korean is subject to debate and change. Tagalog, Ilocano, and Portuguese are often spelled (or misspelled) phonetically in restaurants and on market stalls. Because this is a book about the food that is eaten at the moment in Hawaii, I have chosen simply to adopt the spellings most widely used in grocery stores, restaurants, and cookbooks. However, diacriticals do appear in Hawaiian entries in the Glossary.

Part One

LOCAL FOOD

LOCAL FOOD AS CREOLE FOOD

"If I didn't speak pidgin at home," remarked one of my students in passing when she asked me to recommend her for a National Science Foundation graduate fellowship in biochemistry, "everyone would think I was trying to be a high muckamuck." Pidgin, as it is called in Hawaii, has been the first language of the Islands for the last couple of generations.[1] Initially pidgin was a makeshift language used by plantation workers to cope with the dominant and unfamiliar English. Although it varied a little from ethnic group to ethnic group, in general it had English as its base with touches of Hawaiian, Japanese, Chinese, and Portuguese. Hawaiian pidgin, like other pidgins around the world, offers a glimpse of how languages grow and develop. Linguists insist that pidgins are not debased languages but creative adaptations to new and difficult circumstances. Admittedly these languages were created to cope with a limited range of situations—usually the workplace—but they have their own structure and their own logic.

For the first generation of immigrants, pidgin was a second language. But the children of those immigrants grew up speaking it as their first language. Because they also understood and perhaps spoke their parents' language and English as well, they acquired considerable facility with languages and their contexts. In one of the first novels written in pidgin, *All I Asking For Is My Body*, first published in 1959, Milton Murayama explained that when he was growing up, "We spoke four languages: good English in school, pidgin English among ourselves, good or pidgin Japanese to our parents and the other old folks."[2] "Pidgin" in common parlance, linguists call this second-generation first language a creole, Hawaiian English Dialect. Because it is used in the family and among friends, not just at work, and thus has to express more emotions and ideas, it is more complex in structure and in vocabulary than pidgin proper.

What has this long digression to do with food? A good bit, because the parallels between language and food in Hawaii are well nigh irresistible.[3] Just as my student spoke pidgin to show that she wasn't a "high muckamuck," so she would eat Local Food to show she was Local. And just as Locals can always revert to pidgin to establish their Local credentials with friends or to exclude a newcomer, former Locals back from the mainland join their friends for ritual plate lunches—"almost as a joke" they maintain, though a joke with a purpose.

When the immigrants first arrived on the plantations, the food of their employers was as strange as the language. The newcomers had to create a makeshift cuisine from what was provided and what they brought with them, adapting familiar cooking methods and eating habits to the work schedule of the plantations. Try as they might to preserve their traditional cuisines, these were inevitably transformed. By the time the second generation was growing up, there were signs that a new cuisine was beginning to emerge. By the third and fourth generations, this process of culinary change was accelerating rapidly, and sometime in the 1970s or 1980s, the new fusion food acquired its own name: Local Food. "Also serving Japanese, Local & Continental Cuisine," trumpets the Golden Chinese Coffee Shop. "Wanted: Lowfat local style recipes," pleads the Cookbook Committee of Project LEAN Hawaii from Queen's Medical Center.[4]

Like Hawaiian creole, Local Food first emerged in public, not in private, where ethnic foods continued to hold their own. It was to be found in the lunch wagons on the plantations, in the saimin stands, and in the crack seed stores.

Hawaii's restaurants help create Local Food

How a Mainland City Looks to
a Hungry Local

Like Hawaiian creole, Local Food has its own structure, best exemplified in the plate lunch, which is held together by Asian rice, given shape and meaning by the haole quantities of meat cooked Asian style, presented heaped on haole plates, eaten with Asian chopsticks, with salt, pepper, and soy sauce available for seasoning. Like Hawaiian creole, Local Food has its own vocabulary dominated by such items as rice, fish, soy sauce, SPAM, Portuguese sausage, and crackers. Like Hawaiian creole, Local Food has survived and flourished in the face of official opposition. Just as the School Board has struggled to extirpate pidgin from the schools, so nutritionists have derided Local Food. Favorites such as Portuguese sausage, Chinese sausage, SPAM, sweet and sour pork, kalua pig (pit-cooked pork), laulau (meat and taro leaf bundles), pig's-feet soup, oxtail soup, manapua (savory stuffed buns), haupia (coconut pudding), kal bi (Korean grilled beef), char siu (Chinese roast pork), fried wonton, and Chinese roast duck have all been condemned as irremediably fatty.[5] Like Hawaiian creole, Local food offers a glimpse of how new habits evolve.

And like the language, Local Food survives. Every fall when students set off for mainland colleges, the local newspapers carry stories on how to avert homesickness. The standard remedy? Pack an electric rice cooker, Hawaii-style rice, a plug-in coffee pot for saimin, crack seed, dried cuttlefish, soy sauce, saloon pilots, and guava jelly to spread on them.[6] Local Food survives in part because it tastes good. But it also survives because it, like pidgin, is one of the few experiences that the peoples of Hawaii share.

THE PLATE LUNCH, OR WHAT COUNTS AS A MEAL IN HAWAII

I'm local: L-O-C-A-L!
As brown as one dollar-size opihi shell
I'm as local as the ume in your musubi
As one spaghetti plate lunch with side order kim chee

I'm as local as the gravy on the three scoop rice
As all the rainbow colors on da kine shave ice
I'm as local as one B-1 cockaroach
Flying for your face in one ewa approach[1]

To be Local, as Local comedian Frank De Lima's lyrics make clear, is to eat plate lunches. One popular spot is Masu's Massive Plate Lunch, less than a mile from downtown Honolulu. It is located on a busy junction in Liliha, an older neighborhood whose faded frame houses once housed the servants for the big kamaaina homes farther up the valley. Every month more of these homes are being razed and replaced by concrete and cinderblock, but the main thorough-fares remain chockablock with mom-and-pop stores and plate lunch places.

Masu's doors are open from early morning to early afternoon and let in a steady stream of customers—muscled Hawaiian construction workers; a haole woman with her Local husband and hapa (mixed) 5-year-old child, all in shorts, T-shirts, and rubber sandals (called slippers in Hawaii); an elderly Japanese lady bent with years of work; a couple whose faces reflect the mixed ancestry typical of the Islands in the business dress of Hawaii, silk blouse, hose, and heels for the woman, discreet pink aloha shirt in reversed pattern for the man. The interior is overwhelmingly brown, a faded brown carpet on the floor, brown-veneer tables, yellow ocher plastic chairs, mock paneling on the walls. Even the branches of artificial plum blossoms suspended about the counter are brown with years of dust.

Korean plate lunch offerings

THE INOUYES INVENT
LOCO MOCO

Loco moco, so the story goes, was invented in 1949 by the owners of the Lincoln Grill, a small cafe in the port and plantation town of Hilo on the Big Island.[4] Local teenagers clamored for something different from American sandwiches and less time-consuming than Asian food. Mr. and Mrs. Richard Inouye had rice and hamburger patties on their menu and Mr. Inouye had learned to make sauces and gravies when he worked at the Royal Hawaiian Hotel in Waikiki. So they piled two scoops of rice into a bowl, topped it with a hamburger patty and a fried egg, and then they poured a generous helping of gravy over the whole lot.

The teenagers chose the name. The nickname of the first boy to eat loco moco was Loco (crazy in Portuguese and Hawaiian pidgin). Moco rhymed with loco and sounded good. Loco moco is now served statewide in small Local restaurants.

Lunch wagon selling plate lunches near the University of Hawaii

Dusty or not, people flock in for the values. The menus for the daily plate specials are printed up a month in advance so that customers can call in to reserve their favorite lunches. The manager matches them to the calendar. For Japanese Girl's Day, the plate is piled with cold somen salad, a half roll of maki sushi, charcoal-broiled sirloin steak, teriyaki sauce, fried chicken, fried shrimp tempura, Vienna sausage (the whole can), and tuna potato salad. For Saint Patrick's Day, the Irish Hawaiian plate includes laulau, kalua pig, charcoal-broiled sirloin steak, teriyaki sauce, green kamaboko pasta salad, Emerald Isle fried shrimps, namasu, and shoyu hot dogs, all for not much more than the price of a movie ticket.

Hawaiian music plays in the background competing with the noise of the traffic outside, signed photos of local entertainers and politicians smile down fixedly from the wall, the Masu Basketball Team trophies shine amidst the brown, and the elderly Japanese ladies behind the counter keep dishing out the lunches in their styrofoam divided platters. This is not gourmet dining but it's not going to leave anyone hungry either. Sitting there, it is easy to believe a survey by home economics students at the University of Hawaii showing that the average plate lunch runs to about 1,400 calories.

There is some speculation in Hawaii that the plate lunch evolved from a cross of the lunch wagon and the bento, the traditional Japanese packed lunch that the plantation workers took out into the fields.[2] Certainly lunch wagons were selling meals to the plantation workers from the 1930s on. The major home economics text in the Islands made an example of a fictitious John Ching of Hilo, on the Big Island, who bought his lunch from a wagon for just 20 cents. It was dreadfully unbalanced, consisting of macaroni salad, rice, potatoes, and some vegetables, followed by pie and a soda.[3] The author urged that her model student, Mabel, enhance this, perhaps by sending John off with milk and fruit. But, aware that this was a counsel of perfection, she added the more feasible caution that he should buy only wrapped foods, free from the dust that swirled about the unscreened wagon.

In World War II, lunch wagon business boomed as dockyard and military workers looked for relief from institutional food. After the War, many of the classic plate lunch places that dot the Hawaii scene today got started. By the late 1970s, they were so well entrenched that they survived the arrival of mainland fast-food chains in style. The entrepreneur who brought McDonald's to Hawaii took advantage of its remoteness to adjust the menu to Local taste. In 1976, in defiance of corporate policy, he added saimin, fruit punch, and Portuguese sausage to the regular round of burgers, fries, and shakes.[5] Many of the plate lunch operators such as Diner's, Grace's, and Like Like Drive Inn have established small chains. The most

PART 1: LOCAL FOOD

upmarket of these chains is Zippy's, all shining greenhouse glass, tile floors, classical columns, and paintings of flower arrangements that owe something to the Dutch school. Day and night, you can pick up a takeout meal or place an order for Chinese oxtail soup or Okinawan pig's feet soup while you discreetly people watch: at one table are members of one of the traditional Hawaiian orders in long white dresses and orange head leis, at others are students in tuxedos and long pink satin dresses giggling after their prom, Filipino women in silky polyester overshirts and knit polyester pants just finished with cleaning downtown offices, and a suburban haole family having hamburgers, fries, and shakes after the movies.

Then there are the battered old lunch wagons drawn up wherever there are surfers, or construction workers, or students, or even hungry businessmen.[6] Their owners get up at the crack of dawn to prepare the meals, drive out to a rented piece of wasteland or parking lot, fire up their propane burners, and sell between a hundred and three hundred lunches before heading for home.

As befits their eclectic offerings, plate lunch places go by a variety of names that leave the mainlander slightly dizzy: delis that offer not a trace of pastrami or lox or rye bread or bagels; barbecue places with neither smoked beef nor smoked pork nor ketchup or mustard-based sauce; diners with not the faintest resemblance to the original railroad cars of New Jersey; drive-ins where no parking is available. Kevin's Drive-In, for example, can be found on River Street on the edge of Chinatown fronting on a pedestrian walkway where the permanent tables are filled with elderly Chinese men clicking their mah-jongg counters.

Why the plate lunch survived and what makes it so central to the evolution of Hawaii's Local Food is that it is a *meal*. All sorts of other food are identified

Chinese plate lunch menu

as Local, including the opihi (a limpet eaten raw), the musubi (a savory rice "sandwich"), and the shave ice mentioned by De Lima in the lyric that introduces this essay. But neither opihi nor musubi nor shave ice nor many other favorites are *meals* that leave the eater full and satisfied.

Plate lunches *are* meals because they satisfy a couple of criteria. First, they include rice as the starch, and to the hungry Local, it is rice, not noodles or bread, that makes something a meal. A hefty two or three "scoop" rice (referring to the ice cream scoop used to dole the rice out of the rice cooker; because this is pidgin, the "s" is left off) goes on the divided plastic plate before anything else. Second, the plate lunch includes heaping portions of meat, chicken, or fish, the selection varying somewhat according to the ethnicity of the owners and the clientele. Perhaps most common is a mixture of Japanese (teri beef or chicken katsu, for example) and haole (fried mahimahi, spaghetti and meat sauce all mixed up together, wieners, SPAM). Some plates have a Hawaiian accent offering kalua pig (pit-cooked pork), curry stew, and beef stew. Masu's, for example, has a Japanese-Hawaiian-haole menu. Others offer Chinese flavor with pot roast pork (kau yuk) and shoyu (soy sauce) chicken. Rapidly growing in popularity are Korean plates, with Korean barbecue (Korean grilled beef), meat jun (thin-sliced beef in egg batter), and mandoo (meat dumplings).[7] There may be just one of these meats on the plate, but usually there are two or three. A mixed plate is truly mixed, with meat and fish and chicken all served at once and prepared according to radically different culinary traditions.

Occupying the third hollow on the plate is a scoop of macaroni salad (sometimes replaced by potato salad) and somewhere off to the side, or lurking underneath the rice or meat, will be a gesture toward a vegetable or pickle, a lettuce leaf, shredded cabbage, takuwan (pickled daikon), or the popular kim chee. An optional thick coating of gravy, presumably from a package or can, may be ladled on top of the pile. On the side are salt, pepper, and soy sauce.

In short, the plate lunch is a truly pidgin (creole) food. The vocabulary of the meal (with the exception of the potato and macaroni salads) is overwhelmingly Asian, but the syntax, the way it is put together, with its large portions of meat, its downplaying of vegetables, and the brown gravy, is haole. The way it is served (heaped on a plate instead of in small bowls) is haole. The way it is eaten (a choice of chopsticks or plastic cutlery) is mixed again.

The plate lunch is public food, designed to satisfy clients from diverse ethnic backgrounds. In doing so it exposes consumers, often for the first time, to the foods of other ethnic groups. The haole, or Japanese, or Chinese, or Hawaiian, or Korean dishes that individuals first come across in Hawaii are likely to be the plate lunch dishes, just as the first American dishes that people in other parts of the world encounter are likely to be hamburgers. Thus the spaghetti, chili, hamburger, teriyaki, katsu, shoyu chicken, laulau, and Korean barbecue become the foundation of Local food in the home as well as in public. More important yet, the constitution of the meal and the way it is eaten becomes a model for the meals eaten in many homes in Hawaii: lots of rice, more meat than in Asian countries, and all served on one big plate. One Miss Hawaii described her Thanksgiving dinner for me: turkey, dressing, rice, sashimi, sushi, macaroni salad, jello salad, namasu (cucumber salad), mashed potatoes, and kim chee.

All the following recipes are for plate lunch standbys. Other favorites, for which recipes are given elsewhere in this book, are rice, SPAM, laulau, kalua pig, Hawaiian curry, kau yuk, and char siu.

TERIYAKI SAUCE

"Teri" anything—chicken, burger, steak, fish—is a plate lunch favorite, distinctly different from the Japanese origins that the name evokes. In Japan, teriyaki is made by combining soy sauce and mirin, the Japanese sweet cooking wine, and it is used to marinate fish and as a basting sauce for broiling; the term came from "glazed" (*teri*) and "seared with heat" (*yaki*).[8] In Hawaii, the tale passed down from mother to daughter is that the Local Japanese substituted brown sugar for the mirin and added ginger and green onions.[9] The addition of substantial amounts of sugar to soy sauce would have been natural where mirin was virtually unobtainable but where sugar was king. Ginger and garlic may have been Chinese additions. By the 1960s, and possibly much earlier, Hawaii-style teriyaki sauce had become one of the culinary symbols of the Islands.[10]

2 cups soy sauce
¾ cup sugar, preferably turbinado or Demerara variety
2 green onions, chopped
1 tablespoon fresh ginger, grated
1 clove garlic, minced
1 teaspoon monosodium glutamate (optional)

Mix all ingredients together in a saucepan and stir over low heat until sugar is dissolved. Pour into sterilized bottle. Use this sauce to marinate fish and meat before broiling. It keeps for a week or more in the refrigerator.

Yield: Just over 2 cups

Note: To grate fresh ginger, use the fine side of a grater or, better, one of the handy Japanese ginger graters that can be found in Asian stores. I have also extracted ginger juice successfully in a juicer, but the ginger must be fresh and tender.

. . .

BEEF TERIYAKI

2 pounds beef, thinly sliced
⅔ cup teriyaki sauce
1 teaspoon sesame seeds, toasted in a dry pan until golden (optional)

Marinate beef in teriyaki sauce for at least 1 hour. Broil quickly and sprinkle with sesame seeds, if desired, before serving. Serve with rice.

Yield: Four generous servings, more if other meats are offered

Note: In Hawaii, beef is sold thinly sliced for teriyaki. Should it not be available, choose a lean cut such as top round, partially freeze it to make cutting easier, and then cut into slices about ⅛ inch thick.

KOREAN BARBECUE SAUCE

Korean barbecue is first cousin to teriyaki. The mix of soy sauce, sesame oil, and sugar is appealing.

½ cup soy sauce
¼ cup sugar (or less, to taste)
1 clove garlic, finely chopped
4 green onions, finely chopped
1 inch ginger, peeled and grated
2 tablespoons sesame oil
1 tablespoon toasted sesame seeds

Mix all ingredients and store in a jar in the refrigerator.

Yield: ¾ cup

. . .

KOREAN BARBECUE

(Bulgogi)

2 pounds beef, thinly sliced (as for teriyaki)
¾ cup Korean barbecue sauce

Marinate steaks in barbecue sauce for half an hour. Grill over charcoal or under broiler for just enough time to sear. Serve with rice and kim chee.

Yield: Four generous servings, more if part of a mixed plate

. . .

KAL BI

(Korean Barbecued Short Ribs)

2 pounds beef short ribs, cut into 2-inch pieces
¾ cup Korean barbecue sauce

Place the ribs on a cutting board with the meaty side up. With a sharp knife, score a diamond-shaped pattern, cutting to the bone. Marinate the ribs in the barbecue sauce for several hours or overnight. Broil 6 or 7 minutes on each side over charcoal (or under the broiler). Serve with rice and kim chee.

Yield: Four servings

KIM CHEE

(Korean Pickle)

This hot, spicy family of pickles, usually made with cabbage but sometimes also with daikon, cucumber, ogo, and other vegetables, is addictive. One of Hawaii's most popular relishes, kim chee can be bought in all grocery stores in Hawaii, though many people make it at home. Korean grocery stores carry handsome, but huge, earthenware jars for a season's supply of kim chee. The quantity of this version will serve for an occasional side dish.

> **1 large Chinese cabbage (about 2 pounds)**
> **½ cup sea salt**
> **2 tablespoons red pepper powder (or coarsely ground red peppers)**
> **4–5 cloves garlic, minced**
> **1 inch ginger, peeled and grated**

Trim any tough or brown leaves off the cabbage, cut lengthwise into quarters, and then crosswise into 1½ inch pieces. Place in a large bowl and sprinkle with the salt. Leave for 3–4 hours to wilt without loosing all snap in the stems. Meanwhile, mix the other ingredients to a paste to allow the flavor and color to develop. Rinse the cabbage and drain. Rub in the spice paste and pack into a quart jar. Cover tightly. Then wrap the jar in a plastic bag and seal with a rubber band to prevent the odors from permeating everything around the jar. Kept in the refrigerator, it will be ready in 4–5 days. Serve in small dishes as a relish with meals.

Yield: 1 quart

• ■ •

PORK KATSU

(Breaded Pork Cutlet)

These crisp slices of breaded pork are said to derive their name from the Japanese pronunciation of "cutlet;" they are also called tonkatsu. In Hawaii, boneless chicken is often substituted for pork, and the dish is called chicken katsu.

1 pound lean pork from the loin or trimmed from chops
Salt
Flour
1 egg, beaten in a shallow bowl
Dried bread crumbs
Oil for frying

Cut the pork into eight slices. Flatten lightly with a mallet and salt. Place a handful of flour on one plate or piece of greaseproof paper and a somewhat larger quantity of bread crumbs on another plate. Place each slice in the flour until coated, dip in the beaten egg, and then in the bread crumbs. Heat ½ cup cooking oil in a pan until bread crumbs sizzle when dropped in the oil. Fry the cutlets in batches, allowing plenty of room, until golden brown on both sides. Properly done, they are not at all greasy. Drain on paper towels. Serve with rice and dip in katsu sauce.

Yield: Four servings

· · ·

KATSU SAUCE

½ cup ketchup
3 tablespoons Worcestershire sauce
1 tablespoon soy sauce

Mix all ingredients together, adjust amounts and seasoning to taste, and serve as a dipping sauce.

· · ·

FRIED MAHIMAHI

Although grilled mahimahi (dolphin fish steaks) are gaining in popularity, these fried steaks are a plate lunch standard. Using fresh, not frozen, mahimahi makes all the difference.

1 pound mahimahi, cut into four steaks
Milk
Flour
Dried bread crumbs
Oil for frying, with a little butter for flavor

Dip the fish in the milk, then in the flour, then in the milk again, and finally in the bread crumbs. Heat enough oil to cover the bottom of a frying pan and add a little butter. When the foam subsides, quickly saute the steaks until they are brown on each side. In Hawaii, this is served with rice, but fries or bread and butter also make nice accompaniments.

Yield: Four servings

· · ·

SHOYU CHICKEN

(Chicken Simmered in Soy Sauce)

It was almost certainly the Chinese who introduced this simple but tasty dish to Hawaii, for chicken simmered in soy sauce is a dish typical of Canton, whence most of the Hawaii Chinese came. In English-language cookbooks, it might be called red-cooked chicken (that is, chicken simmered in soy sauce).[11] But as so often in Hawaii, more sugar has crept into the recipe and the dish has been adopted outside the Chinese community, as the common name "shoyu chicken" or "chicken shoyu" suggests (shoyu is simultaneously the Japanese and the Local term for soy sauce). Sometimes the Japanese influence is yet more marked when teriyaki sauce, which is basically sweetened soy sauce, is specified instead of soy sauce and sugar.

> **2½ pounds chicken thighs**
> **1 cup soy sauce**
> **½ cup brown sugar, preferably turbinado sugar**
> **2 cloves garlic, crushed**
> **1 teaspoon five-spice powder**
> **2 tablespoons fresh ginger, finely chopped**
> **4 tablespoons dry sherry**
> **3–4 green onions, chopped, plus a couple more cut in rings for garnish**
> **1 tablespoon cornstarch**
> **Salt and wine vinegar to taste**

Combine chicken, soy sauce, brown sugar, garlic, five-spice powder, ginger, sherry, and green onions in a large pot. Add water just to cover. Simmer until the chicken is tender, about 20–30 minutes. Remove chicken from pot and arrange neatly on a serving dish, skin side up. Keep warm while you prepare the sauce. Reduce the cooking liquid to about 2 cups. In a small bowl, add 2 tablespoons water to the cornstarch and stir to make a smooth paste. Add to the cooking liquid. Bring to a boil and simmer until thickened. Adjust seasoning to taste. Pour the sauce over the chicken. Garnish with rings of green onion and serve the aromatic brown-glazed chicken with rice and a simple stir-fried vegetable or a salad.

Yield: Four servings

OUR DAILY RICE: HAWAII'S STAPLE

Barbara Hoshida, who worked at the University of Hawaii, had a keen sense for food. On her office door she had pinned a cartoon: an Asian mother towered over her child, who was sulking in front of chopsticks and a rice bowl. "Eat your rice," commanded the mother. "Think of all those millions of Americans eating nothing but junk food." Barbara had slyly doubled the joke. In Hawaii, Americans do eat their rice.

Indeed, in the state of Hawaii, every man, woman, and child eats an average of 60 pounds of rice a year (by comparison, mainland Americans use about 9 pounds of rice per person per year as grains, plus more in the form of beer).[1] Once I had occasion to take some university students to lunch. I could see them casting around in an effort to make conversation with this mainland haole. Finally one of them lit on something she really wanted to know: "How often each week do you eat rice?" she asked. In a similar vein, a high school teacher told me that what had most interested his students on a tour of Washington, D.C., was not the Capitol, nor the White House, nor the Smithsonian, but that there was no rice at McDonald's. Without rice, food in Hawaii, however substantial, is not a meal. It is the very foundation of Local Food.

The kind of rice cookery that I took years to master is of little use in Hawaii as I discovered to my cost. Invited to a pot-luck party, I thought to show good will by bringing the rice and to introduce some novelty by preparing a spiced Indian pilau made with basmati rice. The group politely forced down a few mouthfuls—refusing food is considered particularly rude in Hawaii—but it was quite clear that, as far as Locals were concerned, what I had prepared simply didn't count as rice. What does count is Japonica rice. Piled up at the front of the grocery stores, along with the charcoal and the dog food, are 10- and 20-pound bags of this rice shipped from California, while haole rice— Uncle Ben's, Minute Rice, and all those Rice-a-Roni mixes—sits neglected on the regular shelves. Later, those big sacks serve as handy trash bags.

The Chinese, the first immigrants to work on the plantations, demanded rice instead of poi, the Hawaiian staple.[2] At first, their rice had to be imported, but as the Hawaiian population declined, so did the demand for the taro from which poi was made. Taro patches became vacant. Like rice paddies, taro patches are carefully terraced and irrigated, and thus ideal for rice. In the Caribbean, the Chinese immigrants quailed at the thought of constructing rice paddies from scratch and, at least initially, settled for yams and sweet potatoes, but in Hawaii they seized on the old taro patches.[3] Rice was thus one of the first major crops to be grown by the third wave of immigrants to Hawaii, the plantation workers.[4] By the early 1860s, rice was well established. Where the skyscraper hotels of Waikiki now stand, water buffalos once plowed through the rice paddies.

When Hawaii finally succeeded in signing a reciprocity treaty that allowed tariff-free trade with the United States, rice boomed. In 1888, over 13 million pounds of rice were exported to California. A year later, rice from Hawaii, along with the newly built Eiffel Tower, was featured in the Paris Exposition. By 1907, Hawaii had some 10,000 acres in rice and was experimenting with 130 different varieties. Only sugar surpassed rice as a crop.

Rice growing was grinding labor. Farmers planted the rice in May and waited for about a month until the seedlings were 7 inches tall. Then they pulled, washed, and bundled the little plants for hand transplanting into the paddies. A month and a half later the rice was ready to harvest. Families banded together, the wife laboring in the kitchen to produce three or four meals a day for the horde of harvesters. Because the families were working for themselves, not for the big plantations, they thought the labor worthwhile and, indeed, for many it paid off. Some saved enough to return to China and clear the debts

EATING ON A RICE FARM

In the 1920s, Lum Chew Chang Ho used to visit her family's rice farm behind the famous landmark, Diamond Head, in what is now the heavily built-up suburb of Kaimuki.[5] She described the workers' building, with its nets to protect against the mosquitoes, scorpions, centipedes, cockroaches, and lizards; the yard where the pig and her piglets, the rooster, and the cat roamed in the shade of the kiawe and kamani trees; the scarecrows in the fields decked out in Chinese clothes and coolie hats; and the cement square where the horse-drawn threshers separated the grains from the stalks, and the crew, led by aunty in her Chinese pants and top and wooden clogs, worked to bag them for the miller.

But most of all, Lum Chew Chang Ho rejoiced in the food. To catch the biggest, fattest frogs for fried frog legs, her tomboy cousin dived into the artesian well. To ensure a supply of deep-fried, crisp sparrows, they fired volleys of BB shots. To collect the glossy snails for the Moon Festival, she paddled through the clear water of the irrigation ditches with a tin bucket, watching the moonfish, catfish, tadpoles, and mosquitofish swimming around her feet. These snails were kept in the bucket with a cleaver, which was believed to make them discharge their slime and dirt, for 2 or 3 days. They were washed, drained, and the tips of their shells cut off to make them easier to eat. Then they were stir-fried in a wok with oil, garlic, ginger, shrimp sauce or salted black beans, and a minced purple-green herb. Then she could pluck out the meat with a toothpick and suck the succulent juices from the shell.

Planting rice in Hawaii (early twentieth century) (HSA)

that had driven them to Hawaii in the first place. Others started businesses in the Islands: City Mill, where Honolulu residents now go for most of their home improvement supplies, was founded by Chung Kun Ai and Chun Mun Kai as a lumber and rice mill.

The Chinese sold their leases for rice farms to the next wave of immigrants, the Japanese, just then completing their plantation contracts. They had a more difficult time. Their traditional methods, employed on small farms leased from the big estates of Hawaii, could not compete with the large-scale mechanized rice farms that had been set up in Texas, Louisiana, and California. The most likely buyers, the Hawaii Japanese, preferred rice from Japan to local rice even when this was grown with Japanese seed. They refused to shift their loyalties until Japanese rice became available from California, perhaps because it cost less. By the 1930s, less than half a century from the time when Hawaii had supplied California with its rice, Hawaii was absorbing two-thirds of California's rice output.

The local folk struggled to keep the rice industry and the rice mills going. In the 1940s, they replaced horses with rubber-tired tractors for threshing. In the 1950s, they tried combine harvesters, which cost an enormous $7,000 in the money of the day. Although these machines enabled three people to harvest as much rice in half a day as ten people had been able to harvest by hand in 3 days, they were ill-suited to the small paddies in Hawaii. The farmers tried popular specialty rices, such as mochi. It was to no avail. By the 1960s, rice farming was dead in Hawaii. In an ironic turn, it was proving more profitable to grow taro than rice. Not that taro was an easy crop, but it was less sensitive to climate and demand was on the rise. Some, at least, of the rice paddies were turned back into taro patches.

Rice farming might have been dead, but rice was firmly established as Hawaii's staple. When the Gulf War broke out, an acquaintance of mine rushed to buy ten 20-pound sacks of rice. She was not alone. Stores all over the state reported a run on rice, many rationed their customers to one 20-pound bag, and the governor issued a warning against hoarding.[6] A couple of years later, when the poor rice harvest in Japan created a demand for Californian rice, a local newspaper ran a headline alerting its readers to rising rice prices.[7] Letters to the editor bewailed the fact that 20 pounds of rice would now cost as much as $6, prompting tart replies that 60 pounds of rice would still cost less than a tank of gas. White rice, once a luxury for Chinese and Japanese peasants, was now the cheapest food in the market. Meanwhile, Safeway, which like other grocery stores runs rice as a loss leader, offered 20-pound bags for just over $3. Within a day, they were completely out of rice.

TO COOK RICE, LOCAL STYLE

Japanese rice of the Calrose variety is the kind most often served in the Islands. When cooked, the rice should end up moist but not mushy, the grains distinct but clinging, all the better to be lifted on chopsticks. Because it is traditionally eaten with flavorful accompaniments, usually sour, sweet, salty, or some combination of the three, it is cooked without salt. It has a delicious, if subtle, flavor of its own.

How much rice to cook depends on who you are feeding; people in Hawaii eat more than people on the mainland. If you begin with 3 cups of uncooked rice, you will end up with 9 cups of cooked rice. Rinse the rice in several changes of water or place it in a sieve and wash it thoroughly, swirling the grains around. A quick swish will not do; the water must run clear. In Hawaii, you would now follow the instructions on the rice cooker, surely Hawaii's most common small appliance. If you do not have a rice cooker, place the rice in a large, heavy pot and add 3½ cups water. Cover and leave to sit for about 20 minutes. Then bring to a brisk boil, reduce the heat, and cook for about 5 minutes until the sound changes, indicating that the water is absorbed. Turn the heat up for a few seconds to dry off the rice, remove the pot from the heat, and let the rice steam for 10 minutes in the residual heat.

Note: If you do not want the bother of measuring rice and water, simply place washed rice in a pot, put the tip of your middle finger on top of the rice, and add water to come just to the first knuckle.

No one knows more about the history of rice in Hawaii than Rodney and Karol Haraguchi, whose own family history exemplifies the history of rice in Hawaii. They have labored to restore the Haraguchi rice mill in Hanalei Valley.[8] Once it was just one of dozens of such mills in Hawaii, the rest of which have disappeared. Rodney's great-grandfather acquired it from the Chinese in 1924; in it he hulled and polished the rice from their own 75 acres and from that of several of their neighbors. The milling machinery itself, an ingenious assembly of American and Japanese components, is housed in a shed adjoining the corrugated iron storage barn. The rice was poured into a hole in one corner of the main building, falling down on to an elevator that raised it overhead and ran it through a shaker to get rid of dirt and impurities. Up it went again and again to be run through two hullers in succession until a fairly white rice emerged. Finally, to turn it into a shining product, it was passed through a polisher with leather straps, reminiscent of a modern car wash. Milling went on there for several generations, powered first by an overshot water mill and later by a diesel engine, until the last batch went through in 1960.

SORTING OUT RICE

Rice terminology[9] remains confusing and contradictory. This is simply a guide to the names of rices in stores and restaurants in Hawaii, which tend to stock a wider range of rice and rice products than mainland United States stores.

Calrose rice This is a kind of Japonica rice, the type preferred by the Japanese, and the rice most commonly used in Hawaii. The Calrose variety was developed after World War II by agricultural researchers in California to meet specific conditions for fertilizing, pesticides, frugal use of water, and mechanical harvesting. Today there is no true Calrose—it has become a generic term for a number of high-quality varieties that were developed after the original Calrose. In the United States and Europe, the California varieties are the preferred rice for sushi. Hinode, Diamond, and Fukusuke are common brands available everywhere in Hawaii; on the mainland they can be found in Asian stores and occasionally in supermarkets.

When cooked, the grains, which are medium to short in length, swell to a pearly translucence and cling together, making Calrose rice easy to eat with chopsticks. That is why it is sometimes called "sticky rice," but it should be carefully distinguished from mochi rice (see below) and Thai sticky rice (see below).

Long-grain rice This is the type most generally used in the mainland United States and Europe under such names as Carolina rice or basmati rice. It is available in Hawaii but relatively little used, although the Thai variety, jasmine rice, is popular with Southeast Asians.

Mochi rice This is the Japanese, and consequently the Local, term for the short-grain rice often called sweet rice or sticky rice. Uncooked, the short grains are chalky in appearance, somewhat similar to pearl barley. Hawaii's mochi rice comes from California. It is cooked by steaming, not boiling, and it is truly glutinous or sticky. It is most commonly pounded to make confections, popular in Hawaii and all over East and Southeast Asia.

Mochiko This is the Japanese, and consequently the Local, term for a flour made from mochi rice, often called sweet rice flour. It is mixed with water and steamed to make a variety of con-

fections. A popular brand from California is Blue Star, sold in 1-pound boxes. Because it is made with glutinous rice, it does not have the same properties as the regular rice flour sold in Europe and the mainland United States (though not often in Hawaii). Thai stores in Hawaii do carry both kinds imported from Thailand and they are clearly distinguished as glutinous rice flour and rice flour, respectively.

Thai sticky rice Popular in Thai restaurants in Hawaii (most of which serve the cuisine of northern Thailand, one of the few regions in the world where glutinous rice is the staple), this is a long-grain, glutinous rice, not a short-to-medium grain rice like Calrose. It is steamed to make a clinging, aromatic dish to accompany meats, fish, and curries.

Malagkit rice This is a long-grain, purple rice used by Filipinos (and Southeast Asians) to make a variety of confections.

POKE: OR HAWAII'S WAYS WITH FISH

Every morning, just after daybreak, in the old port and plantation town of Hilo on the Big Island a fish auction takes place right on Hilo Bay, in a lean-to with a corrugated-iron roof shaded by the huge umbrella of a monkeypod tree. The fish are laid out on pallets, neatly arranged by species. A dozen or so buyers from the fish markets, grocery chains, and restaurants gather to exchange gossip and jokes, their rubber boots squelching in the puddles on the concrete floor. A notice on the wall instructs them that in the interests of health no one should stand or walk on the pallets. From time to time, one of them takes a knife and scrapes away at the flesh just in front of the tail of a fish, testing its quality. Impressive sleek monsters, the fish are longer than a man is high, shining dark gray. These are deep-ocean fish, the aku and the ahi (tunas), the mahi-mahi, and the swordfish.

Out to sea is the long breakwater that protects the harbor. Coming into Hilo from the air, I had seen the way it broke up the long Pacific swells. A container-ship nudges its way around the barrier to meet the tug that will take it into the docks round the headland. Across the bay, Mauna Kea looms up, the white cluster of international observatories just visible on the summit. The gentle slope of its flanks disguises the volcano's immensity, making it hard to believe that it rises 13,796 feet above sea level in just a few miles. The only excrescence on its flawless outline is a small cinder cone on the windward side. The snow on the summit and the pale full moon setting on its leeward side make this a moment to savor: the quiet fishermen around me, the palms, the little town of Hilo climbing the hill across the bay, and the moon against the mountain. After the high-rises and the hustle and bustle of Honolulu, Hilo seems to lie at the outermost reaches of the world.

The auction starts, and the auctioneer goes from fish to fish, chanting his indecipherable call and slapping stickers with the buyer's name on each fish before moving swiftly on to the next. Partway through, a fishing boat comes in, year to 9,000,000 cans a year within a decade. By the 1930s, Hawaii's sampan fleet was the most modern in the world. One hundred forty fishing boats were operated by Japanese residents, 80% of the Hawaii fishing fleet. The industry was worth over $2,000,000 annually, ranking third in the Islands after sugar and pineapple.

Then came World War II. The government worried about the security risk posed by the fishing fleets, particularly because they were Japanese-owned (even if the Japanese were residents of the United States). Fishing was severely restricted for everyone and banned altogether for Japanese nationals. Japanese fishermen were among the first Japanese to be interned. A few managed to sell their vessels, but most were simply confiscated. Although a black market was quickly established, the fishing industry never recovered. In 1985, the cannery closed; by 1993, only six commercial sampans continued to operate out of Kewalo Basin in Honolulu.[2]

its turquoise blue paint faded and peeling. An elderly man (perhaps the owner), tall for Hawaii but stooped at the waist from years of labor, wearing a T-shirt and pants grimy from his work, pulls a huge fish from his cooler and heaves it up to add to the auction. The auctioneer finishes with the deep-sea fish and is down to the little fish, the reef fish. No dark gray here but stunning reds and oranges, sold in lots of several at a time. Already the buyers are dragging the big fish by the tail out across the concrete to be manhandled into their pickup trucks. Another quarter of an hour and the drama is over for another day. The employees wash down the area with a motor-powered spray. The fisherman returns to his boat, the pickup trucks drive off, and the few spectators wander away to continue their vacations.

Surrounded by its great ocean moat, Hawaii delights in fishing:[3] commercial fishing, recreational fishing, subsistence fishing; fishing in the streams and ponds, fishing on the reef, fishing in the deep ocean; pole fishing, spear fishing, net fishing with hukilau (seine) nets and gill nets and throw nets and bag nets and surround nets; daylight fishing, torch fishing, moonlight fishing, dark night fishing; crabbing and shrimping and lobstering and hunting for limu (edible seaweed) and wana (sea urchins). Families wade out to islands just off the coast, wearing shoes to protect themselves from the wana, and then go fishing. The children look for hermit crabs, fish, *opihi* (limpets), shells, seaweed, and sea cucumbers while the men go spear fishing for *tako* (octopus). Once caught, the octopus wriggles in the bucket. How to kill it? Turn the head inside out and bite the neck.[4]

What happens to all that fish? Some of it is exported, but much goes to local hotels, restaurants, and fish stores. Many Islanders eat fish every day. Per capita consumption of fish is twice what it is in the mainland United States,

Right: Tuna ready for canning, 1950s (HSA)

Opposite: Fishing for dinner at Honolulu Harbor

PART 1: LOCAL FOOD

and the per capita consumption of raw tuna is exceeded only by
Japan. Fish mark the special festivals of the year: tuna prices soar at
New Year, and the demand for fish roe goes up. Hawaii eats fish in
almost every conceivable way: raw, dried, salted, steamed, baked,
grilled, and fried. Hawaii's unique contribution to fish cuisine,
though, is often considered to be poke. (The word "poke" does
not rhyme with "spoke" but with "OK" or often "pokey."[5])

What is poke? At its simplest—and the simplest does not occur
all that often—poke consists of fingertip-sized chunks of raw fish
seasoned with Hawaiian salt, chopped seaweed, and roasted, ground
kukui nut meat. It is a down-home version of the elegant and re-
strained sashimi, also popular in the Islands. Sashimi must be cut
into perfect, even slices to be acceptable. A little raggedness in the
bits of poke is no matter. Sashimi must be arranged meticulously
on thin shreds of daikon. Poke is tumbled onto a plate. Sashimi is
delicately dipped into small bowls of soy sauce and wasabi. Poke is
doused in seasonings from the start. And poke can be made with
cheaper pieces of fish. Beginning with similar ingredients, the two
dishes carry different messages. What they share is a delight in the
sweet taste of really fresh fish, a taste that is favored around the
shores of the Pacific, from the sashimi of Japan to the kinilaw of
the Philippines to the ceviches of Latin America.[6]

Poke now appears in a vast range of variations; besides the simple additions
of Hawaiian salt, a relish of ground kukui nut kernels (inamona), and one of
several kinds of seaweed (limu), other popular additions include soy sauce,
green onion, sesame oil, and chili pepper. "We carry 20 different kinds of
poke," advertised a discount grocery store that opened in the mid-1990s, to
reassure shoppers that their choice would be wider than in the full-price stores.
Such a range of pokes might include classics such as aku limu (tuna with seaweed), aku green onion, aku shoyu, aku onion, ahi (tuna) onion, nairagi
(striped marlin) onion, kajiki (striped marlin), and swordfish shoyu, as well
as the cooked pokes, usually shellfish or tako (octopus)—locally cooked tako,
king clam, crablike, mussel, Korean-style tako, Japan tako onion, and smoked
tako onion. Ake (raw beef liver) poke, aku with blood, and oio lomi (bonefish
mashed) can be found in stores that cater primarily to Hawaiians.

Where does poke come from? It is often described as a traditional Hawaiian
way with fish. True, the word "poke," in Hawaiian, means cut piece or small
piece. The Hawaiians certainly did and do enjoy raw fish, either whole in the
case of small reef fish or river fish, or cut, or lomied (mashed with the fingers),
seasoned with salt, ground kukui nut kernels, and, almost always, seaweed.
At first this sounds like the poke that is so popular today.

HAWAIIAN FISHPONDS

Every day, thousands of
cars pull off the road from
Honolulu to the windward
side of Oahu so that their
passengers can walk the few
feet to the Pali Lookout for
a panoramic view down the
precipice, across the rest of
the island, and out to sea.
Some notice a hook-shaped
protrusion jutting out into
the ocean to the north of
the town of Kaneohe. This is
not a natural spit of land. It
is one of the old Hawaiian
fishponds.

The Hawaiian fishponds
were the grandest in the Pacific.[7] The largest, owned by
the chiefs and managed by
their caretakers, were massive structures, with semi-
permeable walls of lava rock
or coral jutting out into the
ocean (though some were
inland). One of the walls of

a fishpond in the Kona district of the island of Hawaii is about 200 yards in length, 35–40 feet at its base, and about 6 feet high. Their average size was about 15 acres. A fixed sluice grate at one or more places in the seawall allowed fresh seawater into the ponds and attracted the fish at ebb and flow to the nutrients that went past. To stock the ponds, the caretakers sought the fry of certain fish and collected favored seaweeds. They also raised crustaceans, shellfish, and even turtles. The fish were fed with sweet potatoes, taro, breadfruit, mussels, and seaweed.

It is estimated that at the beginning of the nineteenth century, the royal fishponds collectively yielded about 5,000 pounds of fish a day and that the average annual yield per acre was as much as 350 pounds. The harvested fish were forbidden to commoners and the edict was enforced with vigor.[8] But if the chiefs numbered about 5,000 as is sometimes estimated, this meant an average of about a pound of pond fish a day for each of them.

However, neither the most extensive study of Hawaiian uses of fish nor the first ethnic cookbook mentions poke as a fish dish, nor does the definitive Hawaiian dictionary nor the major glossary of pidgin.[9] Recipes labeled "poke" do not occur in cookbooks published before the mid-1970s.[10] Locals who left for the mainland in the 1960s often have no recollection of poke and when they return to the Islands express surprise to be offered it so frequently.

In short, poke as a widely used Local dish is a Local creation, melding the existent Hawaiian taste for raw fish with the existent Asian, particularly Japanese taste for the same, but coming up with a new synthesis. The Hawaiians contributed the name and the seasoning with salt and seaweed, while their taste for reef fish lost ground to tuna, and lomiing or eating whole to cutting in blocks; the Japanese contributed seasonings of soy sauce and the preference for deep-ocean fish, while sashimi continued its more purist ways. Local taste as well as other Asian tastes added the sesame oil and the green onion and the hot chilies sometime during the 1960s or 1970s, poke became the thing to have with a beer after work or to make sure to include among the "heavy pupus" for your party.

SORTING OUT FISH AND SEAFOOD

Fish are listed in the glossary under their common Island names. Because the fishing in Hawaii has been done primarily by the Hawaiians and the Japanese, most names are in those languages. But this does not help fit them into categories recognized outside Hawaii. Many visitors do not find the seafood that they expect in Hawaii. That is because the Islands have a narrow fringing reef that falls off quickly to very deep ocean. Hence many of the types of fish and shellfish found on the continental shelves of the east coast of the United States and of Europe are either in short supply or not to be had at all in Hawaii. There are, however, many kinds of deep-ocean fish.[11]

The tunas. These include aku, ahi, and albacore. Commercially these are much the most important fish in Hawaii. A large part of the catch goes to Japan to be sold for sashimi. The tunas range up to several hundred pounds in weight and their silvery bodies are darker on top than on the bottom. In Hawaii, they are favored for sashimi or poke but are also good grilled or sauteed.

The billfish. These are generally known locally as au and are regarded as sport fish; on the mainland they are better known as marlins and swordfish. Like the tunas, they can be huge and they are sold in the same section of the fish store, ready cut into filets or into long triangular sections that can be sliced as steaks. Their flesh is lighter than that of a tuna and is good barbecued or grilled. They are most common during the summer.

The snappers. These include the opakapaka and kalekale, the onaga, the uku, and the taape. They are smaller than the tunas and the billfish, ranging from 1 to 12 pounds. Many of them are colored bright red, the color of good luck and happiness in many Asian cultures, making them popular at Chinese and Japanese New Year. Serendipitously, snappers are most common in midwinter. Their flesh is white and delicate and they are often baked or steamed. The taape, a recent introduction, is less popular than the other species.

The groupers. Only one of these, the hapuu, is commercially important in Hawaii. It is most common in September and has firm white flesh.

An opah ready for purchase

The jacks. The ulua or papio, the akule, and the opelu are the main representatives of the jacks. The first has white flesh, the other two are oily and moist with a rather coarse texture; all are excellent dried and smoked.

Miscellaneous other ocean fish. The best known are the ono, with its moist, white flesh that is good grilled or sauteed, and the mahimahi, which is usually cut into steaks and fried or grilled.

Squid and octopus. Squid is readily available and popular, though most of it does not come from Hawaii. Octopus is caught around the Islands.

Reef fish. All those delightful and colorful fish that you see drifting and darting beneath you as you snorkel are eaten by someone or other with great relish. Most are small and bony.

Shellfish. Hawaii has some shellfish though not as many as one might expect. Opihi (small limpets) and wana (sea urchins) are all popular, as are small black crabs that are eaten raw. Slipper lobsters are occasionally available. Shrimp and prawns farmed in the Islands are of high quality.

Freshwater fish. As one might expect in small islands, there are relatively few freshwater fish. Mullet, which lives in brackish water, is very popular. Streams used to be full of small oopu, much favored for eating, but these are now scarce.

I give only a couple of recipes for poke. The discussion in this section should be enough to indicate the basic principles. The points to remember are that the fish should be fresh and of fine quality and that the seasonings are there to enhance the mellow buttery taste of the fish, not to overwhelm it.

AHI POKE

(Seasoned Fresh Tuna)

1 pound raw ahi (tuna)
½ cup ogo (seaweed)
Soy sauce

Cut the fish into ¾-inch cubes. Wash the seaweed, taking care to remove any sand if you have collected it yourself, and chop it into ½- to 1-inch pieces. Mix gently with the fish and add the soy sauce to taste. Serve on a chilled platter and supply chopsticks.

Yield: Six to eight servings

Note: Alternative seasonings (not all at once) include salt, coarsely ground red chili peppers, sesame oil, and chopped green onions. Any fish used for sashimi can be substituted for the ahi.

• • •

TAKO POKE

(Seasoned Squid or Octopus)

1 pound octopus or squid, cooked and cut in ¾-inch cubes
Soy sauce
Salt
Sugar
Ogo
Inamona (roasted kukui nut relish), optional

Toss the octopus in enough soy sauce to coat and then season with salt, sugar, and ogo to taste. Serve on a chilled platter and supply chopsticks.

Yield: Six to eight servings

SASHIMI

(Fresh Fish)

Sashimi is offered at parties and celebrations throughout the year and is an absolute must at Christmas and New Year. The buttery taste and texture of the fish contrasts nicely with the sharp condiments.

**1 pound fresh, boneless aku or ahi (tuna), onaga, or
  swordfish
Daikon, red or green cabbage, watercress tips, or lettuce,
  thinly shredded
Soy sauce
Wasabi**

Prepare a serving dish with a bed of the vegetables in a color that will enhance the fish: white or green vegetables such as daikon, green cabbage, or lettuce for tuna, red or green vegetables such as red cabbage or watercress tips for white fish. Cut the fish so that its cross section is no more than 1 by 1½ inches. Then using a sharp, wet knife slice the fillets into pieces no more than ⅛ inch thick. Let the pieces fall into a row like dominos as you slice. Slide your knife blade under the slices and transfer them to the vegetable-covered dish. Give each person a pair of chopsticks and a small dish of soy sauce with a dab of wasabi on the side. They select a piece of fish with a few vegetable shreds and dip it in the soy-wasabi sauce.

Yield: Serves four generously, six or eight with other hors d'oeuvres.

Note: Wasabi can be bought ready-prepared in a tube or powdered in a small can. In the latter case, mix with a little water to make a thick paste. As an alternative, hot, freshly prepared mustard is often served in Hawaii.

. . .

FISHCAKE

A popular way to prepare fish, particularly bony fish, is to make fishcake, which is used to stuff various Chinese noodle dishes or to deep fry in patties. Fish such as ladyfish is cleaned and refrigerated for 3 to 4 days. Then it is split in half and the meat scraped out with a spoon. For each cup of flesh, approximately ¾ cup cornstarch and ¾ cup water or dashi is added to make a taupe-colored paste, which is seasoned to taste with salt and sugar. Sometimes slivered vegetables such as carrots or green beans are added. Because fishcake is time-consuming to make and is widely available in stores, most people buy their fishcake ready prepared.

· · ·

TOFU FISH PATTIES

Tofu fish patties are real home cooking in Hawaii, Hawaii's version of fish cakes or fish sticks. The patties are made of tofu, green onion, and some kind of fish, bound by eggs and fried. Slivered vegetables, such as green beans, can be added. Like all such recipes, the quantities vary with what is on hand, but this is reasonably representative. The patties can be eaten as a snack or hors d'oeuvres, or with rice for a more substantial meal.

1 block tofu (1-pound package), drained and mashed
8 ounces fishcake (or canned tuna or imitation crab
** meat flakes)**
8 green onions, chopped
2 eggs
Optional seasonings (see note)
Oil for frying

Combine all ingredients and mix well. Shape into small patties of about 1 teaspoonful each (these can be floured if you wish). Heat oil in a frying pan and saute the patties until golden brown on both sides. Serve as they are, with rice, or with a dipping sauce of your choice. Mild rice vinegar is one good choice.

Yield: Four servings

Note: Optional seasonings include salt, dashi, sesame seeds, miso, and slivered vegetables or bean sprouts.

· · ·

CRISPY FRIED AKU (TUNA) BONES

I had always assumed that the aku skeletons for sale in Chinatown fish markets were for soup until I came across this recipe by Local fishing-show host Hari Kojima.[12]

Cut aku bones into 2½ to 3-inch pieces. Season with garlic salt and black pepper. Dust with flour, dip in beaten egg, and roll in bread crumbs. Pan fry until golden brown. Nibble on the bones as finger food, sucking off any flesh that is left and crunching the ends of the bones.

. . .

SEARED AHI

(Seared Tuna)

Seared ahi was one of the first of the chefs' recipes from Hawaii Regional Cuisine to become a Hawaii standard. It may well have had Island roots in "half-cooked aku sashimi (takaki)," a dish in which aku fillets were seared on the grill, cut in sashimi pieces, and served with a dipping sauce.[13] In any case, it is quick and simple to make at home, provided you make sure that you heat the pan to a scorching temperature. The combination of charred, smoky outside, silky inside, and cream and mustard sauce is ravishing.

1 pound fillet of ahi
2 tablespoons ready-prepared Cajun spices
Dipping sauce of ¼ cup heavy cream mixed with
  2 tablespoons prepared dijon mustard

Rub the fish with the spices. Preheat a cast iron frying pan over high heat. Without adding any oil, sear the fish on each side for just a minute. Remove from the pan and cut into half-inch slices. In cross section, the outside should be black and crisp, then the tiniest layer of cooked, white tuna, and the bulk of the inside should remain dark pink. Arrange the medallions on a serving tray with a pool of the sauce (or place the sauce in a small bowl alongside). Garnish with fresh vegetables as desired. Serve with chopsticks.

Yield: Four servings

Note: Other dipping sauces of your choice may be substituted.

LIMU (SEAWEED): HAWAII'S SPICE

At eight o'clock in the morning on the Waianae coast, on the dry leeward side of Oahu, the sun is already high. Little rain falls here and the mountains are brown and dry, plunging the 3,000 feet into the ocean. At their foot winds a road, lined by sagging frame houses, abandoned railroad tracks that once carried sugar, fast-food restaurants, and neat frame Samoan churches. At one point on the ocean side, these give way to a hau tree, its slender trunk and spreading shade canopy of hand-sized, heart-shaped leaves casting a shadow toward the slim line of beach. Faced with the litter of beer cans and paper diapers under the hau tree, the eye cannot resist turning out to sea, already an intense turquoise blue, so different from the steel gray of the North Atlantic.

The tide is out. A line of brilliant white surf marks the crest of the reef a couple of hundred yards offshore. And if you squint, just this side of that brilliant white you can make out a figure moving slowly along, a bag slung over one shoulder, stooping from time to time to collect something under the water and stow it in the bag. From this distance, the clothing is invisible. If you ignore the diapers and the noise of the cars on the highway, you could be back in ancient Hawaii. For what you are watching is a limu picker.[1]

The Hawaiian word "limu" originally referred to any plant that could grow in a wet spot. Over the generations, usage gradually narrowed, initially to sea plants and more recently to edible sea plants, or sea vegetables, as some of their enthusiasts prefer to call these marine algae.[2] The Hawaiians had names for over 80 seaweeds, of which 32 can be equated with scientific names. Limu was one of the few vegetable foodstuffs that was available to the first arrivals in Hawaii and it played an important role as a seasoning, equivalent to the herbs and spices of Europe and Asia. It was especially important for women. Their diet consisted primarily of poi (pounded taro); pork, coconut, and all but three varieties of banana were denied them. The women picked limu, gossiping as they cleaned it, glad of the seasoning it brought to their foods.[3] With the arrival of the Europeans and the changing of the Hawaiian diet, the number of species that were commonly eaten gradually declined. The reefs have been picked clean of many of the more popular forms of edible seaweed. Limu pickers have become rarer. No longer do women and children search for limu in the debris thrown up by storms on Waikiki Beach as once they did.

The number of species eaten may have declined, but the enthusiasm for limu remains. It continues to be used for every stage of the meal, from pre-dinner snacks, through soups, salads, main courses, and desserts. It is one of the foods that serves as a common bridge between Hawaii's ethnic groups, most of whom already enjoyed limu in their homelands. Hawaiian-Americans, Chinese-Americans, Japanese-Americans, Okinawan-Americans, Korean-Americans, and Filipino-Americans all eat seaweed. Fresh and dried varieties are available in every supermarket. The most widely used fresh seaweed, or limu as everyone calls it in the Islands, is ogo and it comes largely from the state's three large seaweed farms. It is no small business. In 1989, some 400,000 pounds of marine algae (some of this microalgae) were harvested, with an economic value of almost 2 million dollars. Other farms or wild stocks supply smaller amounts of other selected species.

"Books about seaweeds?" I once overheard the sales clerk saying to another customer in Kitchen Arts and Letters, the specialty cookbook store in New York City. "Those are our worst sellers." Although Americans unwittingly consume seaweed (carrageenan) that is added to chocolate drinks, low-fat burgers, and ice cream, they simply don't choose to eat it knowingly, even when goaded on by health food addicts and natural food hunters. That is, except in Hawaii. There it is enjoyed knowingly and enthusiastically.

SORTING OUT HAWAIIAN LIMU

This list describes just a few of the more common limu in Hawaii.[4]

Limu eleele (*Enteromorpha* spp.). A fine green algae that grows in brackish water. It is collected by catching it in buckets or using nets to strain it from the water. Then it is rinsed, drained and the water squeezed out. Traditionally, Hawaiians allowed it to "miko" (ripen) with a little salt. It can be added to raw fish, saimin, or stew.

Limu huluhuluwaena (*Grateloupia filicina*). In ancient Hawaii, this limu, known as the "pubic hair seaweed" because of its dark, hairlike branches, was reserved for the alii (the nobility). Not readily available in stores, it must be gathered; it is chopped and added to opihi, raw liver, and other dishes.

Limu kala (*Sargassum echinocarpum*). This is the seaweed, or at least a relative of the seaweed, for which the Sargasso Sea that trapped so many mariners was named. It is a tough, yellowish limu that is used to make striking leis. Traditionally the leaves were chopped and added to stuffed fish or fish heads. The most sympathetic use for those not accustomed to this limu is deep-fried as crispy chips to use with drinks.

Limu kohu (*Asparagopsis taxiformis*). Also traditionally reserved for the nobility, the alii. A feathery red-brown seaweed, rich in bromine; indeed so rich in bromine that it is quite dangerous in its raw state: bromine gas, after all, is used in Hawaii to fumigate tented houses to get rid of termites. The Hawaiians rolled it into small balls and dried it in the sun for a day before powdering it into their foods as a relish. You can still buy these balls, which resemble small balls of rusty colored, hairy wool, in the Aloha Farmers' Market. This species is eaten only in Hawaii and is not recommended for the limu neophyte.

Limu lipoa (*Dictyopteris plagiogramma, Dictyopteris australis*). Loved by the limu picker, hated by the surfer because it clutters the waters, this limu grows below the low-tide line. Its fronds, 2–8 inches long, are yellowish, narrow, and curled at the edges. It has a spicy taste, sometimes compared with sage and pepper, and it is used with raw fish.

Limu manauea (*Gracilaria coronopifolia*) and **ogo (*Gracilaria bursapastoris*).** The Hawaiian and the Japanese names are often used interchangeably for these two species, although the aficionado can tell the difference and although the second is probably an introduced species. They are the most common of all the limu in Hawaii: crisp, slightly salty, mild, and adaptable red filaments. The Hawaiians mix limu manauea with other limu or with fish or meats. Because ogo is now farmed in the Islands, it is available in every grocery store. It is prepared as pickle, salad, vegetable, candy, and in diverse other ways, including as a thickener for soups and stews, and an ingredient in poke.

Limu wawaeiole (*Codium edule* or *Codium reediae*) (Rat's-foot limu in English, miru in Japanese, or pokpoklo in Filipino). The rat's foot metaphor is appropriate: these are velvety, dark olive green branches of limu with spongy endings like little feet. This limu is particularly popular with the Filipinos and can usually be found in the Open Markets.

For other recipes that include seaweeds, see the index.

CUCUMBER AND OGO NAMASU

(Cucumber and Seaweed Salad)

In this Japanese salad, the clean taste of the cucumber combines with the crisp, slightly salty sea flavor of the ogo to good advantage. The proportions of cucumber and ogo can be varied to taste and some selection of slivered carrots or celery or fish (raw or cooked) can be added.

2 Japanese cucumbers (or 1½ English or 3–4 American)
1 cup ogo
¼ cup rice vinegar
1 teaspoon grated ginger
2 tablespoons sugar
Salt

Peel the cucumbers if they are waxed or if the skin is coarse, cut in half lengthwise and scoop out the seeds if they are large, and slice thinly. Place in a bowl, sprinkle with salt, and leave for half an hour. Blanch the ogo by placing in a sieve and pouring boiling water over it. Chop it into ¼- to ½-inch lengths. Drain the cucumber and squeeze between the hands until dry. Place the cucumber and ogo in a bowl, reserving a few pieces of ogo as a garnish. Mix the vinegar, ginger, and sugar and pour over the vegetables. Turn gently and test for seasoning. Sprinkle the top with the reserved ogo.

Yield: Four servings

· ■ ·

OGO KIM CHEE

(Korean Spicy Pickled Seaweed)

2 pounds limu manauea (ogo)
1 onion, chopped
1 cup vinegar
½ cup soy sauce
1 clove garlic, chopped
Ground chili pepper to taste
1 inch ginger, grated
Sugar to taste

Clean ogo under water and wilt it by pouring boiling water over. Mix with onion, vinegar, soy sauce, garlic, chili pepper, ginger, and sugar. Leave for a few days to pickle. Serve as a side dish.

▪ ▪ ▪

SESAME-OGO CANDY

An unusual recipe for a seaweed candy where the slightly salty tang of the ogo combines with the sweet nutty taste of the other ingredients to produce an enticing taste.[5]

2 cups brown sugar
1 cup water
½ cup sesame seeds
¼ teaspoon sesame oil
1 teaspoon vanilla extract
4 cups ogo, chopped into 1-inch pieces

Boil the brown sugar, water, sesame seeds, and sesame oil until they form a thick syrup. Continue cooking until they reach the soft-crack stage. Remove from the heat. Add vanilla and ogo. Pour into a shallow, greased baking pan and spread in a thin layer. Allow to cool and then dry in the sun for a few days. Cut into 1-inch squares to serve.

▪ ▪ ▪

LIMU WAWAEIOLE (POKPOKLO) SALAD

(Tomato, Onion, and Seaweed Salad)

Limu wawaeiole (rat's-foot limu), which can be found regularly in Open Markets in Hawaii and sometimes in grocery stores, has chubby moss-green branches. When you bite into them, there is a burst of salty sea flavor. This Filipino salad makes good use of the texture and taste of the limu.

3 cups limu wawaeiole, packed
4 large tomatoes, finely chopped
½ cup fresh ginger, grated
1 onion, chopped
2 tablespoons soy sauce
Salt

Clean limu and soak in boiling water a few minutes to wilt. Drain, chop, and mix with tomatoes, ginger, onion, and soy sauce. Add salt to taste.

Yield: Four servings

· · ·

ΚΑΝΤΕΝ

(Asian Gelatin or Agar)

Knowing how to make kanten (or agar) is useful because kanten (made from seaweed) has some characteristics quite different from gelatin. It is much less slick and wobbly with a texture that is almost crisp and it combines well with vegetable and fruit purees. It solidifies even at the warm room temperature of Hawaii. It will gel substances such as fresh pineapple that gelatin will not. For aspics, though, I prefer the texture and greater transparency of gelatin.

Kanten usually comes in long crinkly leaves or bundles of crinkly strips. Exact amounts may vary but in general to prepare enough kanten to set 2 cups of liquid, take one leaf or several strips of the kanten (about ⅛ ounce), rinse, and soak in water for about 30 minutes until softened. Heat with 2 cups of whatever liquid you are using—water or sweetened fruit juice or vegetable juice—until the kanten dissolves, remove from heat, strain to remove any remaining shreds of kanten, and pour into a 2-cup mold.

For a pineapple kanten, see p. 202.

SAIMIN, MANAPUA, AND MUSUBI: HAWAII'S SNACKS

"I can always get saimin at McDonald's" is the bravado response of the Local teenager, nervous about going off to the distant mainland, still unaware that there McDonald's does not offer saimin. Even in Hawaii, McDonald's saimin is acceptable only to the young and undiscriminating. Mr. Shigeyuki Yoshitake, who grew up in Kaimuki, a suburb of Honolulu just being developed in the 1930s, and whose mother made saimin, lays down the law. "If you want to eat saimin, don't go to McDonald's," he says on the walking tours he conducts with his friend Robert Takane. "It's greasy; it's made with Swanson's chicken broth."

What then is saimin? It is Hawaii's version of an Asian noodle soup: spaghetti-like noodles in a fish or (despite Mr. Yoshitake's strictures) chicken broth, usually topped with shreds of egg, green onions, slices of fishcake and strips of char siu (Chinese roast pork) or canned luncheon meat, often with a side order of a thin skewer of chicken or beef grilled teriyaki-style. There is a desultory ongoing debate about whether its origins are Chinese, Japanese, or Local. "Saimin is a term peculiar to Hawaii. We do not know when or how it was coined. Local Chinese think saimin is a Japanese dish; local Japanese think it's a Chinese dish. One thing seems certain: it's a local [Hawaii] dish."[1] The debate should be desultory, for what is pretty clear is that almost every Asian country has its own particular version of noodle soup. The name may owe something to both the Chinese and the Japanese; the Japanese had adapted Chinese egg noodles (mein), which they called ramen, from the Chinese, and one of their own most common noodles—a thin, wheat-flour noodle—is called somen.[2] In Hawaii, noodle soups made by every nationality tend to get dubbed "saimin." In the 1990s, Thai plate lunch places quite happily offered Thai and Vietnamese "saimin" with their own special touches, such as thin-sliced raw beef and mint and basil leaves.

Mr. Yoshitake recounts how his mother prepared saimin in the 1930s. She put kelp and dried shrimp into a pot of water to boil for broth. Meanwhile, she

made long, thick, wheat-flour noodles from scratch. When the time came for a bowl of steaming saimin, she would quickly cook the noodles in a second pot of boiling water, and then ladle them into a bowl of the broth. For a more substantial snack, she would garnish the bowl with pieces of luncheon meat (SPAM had not been invented then). Many Japanese set up saimin stands, one of the easiest small businesses to start. All that was needed was a two-burner pushcart and permission from a local gas station to use its premises after hours. During the day you made the noodles and broth at home, and then as darkness drew in, you trundled the noodles, a pot of water, and the pot of broth off to the gas station where you had stored a picnic table. For your customers, it was easy enough to plunge the noodles into a pot of boiling water, pull them out and drain them, and ladle them into a bowl of hot broth. Half a dozen such stands were strung out along Waialae Avenue between what is now the University campus in Manoa and the upmarket suburb of Kahala.

Saimin seems to have been one of the first foods to become truly Local, cropping up in cookbooks from the 1930s on. How Mr. Yoshitake, with his high standards for saimin, would sigh over the Hilo Woman's Club. In 1937 the ladies of the club compiled a cookbook that paid special attention to locally available fruits and vegetables—quite an innovation at the time.[3] They also included a handful of Chinese and Japanese recipes. Mrs. Slator Miller ventured her version of "sai men." After thoroughly cooking a pound of macaroni, she suggested adding several strips of fried bacon, the white parts of green onions, a can of mushrooms, a can of tuna, and soy sauce to taste. This was to be steamed for 20 minutes and then served with a green salad—not a dish the Chinese or the Japanese would have recognized. But it exhibits the perils of attempting new foods. As children, we gobbled up my mother's attempts at spaghetti—a plate of spaghetti, ringed by crisp bacon and plump sections of English sausages, and accompanied by tomato ketchup—just as I suspect Mrs. Miller's family relished the "sai men." But by the time the cookbook reached its eleventh printing in 1974, Mrs. Miller's "sai men" had been dropped from the much-expanded repertoire of Japanese recipes.

Saimin stands became, and in many cases still are, neighborhood institutions: family-style food at very reasonable prices to be eaten with chopsticks in one hand for the solids, a ceramic Chinese soup spoon in the other for the broth. Eating saimin is not quiet or refined—slurping is not only in order, it shows appreciation. Saimin is not considered a full meal because it contains no rice. A saimin stand is where you go to warm up when the temperature sinks into the 60s, to pass the time after a movie, to seek an acceptable haven away from the bosom of the family, or simply to get a great snack. It will even serve for breakfast. When in the early 1990s the Marriott concession at the University of Hawaii added a saimin bar to their standard breakfast offerings of miso soup, rice or hash browns, eggs, Portuguese sausage, bacon, and SPAM, the students flocked to it.

Closely related to saimin in the grammar of Local Food are two other filling snacks, neither quite enough to count as a meal, but each filling the niche that a hot dog fills on the mainland: one is manapua, the other musubi. There is no debate about the origin of manapua: it is Chinese, one of the many kinds of dim sum. But in Hawaii manapua has taken on a life of its own, independent of the restaurants that serve dim sum. It is the size of a large doughnut, made of creamy white dough, slightly shiny on the outside, soft and fluffy inside, and filled with a slightly sweet pork mixture.[4] Its Chinese name is *char siu bao* (from the filling of Chinese char siu pork); manapua comes from Hawaiian words meaning delicious thing filled with pork.[5]

Manapua men used to hawk their wares around the towns and camps of Hawaii, a yoke across their shoulders with containers of manapua suspended from either end. They are now long gone, though manapua is not. Now you can buy it in "valuepacks" in the grocery store and heat it in the microwave. Unlike saimin, it appears to have changed relatively little over the years; the savory filling of sweetened pork was unchallenged until recently. That may be changing as Vietnamese fast-food places offer their version of manapua, made with an egg, bean thread, and pork filling.

The musubi, at its simplest a ball of rice of about the size that can be held in the cupped hands, has become something of a Hawaii mascot, regarded with friendly affection much as one might regard the family mutt—not something

for show but always around and always welcome. You can buy musubi magnets for your refrigerator, musubi cushions for your couch, musubi pins for your jacket, and musubi T-shirts.

The musubi was brought to Hawaii by the Japanese who came to work on the plantations. In Japan, they had eaten it for lunch in the fields or taken it on journeys, placed in a lunch box, a bento. There it was also an appropriate offering for the dead. Tradition had it that the customary flattened triangle shape was in memory of three sailors who had drowned; that way each of them could take a bite from a different side.[6] Unlike sushi, musubi is neither vinegared nor sweetened. Often an *ume* (a pickled fruit usually translated as pickled plum [see the section on crack seed] is tucked in the middle, or perhaps soy-flavored tuna or takuwan (pickled daikon). Nori is frequently wrapped around the outside.[7]

In Hawaii, the musubi has become a standard minimeal that can be picked up in any convenience store, drug store, or grocery store, along with the more elaborate packed lunches known as bentos. One firm alone, Tokyo Bento, is reported to sell between 3,000 and 4,000 musubi a day. No wonder: they cost just a dollar or so apiece and are something between a filling snack and a meal. The musubi is gradually transcending its humble origins, now being enlivened with SPAM, hot dogs, fishcake, eggs, or even spicy Mexican chorizo (a musu-burrito, no less) placed on the outside to form a kind of reverse sandwich. The exact shape of the musubi may vary; one favorite is a triangle about ¾ inch thick, with its angles rounded, another a bar about an inch in diameter and 4 inches long, made either with an empty SPAM can or with the "plastic precision musubi maker" available in the drug stores for a few cents.

Like sushi, though, it is important not to refrigerate musubi because the rice hardens, and the texture that is an important part of the pleasure of eating a musubi is lost. When, in the mid-1990s, the Health Department decided to insist that all food on sale in public places must either be refrigerated or heated above a certain temperature, the public and the sushi and musubi makers were united to challenge this "bento bashing."[8] The measure, at least in its strong form, was defeated.

SAIMIN

(Noodle Soup with Toppings)

Saimin is a simple dish, but as with so many simple dishes, if it is made with fine ingredients, put together with care, it is an excellent dish.

Prepare your broth. You can use dried shrimp and a piece of kelp, or Japanese dashi mix, or chicken stock, preferably homemade. Meanwhile prepare a selection of toppings: cold char siu (roast pork), cut in strips; thin slices of pink-and-white kamaboko (fishcake); thin omelettes rolled and then shredded; chopped green onions. Your imagination is the limit, but a certain restraint is in order. Take freshly made saimin noodles, which in Hawaii you can buy in any grocery store or in the many small noodle factories in Chinatown: local books do not offer a recipe for these noodles on the reasonable assumption that you would be mad to make them at home when they are so readily available. On the mainland fresh chow mein noodles would make a good substitute, or in a pinch, spaghettini. If you want to make your own, the recipe in Chinese cookbooks for Chinese egg noodles is best. Have ready a pot of boiling water and dip the noodles in for just a minute or two. (If they are dried, follow the directions on the packet.) This cooks them and rinses off the floury covering so that the soup will stay clear. Place the hot broth in big Asian flanged soup bowls, ladle the noodles from the boiling water to the broth with a strainer (a Chinese strainer does well for this), and add the toppings. Serve with a Chinese ceramic spoon and chop sticks if the toppings are substantial.

TERIYAKI MEAT STICKS

Frequently saimin is served with a couple of thin bamboo skewers of barbecued meat or chicken (teriyaki or its Korean equivalent) on the side. You fetch up some noodles with your chopsticks, wash them down with a spoonful of broth, and then nibble on the chewy-crisp meat on the skewer.

½ pound beef (sirloin tip or rib eye)
¼ cup soy sauce
1½ tablespoons sugar
½ tablespoon sherry
½ teaspoon minced fresh ginger
1 clove garlic, minced

Slice beef diagonally across the grain into strips 2 inches long, ½ inch wide, and ¼ inch thick. Combine remaining ingredients and marinate meat slices in the mixture for 30 minutes. Thread meat on thin bamboo skewers. Place over charcoal grill or under broiler until done.

Yield: About twelve skewers, plenty for four bowls of saimin

Note: To make chicken sticks, use chicken breasts and follow the same procedure.

• • •

MANAPUA

(Savory Stuffed Buns)

Manapua make a wonderful snack or light meal; the light, very slightly sweet bread dough with its stretchy skin encases a tasty filling. The recipe for manapua may look complicated but for anyone who has ever made a loaf of bread, manapua should pose no problem. In fact, they pose fewer problems, because they always turn out light and puffy, never heavy, if you follow the instructions. The filling can be made the day before, the dough can be left unattended most of the time, and a few minutes more or less of cooking time will not spoil the product. Moreover, manapua keep well in the refrigerator or freezer and reheat perfectly in a steamer or microwave.

For the bun:

1 package dry yeast
3 tablespoons warm water
Approximately 2 cups lukewarm water
1½ tablespoons cooking oil or shortening
¾ teaspoon salt
¼ cup sugar
6 cups sifted flour
½ tablespoon sesame oil

Preparing the dough:

Sprinkle the yeast over 3 tablespoons of lukewarm water and allow to stand until yeast softens. Heat remaining water to lukewarm, add the oil or shortening, sugar, and salt, stirring until melted or dissolved. Cool. Add the yeast mixture. Place the flour in a large mixing bowl or in a heavy-duty mixer and add most of the liquids. Begin kneading. Add remaining liquids to make a very heavy dough. Continue kneading or mixing until you have a smooth ball that is beginning to show signs of long strands on the outside, indicating that the gluten has fully developed. Remove from bowl and rinse out. Pour the sesame oil into the bowl, return the dough, and turn it around until covered with a thin layer of the oil. Cover with plastic wrap. Allow to rise until double in bulk—in a warm room this will take only an hour or so. There is much to be said for placing the dough in the refrigerator and allowing it to rise for 3–6 hours, which develops the flavor. At this point you can proceed with the filling or you can gently deflate the dough and allow it to rise for a second time, which will further enhance the flavor.

Stuffing and steaming the buns:

Heat a steamer with plenty of water. I use a large pot that will take three manapua at a time. Cut twelve 3-inch squares of waxed paper and coat one side with nonstick cooking spray. Punch down dough and divide into twelve pieces. Roll each into a ball. Then flatten into a circle about 6 inches in diameter. You can do this by patting the dough or by using a rolling pin. Make the dough as thin as you can without puncturing it and try to keep the edges thinner than the center. They are going to be folded and tucked under and you want to avoid a lump of dough at the bottom of the bun. Place the circle of dough in the palm of your left hand (or right if you are left-handed). Spoon in a couple of tablespoons of filling, cupping the dough around it. Then with the thumb and finger of the right hand, pinch the edges of the dough as if you were making a fluted edging on a pie crust. When you have gone all the way round (you will need to rotate the dough through 180 degrees), you should have a nearly closed sphere of dough. Take your folds and pinch them together, twisting them as you do so. The manapua is now complete. Local manapua are usually served fold-side down, and Vietnamese manapua with the twirl of dough on top. The choice is yours. Place the completed manapua on a square of greased waxed paper while you complete the others. It will plump up into a satisfying globe with a taut exterior. Place the manapua in the steamer on their squares of paper about 1–2 inches apart because they will expand. Cover the steamer and steam vigorously for 15 minutes. If you are using a metal steamer, place a folded tea towel across the top of the steamer, holding it in position with the lid. This will prevent steam from dropping down on to the manapua and spoiling its tight, shiny surface. If you are using a bamboo steamer, this is not necessary. Remove the steamer from the heat, and allow to rest for 5 minutes before opening so that the buns do not deflate rapidly. Then open and lift out your beautiful puffy buns. Serve hot.

Yield: This recipe makes twelve buns

Notes: (1) Manapua keep well in the refrigerator for several days and can be reheated by steaming for 15 minutes or by microwaving for 1 minute on full power. They also freeze successfully. (2) Baked manapua. A popular alternative is to bake the manapua. Heat the oven to 350 degrees. Brush the top of the buns with a little oil, place on a baking sheet, and bake for about 20–25 minutes. This gives a quite different, but also appealing, texture to the bread. (3) If you want the typical red stamp on the manapua, make a crosswise slit in the end of a chopstick and wedge the cuts open with two toothpicks. Dip the chopstick in red food coloring and stamp on top of bun (red is the color for good luck). (4) Manapua in Hawaii are traditionally large, a good fistful of eating. You can make them halfsize for hors d'oeuvres or smaller appetites. The casing will need to be a little thinner and the filling may show through the translucent white dough, but the taste is every bit as good.

Manapua fillings:

While the dough is rising, prepare the filling in sufficient time for it to cool in the refrigerator. The ratio of filling to bun is not high, so you want a well-flavored filling to offset the mild taste of the bread. A little texture in the meat or in added crunchy vegetables also makes a nice contrast. You will need about 2 tablespoons of filling per bun. This means that for twelve buns, you will need about a pound of meat and a cup of vegetables. Vary these proportions to get the filling you like.

(1) *Traditional char siu filling*

This is a sweet filling, usually colored a rather startling red in Hawaii.

> **1 pound char siu, diced**
> **2 tablespoons prepared an (red bean paste)**
> **4 green onions, chopped**
> **1 bunch Chinese parsley, chopped**
> **2 tablespoons soy sauce**
> **1 teaspoon sugar**
> **1 teaspoon salt**
> **Red coloring (optional)**

Combine all ingredients in a saucepan and cook for a few minutes to meld the flavors. Adjust seasoning. Allow to cool before stuffing buns.

(2) *Pork and mushroom filling*

This recipe is adapted from one in the Maui Extension Homemakers Council cookbook, *Still Many More of Our Favorite Recipes*. The use of canned meat and the substitution of jicama for water chestnuts are both typical of the Islands.

> **½ pound pork, diced**
> **1 cup ham or canned meat, diced**
> **½ cup mushrooms, chopped**
> **1 bunch Chinese parsley, chopped**
> **2 green onions, chopped**
> **2 tablespoons soy sauce**
> **½ teaspoon five-spice powder**
> **Salt to taste**
> **½ cup chop suey yam (jicama), chopped**

Fry pork until browned. Add the ham, mushrooms, Chinese parsley, green onions, soy sauce, and five-spice powder and cook for a few minutes. Adjust seasoning. Add the chop suey yam and allow to cool before stuffing buns.

(3) *Pork and black bean filling*

This is not a traditional Hawaiian way of making manapua but uses Chinese ingredients for a tasty filling.

1 tablespoon cooking oil
1 tablespoon ginger, finely chopped
1 tablespoon garlic, finely chopped
1 pound ground pork
1 hot green chili, finely chopped
1 tablespoon sherry
1 tablespoon sugar
3–4 tablespoons black bean paste
¼ cup water

Heat the oil in a large pan, add ginger and garlic, and fry just until fragrant. Add the pork and stir until cooked, breaking up any lumps. Add the chili, sherry, sugar, and black bean paste and stir. Add water and cook until flavors are amalgamated and the pork mixture is dry; skim off any excess fat and adjust seasoning to taste. Allow to cool.

(4) *Sweet manapua*

Use 2 cups an (sweetened red bean paste) to stuff the manapua.

. . .

MUSUBI

(Savory Rice Sandwiches)

Musubi are very simple preparations that fit into the same slot in the menu as sandwiches or hot dogs—snacks to eat on a picnic, a hike, at a sporting event, at midmorning for a hungry teenager. They have great potential.

4 cups cooked Calrose rice
4 one-inch-wide strips of nori
4 ume (Japanese pickled "plums"), pitted, optional

Divide the rice in four parts. Wet your hands and pick up one portion, cupping it in your hand. Press the ume, if you use it, on top. Gently fold the rice over the ume into the shape you want: a ball, a fat triangle. Pick up the nori and wrap around the musubi. You can use just one strip or several, to your taste. Dampen the ends of the nori to seal.

Yield: Four musubi

Note: Do not refrigerate because the rice will harden and no longer have a pleasing texture. To carry the musubi with you, cover with plastic wrap.

Variations: Add a slice of canned meat, preferably simmered in a little soy sauce and sugar, before wrapping in nori. Or add a slice of smoked salmon.

SEA BISCUITS, KANAKA PUDDING, AND SALOON PILOTS

O. A. Bushnell, professor of medical microbiology and medical history at the University of Hawaii, wrote a deeply informed novel, *Molokai*, based on a true story.[1] The narrator—perhaps modeled on the German bacteriologist Eduard Arning—has just arrived at the leper colony on the Kalaupapa Peninsula on the north shore of Molokai. Fresh from his studies in Germany with the great Dr. Koch, he is fascinated with the disease that is, in the early 1870s, the scourge of the Hawaiians. He is being entertained by the priest who has gone to live out his life with the unfortunates exiled to this desolate patch of land—in real life, Father Damien from Belgium.

> The priest came with portions of our breakfast. "I have only one dish. We use sea biscuits for plates." On his one dish he had laid out three large round crackers, flat and dry as shingles. Upon them, arranged just as they must have fallen from the sugar loaf as he chipped at it, were the moist nuggets and crumbs of raw brown sugar. Never in my life had I been served such poor fare.[2]

I imagine them sitting around the rough wooden table in the small wooden house in one corner of the peninsula, with the incessant trade winds blowing in off the ocean. The cliffs that cut Kalaupapa off from the rest of the island, cliffs that even today can be scaled only on foot or on muleback, are bright now but will soon be casting dark shadows. The land at their feet is brown and scrubby. The waves crash against the rocky beach. Ships cannot land there. The lepers, thrown overboard, swam to their prison if they could. Not all made it. Supplies too were hurled overboard because little or nothing grew on the bright, desolate peninsula.

Sea biscuits seem an appropriate meal. Sea biscuits (or hardtack or crackers) are unleavened bread, the oldest and most primitive of breads, going back deep in human history. Until the middle of the sixteenth century, the English

Saloon pilot crackers

word "biscuit" simply meant bread, a bread that was baked without salt or leavening, a bread that was baked twice to improve its keeping qualities.[3] After navigators began pushing out from Europe in the fifteenth century, sea biscuits became one of the first mass-produced foods, turned out in quantity by commercial bakers for navies and for crews of merchant ships. Sea biscuits must have fed Captain Cook's crew in the eighteenth century when he became the first European that we can be certain encountered the Hawaiian Islands. Sea biscuits were the fare of the sandalwood traders and the whalers and the missionaries from New England who arrived in Hawaii in the nineteenth century.

In the course of the nineteenth century, as techniques for making sea biscuits were improved and as tin cans for transporting them were invented, each region produced its own specialties, often finer in texture because of the addition of shortening and the use of mechanical mixing methods. In England, the great biscuit firms—Jacob and Peek Freans—began making their fortunes.[4] In New England, in 1828, less than a decade after the missionaries arrived in Hawaii, Timothy and Charles Cross began making Vermont Common Crackers in Montpelier, Vermont. Given the simple ingredients, one kind of biscuit differed from another chiefly in texture, depending on how they had been kneaded and rolled. Indeed, as anyone who has ever tried making homemade crackers can attest, it is difficult to achieve an appealing texture by hand. It is for this reason that Mr. G. F. Zimmer, who contributed the article on "biscuits" to the classic eleventh edition of the *Encyclopaedia Britannica*, was not a cook but a member of the Institute of Civil Engineering, and author of the *Mechanical Handling of Material*. He said not one word about the history, ingredients, or taste of biscuits.

In Hawaii, indeed across the Tropics, sea biscuits served well. Their low moisture content made them slow to spoil even in the tropical heat. After tin cans were available, the biscuits lasted even longer. (Even the tin cans in which they were packed were useful. Home economics teachers urged their use as makeshift ovens for baking meat loaf.[5]) Hawaii still imports biscuits from around the world, though the cracker industry has now expanded beyond Europe. The Jacob's Cream Crackers that I can buy in Chinatown in the hermetically sealed metal cartons of traditional blue and black design are made under license in Singapore and endearingly titled "Krim Krakers."[6] The "Cabin Crackers," made by Lee's All Vege Biscuits in handsome, shiny, rectangular, 10-pound tins with yellow labels, that I can buy in Laie on the northern corner of Oahu are shipped there from Fiji for the Fijians who perform in the Polynesian Cultural Center. Or they can opt for huge plastic buckets—the kind that spackling usually comes in—full of soda crackers.

Because the basic ingredients for crackers are simple, people in Hawaii began to make their own. The Hawaiians, for example, mixed flour, salt, and water, shaped patties, and baked them over the embers of guava wood, a minute or so on each side until golden brown. They used these homemade crackers (*pelena*), without butter or jelly, as a substitute for poi.[7] They were not the only ones to try making crackers. It was an obvious opening for small businesses. To this day, there are two companies turning out crackers in Hawaii.

Hawaii has its own name for crackers or hardtack: saloon pilots. Their name betrays their nautical origin. Sea biscuits were known as pilot bread from New England through the West Indies.[8] New England seamen must have brought the use of the word "pilot" for a sea biscuit with them to Hawaii. My suspicion is that "saloon" was added as the crackers became richer and finer than the original hardtack, because the saloon on a ship was usually reserved for the better-off passengers. Along with salted meat and fish and pickled meats, saloon pilots are one of many symptoms of the atavism of Hawaii's food. Neither crisp and tender like soda crackers, nor elegantly spotted with brown like water biscuits, their thickness, their chewiness, and their relative lack of salt make saloon pilots closer to what I imagine hardtack must originally have tasted like.

But Bushnell's story of the sea biscuits is not over. The priest turned to the third person in the group, Keanu, a Hawaiian or *kanaka*, as the Hawaiians called themselves. Like the other two, he was not a leper. Convicted of murder, he had agreed to let the doctor try out on him the potentially deadly experiment of implanting leprous tissue.

SALOON PILOTS AT DIAMOND BAKERY

Soon after World War I, a group of friends—Hidegoro Murai, Kikutaro Hiruya, and Natsu Muramoto—were looking for a business opportunity. Because no good crackers were then being made in Honolulu, they hatched a plan to found a bakery. On 12 October 1921, they opened their doors. But business did not flourish, perhaps because they knew little or nothing about commercial baking: one had worked for a large estate, one was a cook, another was raising children. They struggled on for 16 years while debts mounted, finally joining forces with Sam Dunphy, who did have some professional experience. From then on, business increased steadily. Today Diamond Bakery bakes over 40,000 pounds of cracker dough each week and distributes all over the Pacific.[9]

"If I have some tinned milk we could make us *kanaka* pudding—a real celebration."

"'*Kanaka* pudding?'"

"You do not know what it is? It is the people's favorite dessert. Keanu, tell him what is *kanaka* pudding." . . .

"You soak 'um—da beeskeet, I mean—all crumble' up—you soak 'um in da tea." . . . "Da cracker—when he get all sof'—you squeeze 'um—squeeze out da tea . . . An' den, s'pose you get sugah, can-creem —you poah 'um on top da sof' beesket . . . You get *kanaka* pudding."[10]

Here then the trio sit, eating sea biscuits topped by some raw sugar and dreaming about how they could make them into kanaka pudding if only they had a little canned milk. The sugar, by this time, was not such a luxury in Hawaii, which was growing sugar and hoping for big export markets in California. Tinned milk was a recent invention: Gail Borden had patented sweetened condensed milk in the mid-1850s; Nestlé was under way a decade later.[11]

At least until World War II, and perhaps longer, this was a favorite dessert of all social classes in Hawaii. Hawaiians softened crackers in hot water and enjoyed them with sugar or condensed milk and possibly a little butter as well.[12] Children in the public schools were praised for eschewing candy and thriftily choosing to buy crackers for dessert.[13] And the kamaainas, at the other end of the social scale, spread saloon pilots with condensed milk or soaked them in coffee, milk, and sugar and then set them on a saucer and added lots of butter.[14]

At first, using crackers as a pudding seemed strange because I associate them with savory foods, above all with cheese. In England, I do not recall ever having seen them eaten any other way. Yet the nearest thing in Hawaii appears to be the plantation habit of smearing them with bottled mayonnaise. As I thought about it, though, crackers took their place in a continuous spectrum of baked flour goods: leavened breads have more water; pastries have more water and fat; cookies have more water, fat, and sugar. The line between crackers and cookies is a thin one. In England, the very word "biscuit" can refer to either a cracker or a cookie; that is, to either a sweet or a savory baked good with a low moisture content. Salty crackers grade into mildly sweet digestive or arrowroot biscuits and they in turn to intensely sweet shortbreads and chocolate biscuits. Hawaii's kanaka pudding is not so very different, either, from the icebox cake made of slightly sweet chocolate cookies smothered in whipped cream popular in the Mainland United States.

So there you have it: the people of Hawaii took their own sugar, the humble ship's biscuit, and canned milk and turned it into a dessert that has remained popular until the present, albeit one of those simple, homestyle desserts that seldom makes it into the cookbooks.

NIIHAU PUDDING

This complex recipe for a cracker dessert—though still recognizably the same thing as kanaka pudding—is given by Dora Jane Isenberg Cole and Juliet Rice Wichman in their *Early Kauai Hospitality*. A variant of bread pudding, it is named for the small island of Niihau.

"Take one or two round saloon pilot crackers (hard tack) for each person to be served and soak them well in milk in a shallow, well buttered roasting pan. When well soaked, pour off any extra milk, being careful not to break the sodden saloon pilots. Then take generous spoonsful of soft butter and spread on each cracker, followed by a heaping tablespoonful of raw sugar [brown or better demerara sugar if not in Hawaii]. Cover the crackers well. (This can be done ahead of time, but don't let it dry out). About a half an hour before serving, put the pans in a hot oven (375–400) and bake until the sugar has melted and the cracker surface has become slightly crusty. Serve hot with thick cream."[15]

COMING TO TERMS WITH SPAM (AND VIENNA SAUSAGE AND CORNED BEEF AND SARDINES)

"SPAM[1]?" shuddered an acquaintance from Wisconsin. "You mean the SPAM we ate in the War?" Yes, that SPAM. In Hawaii, there is no dodging the question of SPAM (or of other canned meats and fish, for that matter). SPAM is an important protein for much of the state's population. SPAM is the subject of a whole cookbook, Ann Kondo Corum's only partially tongue-in-cheek *Hawaii's SPAM® Cookbook*.[2] SPAM sells out on grocery shelves and was hoarded during the Gulf War. SPAM is made into SPAM and eggs, SPAM and rice, SPAM sushi, SPAM musubi, and SPAM wonton. No SPAM? Then substitute luncheon meat or canned corned beef, Vienna sausages, or Holmes sardines.

To take on SPAM is to pick at all the ethnic and economic seams of Hawaii. To newcomers, to nutritionists, to those with pretensions to gourmet status, SPAM is an embarrassment, serviceable during wartime rationing perhaps, but too salty, too fatty, too overprocessed to be eaten in these enlightened times. It contains—horrors—256 fat calories for every 4-ounce serving. Its manufacturer—can you imagine?—advertises not recipes but SPAM carving contests.[3]

As a child in postwar Britain, I too was less than enamored of SPAM. It turned up regularly for school lunches in the form of SPAM fritters, slices of SPAM dipped in a batter and deep-fried (surely one of the worst things to do with an already fatty meat), one more in the series of horrors produced by the school cooks, whose efforts exemplified the popular reputation of British food. Blessed with sympathetic parents who regarded as so much rot the theory that choking down bad food develops moral fiber, I was granted the privilege of small helpings. But on leaving school, SPAM was one food I happily forgot.

That is, until I came to Hawaii. Even now, I can't say that I yearn for SPAM fritters, or that I regard SPAM sushi as a great innovation, or that SPAM is on my weekly shopping list. But SPAM is so satisfyingly easy to dismiss that I have become uneasy about my smugness. I'm no longer sure that a well-fed urbanite like myself, with a full freezer and supermarkets just down the road, should be too sniffy about canned meat. My alternatives to SPAM are fresh meats, not dried and salted meat and fish. I do not have to spend hours fishing, calm or storm, but simply pop down to the local market. I do not have to worry about my fish going bad in the tropical heat, I just stick it in the refrigerator or freezer. I am not concerned that fresh fish costs more than SPAM because I can afford it. And what I suffer from is an excess, not a deficiency, of fat in my diet.

Such considerations make me a little more aware of why in remote Pacific islands (and before that among the poor and in far-flung parts of the world), SPAM, like other canned meats, had such appeal. When scientists discovered how to electroplate a neutral tin lining on to steel cans in the 1870s, and canned meats first began to appear, they were hailed as a great innovation. The rapidly growing towns in Europe and the eastern United States were full of people hungering for something other than the endless salt meats that, given the lack of refrigeration and mass distribution, were the lot of most of the population—if they had meat at all. Entrepreneurs opened up canning operations on the distant ranges of the American West, Australia, and Argentina, where there was plenty of beef and mutton but no one to sell it to. The editors of the second edition of Mrs. Beeton's classic *Household Management*, published in 1888, inserted a new chapter on canned meat.[4] If canned Australian beef was already on British tables, could canned wallaby and parrot be far behind? For good measure, they added recipes for roast wallaby and parrot pie to the chapter on foreign and colonial cooking.

"It must be a local delicacy."

Ultimately, though, the editors' enthusiasm for the first canned meats was muted. Canned meat, they decided, was overcooked, fibrous, and lacking in flavor. They owned, though, that it might be a useful stopgap for the working poor who could not afford fresh or refrigerated meat and a handy staple on board ship. And—what they did not say and neither knew nor cared about from their British perspective—for the same reasons, plantation workers and Pacific Islanders would welcome it as an addition to their diet. In the fishing villages and the plantations of Hawaii, canned luncheon meat and sardines became a regular part of the diet.

Meanwhile, the Hormel Company set about designing a canned meat that was neither tough nor bland. To beat the toughness, they ground pork up finely; to give it savor, they spiced it up with salt, sugar, and a variety of other flavorings. They held a competition for a catchy name: in 1937, a certain Keith Daugneau submitted the winning entry—SPAM (spiced ham)—and walked off with the $100 prize. SPAM joined and then overtook sardines, luncheon meat, corned beef, and Vienna sausages as a favorite. All keep well, are quick and easy to prepare, can be stretched with vegetables, and taste good with rice. In World War II, when offshore fishing was prohibited, SPAM helped fill the gap.

Hawaii gives SPAM (and the other canned meats) an Asian or Pacific twist. It is perhaps most commonly fried and served with rice (and maybe eggs) for breakfast, lunch, and dinner. Victor Hao Li, the urbane former president of the federally funded East-West Center, suggested "Begin the day with thickly sliced Spam, fried crisp on the outside, served with rice and sunny-side eggs plus a streak of oyster sauce across the top. (In truth, this really is better than jook.)"[5] Or it can be made into a musubi, as does John DeSoto, a Council member of the City and County of Honolulu. If his name is anything to go by (and given the high intermarriage rate, this is far from an infallible guide in Hawaii), DeSoto is not Japanese, but he offers what is in effect a recipe for SPAM musubi, demonstrating his bonds with his constituents. He explains that "When I was a kid, we always had rice and nori and SPAM around the house, and we would eat those things in various ways. But when there were leftovers, we put them together, creating a kind of sandwich. Since this particular one featured SPAM and since this is a family recipe, we called it a DeSPAMwich. Besides being good to eat, the DeSPAMwich taught me a valuable lesson: To make something good you don't always have to use conventional things in conventional ways. Sometimes, by using what is available and a little imagination, you can create something just as good, sometimes even better."[6]

SPAM can be wrapped in ti leaves or foil and left roasting in the ashes while you go fishing. It is relished cooked in a little soy sauce, sugar, mirin, and ginger and served on toothpicks for cocktails. It is a common stuffing for deep-fried wonton. It can be mixed with Chinese fishcake. It can be used to stuff aburage; you can make SPAM lumpia with kamaboko, green onion, and eggs. Just as good is SPAM fried rice or chow fun or stir-fry. It is standard as a topping for saimin. If your taste runs to the Japanese, SPAM can be used to stuff lotus root or cooked with miso or daikon, and, of course, it makes excellent tempura. Or if it runs to the Korean, you can skewer squares of SPAM with squares of kim chee, dredge them in flour, dip in beaten egg, and deep-fry to make SPAM and kim chee jun. Needless to say it also combines happily with haole foods to make omelettes, meatballs, burgers, quiche, or macaroni and cheese. Sometimes it is even eaten on white bread as a sandwich.

Locals, then, understandably regard SPAM as thrifty and tasty, a food of childhood, a food of family meals and picnics at the beach, a food of convenience. A food of convenience, moreover, with a certain status, harking back to the time when buying something canned conveyed affluence and keeping up with the times. Even the fact that it can be carved is endearing because it makes SPAM easy to shape for sushi and musubi. It is the motherhood-and-apple-pie of Hawaii, not specific to any ethnic group, and hence invoked by politicians to show just how deep their Local roots go. The governor can refer to his State of the State address to the Legislature as a "SPAM-and-rice kind of speech" and have the quip reported approvingly in all the newspapers. Locals get through over 4 million cans every year; that is more than four cans for every man, woman, and child in the state, making us the SPAM champions of the country: over three times more SPAM than any other state in the Union. No wonder that when Hormel came out with Lite SPAM they used Hawaii as one of their test sites.

Maybe now that the standard of living has risen in Hawaii, politicians should be moving away from the inverse snobbery of SPAM, and Locals should be cutting it out of their diet. But for what? For a fast-food hamburger covered with glutinous sauce on a slimy bun, accompanied by french-fried processed potatoes? Surely, for both flavor and health, the SPAM musubi, with its good rice, its wrapping of nori, and the sliver of SPAM with a touch of salt and sugar and soy sauce, is a better bet. Shudders or not, in Hawaii SPAM continues to be something to be reckoned with.

SORTING OUT SUSHI

Many, if not most, Locals consider any gathering incomplete without sushi, whether it be a party, a picnic, New Year, or Thanksgiving. Sushi is worthy of an entire treatise to itself, encompassing a plethora of ways of serving rice flavored with sweetened vinegar. It ranges from the sophisticated (a sliver of rice covered with flying fish roe) to the basic (chunks of hot dog buried in sushi rice). Californians are apt to look down their noses at Local sushi—"Come to California," they insist, "where you can get real sushi." Why avocado sushi is more real (as opposed to more upmarket) than hot dog sushi escapes me. Many Locals find mainland sushi bland and oversweetened compared with the tangier, vinegary flavor preferred in the Islands. Similarly, much, though not all, Japanese sushi is tangier than Hawaiian, except when topped by the delicate sashimi.[1] A Japanese-American acquaintance told me that her nephews and nieces, visiting from Seattle while their mother recuperated from an illness, complained that Island rice was bland and unsalted. Rather than salt the rice, she prepared them sushi rice, which apparently did the trick.

Many kinds of sushi are better savored at a sushi bar or bought from a specialty shop than made at home. Some of the major varieties encountered in Hawaii are the following:

Nigiri sushi (finger sushi). The sushi rice is shaped by hand into flattened oblongs and topped with seafood such as shrimp, cooked octopus, sashimi, or fish roe, or with omelette, cucumber, pickled daikon, or even Korean barbecue.

Inari sushi (cone sushi). Fried bean curd (aburage) is cut in half to form cones, simmered in a broth, and stuffed with sushi rice and vegetables such as finely cut carrots, string beans, or mushrooms.

Maki sushi (rolled sushi). Nori (dried seaweed sheets) is placed on a bamboo mat, spread with sushi rice, stuffed with slices of carrot, watercress, mushrooms, gobo, seasoned eel, or kamaboko, rolled up, and cut into 1-inch servings.

Egg roll sushi. Similar to maki sushi except that a thin layer of omelette is substituted for the nori.

Temaki sushi (hand-rolled sushi). Sushi rice and a choice of flavorings such as tuna, fish roe, crab, crab sticks, SPAM or luncheon meat, cucumber, avocado, or sprouts are rolled in half sheets of nori to form a small cone and dipped in soy sauce, mustard, or wasabi before eating.

Pan sushi. Sushi rice and filling layered in a cake pan and cut into squares to serve.

PAN SUSHI FOR TWENTY-FOUR

Sushi's reputation is that of an upmarket food, best prepared professionally. There are humble versions of sushi, however, easygoing dishes that working wives put together after a day in the office or the classroom. What I give here is a very simple pan sushi that might be taken on a picnic for the extended family at the beach or one of Honolulu's parks on a Sunday, or to a tailgate party before a University of Hawaii football game on a Saturday.[2]

For this you will need 12 cups of cooked rice, sushi sauce, and topping.

Rice:

> **4 cups Calrose rice**
> **5 cups water**

Cook the rice, following instructions on p. 33. While the rice is cooking, assemble the sauce and the topping.

Sushi sauce:

> **1 cup rice vinegar**
> **¾ cup sugar**
> **2 tablespoons mirin**
> **1 tablespoon salt**

Combine all the ingredients and heat until the sugar and salt have dissolved.

Yield: Two cups (sufficient for 12 cups of cooked rice)

Topping:
2 8-ounce cans tuna, drained
2 tablespoons mirin
¼ cup sugar
¼ cup soy sauce
4 eggs
1 tablespoon water
Red or green shrimp flakes (to taste)
Pickled red ginger

Cook tuna with mirin, sugar, and soy sauce for a minute or two, stirring constantly. Set aside. Beat the eggs with a tablespoon of water. Film a frying pan with a couple of drops of oil and spoon in enough of the egg mixture to make a very thin omelette. Turn. When fully cooked, place on a cutting board and cut into ¼-inch strips (the Japanese use a special rectangular pan, but an ordinary frying pan will do).

To assemble: While the rice is still hot, turn it into a large, shallow container. (There is a beautiful wooden tub that is sold especially for this; the wood helps absorb the moisture. But you can use a shallow bowl.) Toss the rice with the sushi sauce, fanning it all the while to help it cool quickly. Have ready a 9 by 13 inch pan lined with waxed paper. Sprinkle shrimp flakes to make an even dusting across the paper. Sprinkle the egg strips on top of this and then the tuna. Top with the sushi rice. Cover with another layer of waxed paper and press down gently. Remove paper. Cool rice, then invert on serving tray. Cut into even, bite-sized pieces and garnish with pickled ginger.

SHAVE ICE: NO MERE SNOW CONE THIS

One October morning in the fall of 1991, I happened to spot a handwritten notice in the window of a mom-and-pop storefront on School Street. It proclaimed the fortieth anniversary of the opening of the B & S Store in 1951, years before statehood, and long before the noisy freeway isolated School Street from downtown Honolulu just a few blocks away. The Higas, it announced, were looking forward to their fiftieth anniversary in 2001. Pinned to the faded brown door that opened into the shop were fan-shaped pieces of paper, each covered with writing yellowed almost to invisibility by the insistent sun. Peering more closely, I could see that these were flattened paper shave-ice cones, each message praising the store's outstanding product. Next to them was a clipping from the local newspaper, showing that readers had ranked B & S third on Oahu for shave ice, just behind the better-known Matsumoto and Aoki Stores in the surfing town of Haleiwa on the North Shore.

Shave ice paper cones with special messages for the store owner

This section of School Street hardly seemed a likely spot to run across anything prizewinning. Drivers pass B & S without even noticing. Even walkers stroll past the storefront, its small window unobtrusive among the sagging green-and-white frame houses, thrift stores, luau supply stores, and weedy vacant lots that make up the street. The traffic roars on the freeway, heat and dust swirl up from the sidewalk, and cars line up on the on-ramp, their exhausts spewing out yet more heat on one of the hottest days of the year.

Stepping into the darkness, a relief from the blazing sun on the concrete pavement, I found the owner, Mr. Higa, a small man with a shy, intelligent face, sitting behind the counter, fanning himself with a heart-shaped fan of palm fronds, with shelves of gum and soy sauce and crackers and canned meat arrayed behind him. To his right was the shave ice machine. It belongs in a museum of industrial art, a marvelous creation of silvered wheels and neatly punched ratchets. I placed my order, and Mr. Higa went off to the freezer, heaved out a fresh block of ice, and placed it at the bottom of the machine on a metal plate punctuated with sharp angled blades. Then he adjusted the plate so that the ice was held fast by a fixed, toothed upper plate. As he pressed a foot pedal, the wheels started to turn, the lower plate rotated, and the blades shaved transparent slivers of ice.

In the old days, the ice was shaved by hand, Mr. Higa said, stopping for a moment and gesturing as if he were planing a piece of wood. He remembered it from his childhood in Japan, where his parents, immigrants to Hawaii from Okinawa, had sent him home to be educated. His machine is one of the oldest in the Islands, acquired over 40 years ago when he first opened the store. Originally it was hand cranked, but many years ago he attached a rubber belt and a small electric motor to the main wheel. There are only two or three such machines left in Honolulu, he added proudly, and they produce the lightest, finest shavings of ice. The newer machines don't do that, neither the pneumatic-looking machines manufactured in the 1950s nor the big modern ones.

As he spoke, Mr. Higa caught the ice in his cupped hands, eased it into a paper cone, and deftly mounded it into a snowy pile twice the height of the cone. Rough handling would have crushed the ice and destroyed the feathery texture that is crucial to a good shave ice. He asked me what flavor I wanted, gesturing to a row of bottles, filled with crimson and turquoise and aquamarine and lemon yellow liquids and topped with metal spouts. His wife mixes up these syrups, he continued, using sugar, flavor extract, color, and acid for preservation, all bought from a local supplier. I opted for pineapple. He poured the brilliant sunflower-colored syrup all over the ice, its color fading slightly as it sank in, handed me a wooden ice cream spoon, and I relished the icy sweet taste melting on my tongue. Newcomers sometimes make the mistake of confusing shave ice with snow cones, but a quick taste is enough to dispel such nonsense. The shaved ice is smoother on the tongue, the flakes of ice hold the syrup in suspension so that it does not end up in a pool at the bottom of the cone, and you cannot detect the difference between the ice and the flavor, which are melded into one delicious, cooling sensation. Had I wanted something more substantial, I could have asked for a spoonful of sweetened azuki beans in the cone or ice cream on top. But even the most basic form, and even the suspiciously synthetic flavors and colors, are wonderfully refreshing in hot weather.

Shave ice (or ice shave as it is called on the outer islands) can be found in mom-and-pop stores, beachfront lunch wagons, and crack seed stores all over the Islands. What marks the name as pidgin is the dropping of the final "d," just as the "ed" is dropped in crack seed. Surfers pick it up after hours on the waves, hikers on their way down from the mountains, and children on their way

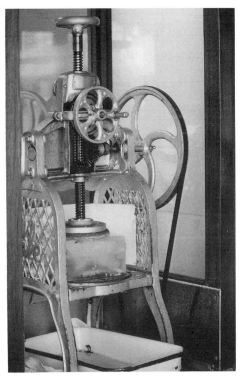

SHAVE ICE

PLAIN ~/ FLAVORS
w/ ICE CREAM
or
AZUKI BEANS
or
ICE CREAM + BEANS

	Small	Large
	.80¢	.90¢
	1.10	1.20
	1.15	
	1.20	

FLAVORS
ALL SYRUPS ARE HOMEMADE

CHERRY	ROOT BEER
LEMON	COCONUT (pink)
GRAPE	PASSION FRUIT (Lilikoi)
LIME	PINEAPPLE (blue)
ORANGE	VANILLA (LT. BROWN)
BANANA	STRAWBERRY

HAWAIIAN DELIGHT — Pineapple, Banana, Coconut
VOLCANO — Lilikoi, Banana, Splash of Strawberry
RAINBOW — Lemon, Strawberry, Pineapple

home from school. The flavors and colors are riotous: new ones are constantly developed: banana, bubble gum, lilikoi, li hing mui, green tea, coconut (which for some reason is a vivid blue), strawberry, vanilla, lemon-lime, coke, cherry, grape, watermelon, root beer, and fruit punch. In the 1950s, children used to order the ice by color, knowing what flavor each color represented; a mix of colors was called *kalakoa*, Hawaiian for calico, and hence for variegated colors as in the leaves of the croton plant.[1]

Before that, in the hot, red, dusty plantation camps, any ice must have made a welcome treat after a long day in the fields. One popular concoction was "ice cake," a very simple preparation of ice cubes made with a mixture of water and condensed milk or fruit juice. Shave ice, which the Japanese brought to the Islands, probably in the 1920s or 1930s, was more sophisticated. It remains popular in Japan, which is still the source of shave ice machines and where you can buy a variety of different kinds: fruit, snow (with condensed milk), *calpis* (with fermented goat's milk), and azuki beans. In all of them, syrup is essential, but the ordering of the ingredients—whether the ice or the syrup or the additional ingredients are added first or last—varies from region to region.[2]

Left: A classic shave ice machine

Right: Types and flavors of shave ice

A halo-halo stand at a Filipino festival

In the Americas, however, shave ice is identified with Hawaii. A sign in the scruffy West Texas border town of Del Rio advertises "Hawaii shave ice—25 flavors." A sparkling new shopping mall in Queretaro, Mexico, its marble floors, Ralph Lauren shirts, and Benetton sweaters a sharp contrast to the dusty streets outside, boasts a shave ice stand, complete with a Japanese machine distributed by a company from Oakland, California, selling *aloha de limón*, *piña Hawaiiana*, *naranja Waikiki*, and *aloha de uva* (lime aloha, Hawaiian pineapple, Waikiki orange, and grape aloha).

All this I have learned since my conversation with Mr. Higa. Then, entranced with his machine, I asked Mr. Higa if I might take a photograph. He was delighted, though he drew the line at appearing in the photograph himself, and bustled off to the back of the store to turn on the fluorescent lights. In return, he asked me to sign one of his paper cones because I had come to Hawaii all the way from England. I was honored. I added my signature to those of a host of others: the head of the fire company; the then Superintendent of Education; visitors from Japan, the mainland, and Canada; the Cincinnati Reds; and a compatriot who had somehow found his way to the B & S Store on School Street, His Reverence, the Episcopalian Bishop of Chester, England.

ICE CAKE

(Plantation-Style Flavored Ice)

Once in a while, community cookbooks, although they usually go for the impressive or the voguish, give a glimpse of simple, everyday food, the kind that hardly needs a recipe. Such a glimpse occurs in the original *Plantation Village Cookbook*, a part of the fund-raising effort for a plantation village museum.[3] Sei Kaneshiro contributed instructions for making ice cake. He reported that plantation residents made it in old-fashioned aluminum ice cube trays with handles to release the ice. One can of condensed milk was mixed with five cans of water and a can of syrup, both measured out with the empty condensed milk can.

SHAVE ICE

(Fruit-Flavored Syrup over Shaved Ice)

In Hawaii, shave ice is thought of as a snack and thirst quencher, but I see no reason not to think of it as akin to sorbets and sherbets, in cone-shaped martini glasses or dessert dishes. If you have prepared syrup and containers of ice in the freezer, it does not take long to shave enough ice for half a dozen people.

It cannot be overemphasized that shave ice is *not* crushed ice.[4] Ice crushed in a blender gives a quite different texture and even (because of the way it distributes the ingredients) a different flavor. Home shave ice machines can be purchased relatively inexpensively from Asian stores and from specialty mail-order catalogs. They are made in Japan, simple plastic frames with plastic containers for freezing the ice and an embedded razor blade for shaving it—none of the glamour of Mr. Higa's machine. But they do the essential thing: they shave, not crush, the ice. When you pour a syrup or syrupy fruit over the ice, it holds the syrup.

Having first purchased your shave ice machine, you use the plastic containers provided to freeze water, place the frozen block in the machine, and turn the handle to shave the ice. To complete, you can use any commercially available syrup, and there are many of high quality that can be obtained. For homemade coconut syrup, see p. 195.

. . .

AN MITSUMAME

(Japanese Mixed Fruits and Confections with Shaved Ice)

An mitsumame, a mixture of cubes of gelatin, tiny rice-flour dumplings, sweetened red bean paste, and a variety of cubed fruits gently tossed with syrup and shaved ice, is a dessert rather than a drink and a celebration of contrasting textures rather than a bombardment of sweetness. It is not commonly encountered in public in Hawaii, but I have included it because it is so closely related to (and perhaps the source of) related icy dessert drinks from across Southeast Asia that are also to be found in Hawaii. The Filipino halo-halo is particularly common, but Thais and Vietnamese have their own versions as well.

The members of the committee of the Japanese Cultural Center of Hawaii who put together the book on the legacy of the Japanese in Hawaii began by describing an mitsumame as "fruit cocktail with agar-agar and red beans."[5] Do not be deterred by the image of pallid canned fruit cocktail mixed with kidney beans that this evokes; the mixture of fresh fruits, slippery cubes of gelatin, rice-flour dumplings, and sweet, floury bean paste with a texture something like that of marzipan, in a cool mix of syrup and shave ice makes a light, tasty, and colorful ending to dinner on a warm night. Prepare the rice-flour dumplings, the gelatin, and the syrup in advance and it can be assembled quite quickly. For the best appearance and sensation, make sure that the solid ingredients are all cut to the same ½-inch size and that the fruits are of nicely contrasting colors.

> **2–3 cups fruit cut into ½-inch cubes and chilled (melons, mangoes, lychees, apples, Asian pears, etc.)**
> **1 12-ounce can azuki-bean paste**
> **1 recipe dango (rice flour) dumplings (see p. 92)**
> **1 recipe kanten (gelatin) cubes (see p. 49)**
> **1 cup syrup made from boiling together 1 cup water and 1 cup sugar**

Combine solid ingredients in a large glass bowl. Add syrup and toss gently. Add enough shaved ice to pack and chill the contents and gently mix again. Ladle into chilled individual glass bowls and eat with small spoons.

Yield: six servings

• ■ •

HALO-HALO

(Filipino Mixed Fruits and Confections with Shaved Ice)

An mitsumame is similar to another dish popular in the Islands, the Filipino halo-halo (from the Tagalog meaning "mix-mix"), an exuberant conglomeration of sweetened beans, jackfruit, young coconut, and fruits, all mixed in ice and covered with a syrup or condensed milk.[6] In the 1920s when ice plants became operational, the Japanese "refreshment parlors" in the Philippines began serving *mongo con hielo*, sweetened red beans, shave ice, and evaporated milk. In Hawaii, halo-halo can be found in Filipino restaurants and festivals. It can contain from three to twelve items, including coconut (in various forms), sweet potato, *ube* (purple yam jam), sugar palm fruit, jackfruit seeds, red azuki beans, bananas, flaked rice, *leche flan* (crème caramel), and cubes of gelatin. It's a combination of soft, slick, and gelatinous textures unfamiliar to Caucasians but well worth exploring. In Filipino stores in Hawaii, you can often find a shelf with bowls of these different ingredients all ready to be combined and topped with shaved ice. Preparing them oneself is difficult for the home cook far from the Tropics. A compromise is perhaps the best that can be hoped for, and this can be achieved by buying a jar of Filipino halo-halo mix, which contains a selection of these ingredients in a sugar syrup. In Hawaii, this is in every grocery store. Elsewhere you will need to find an Asian specialty store. Empty into a bowl, cover with finely shaved ice, and then pour condensed milk over the top. Addictive.

CRACK SEED: THE MEI AND THE UME

Facing the parking lot on the ground floor of the largest shopping mall in the Pacific, the Ala Moana Center between downtown Honolulu and Waikiki, is a crack seed store. The enticing aroma of anise wafts out, battling the smell of hot gasoline. Inside, it has a typical crack seed store layout: a large central plinth laden with tall glass candy jars and shelves around the walls with further jars.[1] The jars are full of preserved fruits, red and brown and green and black, some of them gleaming with syrup, some frosted with sugar, and yet others wrinkled and dusted with salt, as many as forty or fifty different varieties. Their names are poetry: li hing mui, Maui-style sweet plum, mui plum, preserved chuan pei, chen pi seedless, mixed fruit, dried whole fruit, apricot poo ton lee, red olive, green olive, candy ginger, Hilo slice ginger, lemon juice ginger, wet li hing mango, seedless mango, dry mango, red mango, wet lemon, shredded mango, guava peel, sweet sour seed, sweet sour lemon, ginger, licorice peach, wet ling hui, pickled mango, kam cho ginger, lemon strip, dried mango with skin, wet lemon peel, lemon peel, tender plum, sweet whole plum, dried slice olive, rose plum, preserve kumquats, baby seed, honey mango, sweet whole seed, cherry seed, rock salt plum, seedless plum, sweet sour prune, kam cho harm mui, sweet sour apricot, kam chao whole lemon, kam chao slice lemon.

This collection of preserved fruits is what in Hawaii goes by the Chinese name of *see mui* (pronounced see moy) or, much more commonly, by the Local name of "crack seed": "seed" for the stones of the fruits that are often left in, "crack" for the habit of cracking the stone to expose the kernel, enhancing the flavor. (In English, this would be "cracked," but pidgin drops the last consonant). Seed is the generic name; the specific names are given in a random mixture of English and Chinese.

Picking a jar at whim, I asked the sales girl for 4 ounces. She opened the jar, filling the store with a rich anisey-fruity smell.[2] I left the store, opened the plastic bag, took out a dull pink, wrinkled object about the size of a gumdrop, and bit into it. Whatever this was, it was not, definitely not, candy. It tasted of

PART 1: LOCAL FOOD

nothing but salt, too salty to eat, almost pure salt, surrounding a small hard seed. This, I was to discover, was li hing mui. (The name apparently meant traveling plum, because soldiers used to carry the dried fruit with them.)[3] By sheer chance, I had lit upon one of the saltiest of the tribe of crack seeds. Other seeds were a little easier on my haole taste buds, the proportions of sugar and anise to salt being higher, the fruit around the seed being a little less dehydrated. Sweet sour seed, about the same size, but dark brown and looking as if it had been rolled in half-dried lawn mowings, is much softer and, as the name suggests, quite sweet. In a rock salt plum, the flesh covering the stone is sparse but it is not dry as bone, and the salt is not overwhelming; an anise flavor comes through. It makes a very satisfying morsel to suck on. The term "seed" even stretches to seedless seed. Mango strips, for example, are slices of green mango, skin still on, colored red, somewhat chewy, and tasting of salt, sugar, and anise, but without a seed. Shredded lemon peel comprises a collection of grayish strips about an inch long and one-eighth inch on the side that are soft to the bite with the familiar anise flavor heightened somewhat by the bitterness of the peel. In short, variations in texture are as important as taste in distinguishing different seeds.

Chinese immigrants from Canton brought crack seed to Hawaii in the nineteenth century. But you will not find recipes for seed or references to seed in Chinese cookbooks, any more than mainland cookbooks will enlighten you about M&Ms or licorice whips or Baby Ruths. Instead you have to turn to the work of anthropologists and food historians such as E. N. Anderson, who was

THE YICK LUNG COMPANY

This venerable Hawaii crack seed company is run, not, as you might expect, by families with the name of Yick or Lung, but by the third generation of the Yee family, who explain that the name means "profitable enterprise" in Chinese.[4] Their grandparents came to Hawaii from China in 1898 and founded the company a couple of years later. They imported the salted "plums," the li hing mui, from China.

The Yees discovered that local people liked a variety of sweet and sour tastes and began making different "sauces" to vary the flavor. They added new items to the list, such as mango and cherry seeds. One brother ran a store on Lusitana Street on the slopes of Punchbowl Crater just north of downtown Honolulu, the other peddled the seed from a horse-drawn carriage. Indeed, the family claims that it was their grandfather who gave seed its local name when he noticed that, after they had sucked off all the meat, some people enjoyed cracking the seed to eat the bitter-tasting kernel inside. Now, almost a century later, the company has plans to export to Europe and Asia.

kind enough to expand for me his discussion of Chinese preserved fruits in *The Food of China*, as well as to take me to his garden to see the plant that provides the seed.[5] In China, seed was made from the fruits of *Prunus mume*, often called a plum tree. In fact, it is not a plum at all. It is a quite distinct species, closer to an apricot, known to botanists, plant experts, and the nursery trade as the oriental flowering apricot. It belongs with *Prunus armeniaca* (the ordinary apricot) in the section *Armeniaca* of the genus *Prunus*, not with *Prunus salicina*, the plum or li in Chinese. In California, the trees are grown as ornamentals; presumably the apricot-colored, sour fruit goes largely to waste. But the Chinese dried and pickled it in a multitude of ways (think of plum sauce, for example), creating the *suan mei*, or soured fruits, for snacks or accompaniments to meat.

I have never encountered seed in a meat dish in a Chinese restaurant in Hawaii, nor have I seen reference to it in any of the Local Chinese cookbooks. But *everyone* in Hawaii, not just the Chinese, snacks on crack seed. During World War II, when imported seed was hard to come by, a whole genre of substitute homemade seed sprang up, using local ingredients. As far as I know, *Prunus mume* has never been grown commercially in Hawaii. But the tamarind tree (see p. 189–190), for example, has acidy-sweet pulp in its long leguminous pods—a little like the flesh of a dried apricot—that reminded Locals of the mei.[6] The most popular substitutes, though, were prunes and mangoes, often spiced up with the addition of some commercial seed, particularly li hing mui. Those days of scarcity are over; half a dozen firms in Hawaii manufacture or import seed.

Today children pick up crack seed, along with manapua and shave ice, to chew on as they make their way home from school. They might also find American and European candy; legumes of many kinds, such as deep-fried green peas hot with horseradish flavoring, crunchy fried horse beans (broad beans or fava beans), peanuts boiled with anise, boiled soybeans to be popped out of the pod for eating; mochi crunch (arare crackers) in all kinds of shapes: golden, shiny, and flecked with sesame seeds or *nori*; dried fish, such as shredded codfish, flattened squid, tiny anchovies, dusty pink dried shrimp. If there is no crack seed store nearby, they have only to go to any convenience store, its neon lights casting hard shadows and the smell of hot dogs rotating on spokes replacing the aroma of fruit and licorice, and take a prepacked cellophane package from the end of one of the display shelves. Homesick students away on the mainland call and beg "Send seed." They may not know it, but it is possible to buy seed on the mainland. Asian stores usually carry a small selection of prepacked seed. Recently hygienic modern alternatives to the old crack seed jars have begun to appear, big plastic bags full of individually wrapped and labeled seed imported from Taiwan and Singapore. But they offer neither the range of a Hawaiian crack seed store nor Local varieties such as mango seed.[7]

Crack seed can be bought in any amount

PART 1: LOCAL FOOD

Crack seed in Hawaii might be compared with pizza on the mainland. What was, in its home country, a recognized but minor kind of food, has exploded into a cacophany of variants and a much greater importance. It might also be compared with candy. As countless varieties of candy are made from sugar and a few flavorings such as chocolate and nuts, so countless varieties of crack seed have been spun out of the basic ingredients of fruit, salt, sugar, and anise. New combinations are constantly being developed: two recent entries are dried cranberry li hing mui and li hing mui gummi bears.

The more I learned about the *mei*, the more intriguing it became, cropping up all over the place not only in Chinese cuisine but also in Japanese. As common as crack seed in Hawaii is the Japanese *ume*, the cherry-sized, pink "pickled plum." I have never seen the two associated. But the *mei* is none other than the plum from which the *ume* is made—the names, of course, have the same origin. The Japanese in Japan and in Hawaii nibble on it for breakfast, put it in the middle of their lunch musubi, and drink "plum" wine made from it for celebrations.

But there is more than just cuisine to the *mei*. In the Asian galleries of the Honolulu Academy of Art, surely one of the most beautiful art galleries in the United States with its low, sweeping roofs and interlocking outdoor courtyards, is an exquisite six-fold screen composed by Kiitsu Suzuki (1796–1858) around 1850. It depicts fragile white "plum" blossoms on a gnarled branch with red camellia blossoms in the background. It is but one of thousands of such depictions in Chinese and Japanese art. The tree defies the bitter winter, its habit of blossoming in January and February making it a potent symbol in Taoism. Plum blossoms and crack seed. Something to think about as you lick the salt off a li hing mui.

Crack seed, like candy, is more often bought in a store than made at home. But the following recipes are common in Hawaii cookbooks. I imagine that such recipes were first developed to stretch scarce supplies of seed, perhaps during World War II.

MANGO STRIPS

(Five-Spice Flavored Preserved Mango)

Mango seed not only tastes good, but helps dispose of that enormous crop from the tree in the backyard. It is always made from green mangoes; the seed is easy to cut through, and the flesh is still firm and tangy.

1 gallon of strips about 2 inches long and ¼–⅓ inch square cut from green mangoes (a few odd-sized pieces don't matter, except aesthetically)
1 pound brown sugar
2 cups white sugar
¼ cup lemon juice or lime juice
½ cup water
1 tablespoon salt
2 teaspoons five-spice powder (or to taste)
½ teaspoon red coloring (optional)

Cut the green mangoes and leave in a salt solution overnight. Drain and spread the mangoes on a tray and leave in the hot sun for a day or two until they are partially dried out. (In less sunny spots, partially dry on the lowest setting in the oven or in a dehydrator.) Bring brown sugar, white sugar, lemon juice, water, and salt to a boil and stir until sugar is dissolved. Add the mangoes and simmer for 15 minutes (you are aiming for a tender but firm consistency, with almost no liquid left). Add spices and coloring and cook for 5 more minutes. Store in sterilized jars. Serve when and as you would candy.

Yield: 1 gallon

Note: Mango shreds and mango seed are equally popular. For the first, shred the mango; for the second, cut small green mangoes in half through the seed. Then proceed in the same way, adjusting the drying and cooking times appropriately.

· · ·

PRUNE WET SEEDS

(Five-Spice Flavored Prunes)

Prunes, readily available and with a sweet-sour taste, are also popular for homemade seed, though the recipes usually require that you already have two commercially produced seeds, lemon peel and li hing mui. With these, the recipe is simplicity itself. Outside Hawaii, li hing mui can be obtained in Asian stores, and possibly lemon peel too. If not, you can use the salted lemons in the recipe that follows (if you are patient enough to wait a year).

1 tablespoon five-spice powder
2 tablespoons whiskey
1½ cups lemon juice
3 tablespoons salt
3 whole cloves
1 pound brown sugar
8 ounces lemon peel from crack seed store (wet or dry)
8 ounces li hing mui from crack seed store
Eight 12-ounce packets of pitted prunes

Mix five-spice powder, whiskey, lemon juice, salt, cloves, and brown sugar in a large bowl. Stir in the lemon peel, li hing mui, and prunes. Let stand for 5 days, shaking occasionally. Store in sterilized jars. These are usually eaten like candy, but they are also good (though not traditional) inserted in the middle of a pork loin roast.

. . .

SALTED LEMON

On lanais in Honolulu, it is common to see large jars of these lemons sitting in the sun. Apart from being used to make prune mui, they make an excellent drink when water and sugar are added. To use as a traditional remedy for a cold or cough, infuse in boiling water for 20 minutes and sip the water.

Salted lemons are easy to make, though you have to wait for the better part of a year. Exact amounts are not important, but it is important to realize that the lemons will shrink to ¼ their original weight. This recipe also works well with limes.

Wash whole lemons and pour boiling water over them to sterilize. Pack into large, sterile glass jars, layering with salt. Cover jars and place in a sunny place. Every 4 months, open jars and add more salt to avoid spoilage. They will be ready in 8 months to a year.

PEACH UME

(Pickled Green Peaches)

A substitute for the Japanese pickled "plum" or ume.

1 gallon green peaches
1 cup salt
6 cups vinegar
3 cups sugar
½ bottle red food coloring

Wash the peaches and soak in salt and enough water to cover for a day and a half. Drain and place in the sun to dry for a day. Heat vinegar, sugar, and food coloring until sugar is dissolved and allow to cool. Put dried peaches in a sterilized glass gallon jar and pour the syrup over them. Allow to stand at least 1 week.

. . .

BOILED PEANUTS

Finally, a recipe for boiled peanuts, not a seed at all, but an equally popular tidbit, widely available in the mom-and-pop stores that still flourish in Hawaii.

1 pound raw peanuts in the shell
2 tablespoons salt
1½ pieces star anise

Place peanuts, salt, and anise in a pot, cover with water, and simmer for a couple of hours. Turn off the heat and allow to cool in the water. Drain and serve.

THE MATTER OF MOCHI

"Do you like butter mochi?" asked my friend, cutting in to a large pan filled with what looked like light brown cake. "At least once a month I get a craving for it and just have to fix a panful." She handed me a square the size of a brownie on a napkin. I nibbled at it: dense, rich, sweet, and a little greasy, as the spots on the napkin showed. Chewy too; it might look a little crumbly, like cake, but when I bit into it it was the chewiness that I noticed: not like anything I had ever had before, but good, I decided. She passed along the recipe neatly typed on an index card: it was made with sugar, eggs, butter, coconut milk, and mochiko, as sweet rice flour is known in Hawaii.

Butter mochi was just the beginning. Shortly thereafter, a colleague offered me something that looked like a candy, colored pale rose, with a white dusting on the outside. I picked up a piece, finding it very soft. Indeed its texture, its color, and its powdered exterior made me expect something like the Middle Eastern confection known in the English-speaking world as Turkish delight—the real Turkish delight, that is, not the jellied kind in the middle of chocolates, but the kind that can be bought from Greek and Lebanese stores.[1] I bit into it expecting it to be sweet, even if not flavored with Middle Eastern rose or orange blossom water. Instead it tasted of nothing, and the coating was a raw flour of some kind, not confectioners' sugar. Only the texture resembled Turkish delight. What I was tasting, my colleague told me, was mochi. Then a student brought a dark brown ball about the size of a grapefruit wrapped in red paper to class, cut it into wedges, and passed it around. It was sweet and gummy-chewy. This, I was informed, was gau (see p. 122). And at a fair, I came across skewers with three balls, pale golden in color, that had been deep-fried. Chewy and sweet again. This was cascaron.

What I was encountering, I gradually realized, was that whole tribe of confections, made of sweet rice flour, that are common across East and Southeast Asia. Why had I never encountered them before I came to Hawaii? Because, I think, it is the general impression of restaurateurs and cookbook writers that these confections do not go down well with non-Asians. They can't be easily accommodated in our customary food slots. Unsweetened, they don't fit the notion of dessert or candy. Sweetened, they are too dense and chewy to be cakes, too heavy to be candies. Even in Hawaii, cooks are not quite sure where to place them in cookbooks organized in conventional Western ways. When I checked my collection of spiral-bound community cookbooks, I found recipe after recipe for butter mochi, showing that my friend was not the only person who craved it. But sometimes it was in the cake section, at other times it was under "other" along with the recipes for mochi, dango, nantu, and all the other slightly sweetened, steamed chewy confections of rice flour so popular in the Islands. Where sweet rice flour has entered Western eating habits, it has been in savory form as arare or mochi crunch, savory snacks flavored with salt, soy sauce, and seaweed that fit easily into the category that stretches from potato chips to trail mix.

This neglect of sweet rice flour confections is a pity, though, because they have their virtues. The Japanese mochi is the most austere and is to be enjoyed for its texture as much as its taste: I have seen it advertised as having a "sublime neutrality" and being favored for its "gum-hugging, yummy-smooth edible elasticity," an excellent description. Honolulu boasts a number of mochi factories, small family-run affairs, where wooden trays of mochi mixture are stacked high and steamed over fires. To pick up a selection of these, delicately tinted in pinks and greens, some stuffed with sweetened bean mixtures, is a pleasure in itself, even before enjoying the contrast of powdery coating and pliant, delicately flavored interior. Taken with a cup of tea, they are delightful.

But back to butter mochi. It puzzled me; its mixture of sugar and butter and eggs with coconut milk and sweet rice flour seemed a hybrid of West and East. True, in her *Ethnic Foods of Hawai'i*, Ann Kondo Corum put "custard mochi" in the section on Japanese cooking and listed sugar, eggs, butter, sweet rice flour, and milk as the ingredients, almost identical to my friend's butter mochi except for the substitution of milk for coconut milk.[2] Even so, neither the mixture of ingredients nor the cooking method seemed typically Japanese, even though, given that the Japanese reportedly adopted both sponge cakes (castera) and deep-frying (tempura) from the Portuguese, it is always possible that they also modified their traditional recipes for rice flour under Western influence. I was more inclined to suspect, though, that butter mochi was the brain child of one of the home economists employed by the gas and electric companies. Faced with the prospect of increasing the use of ovens in Hawaii, where most of the population had cooked successfully for generations without them, what better solution than to invent a Western cakelike dessert using Asian sweet rice flour?

There is another possibility, though, and that is that the origin of butter mochi is the Filipino dish known as bibingka. Corum's recipe for bibingka includes sugar, eggs, butter, evaporated milk, shredded coconut, and sweet rice flour, baked in a pan lined with wilted coconut leaves.[3] Bibingka is a festival food in the Philippines, a must for Christmas, New Year, and other fiestas. Traditionally it was prepared with a wet rice flour, made by grinding rice that had been soaked overnight, coconut milk, sugar, eggs, and natural yeasts, and it was cooked over a fire in a closed container with embers on the lid. A fresh white cheese or salted egg could be placed on top of the dough halfway through the cooking. Today, baking powder is used instead of yeast, and bibingka is baked in an oven.

If butter mochi is a descendant of bibingka, then the trail stretches still farther across Asia to the Portuguese settlement of Goa on the west coast of India, where bibingka is a well-known dessert. In the nineteenth-century *Indian Cookery Book* are two recipes for "Portuguese Cocoanut Pudding." One is titled "Bole Comadree" and consists of rice flour, sugar, egg yolk, coconut meat, and milk. The second is "Bibinca dosee, or Portuguese Cocoanut Pudding" and consists of a sugar syrup into which is stirred rice flour and coconut milk boiled until thickened and then baked until light brown.

Hawaii cookbooks are full of versions of butter mochi–like bibingka, though usually without the eggs.[4] Perhaps the most likely explanation is that both stories have something to them. Mochiko, ovens, home economists, coconut milk, Filipinos, and Japanese all intermingled to produce Hawaii's own butter mochi, a hybrid dish acceptable to different palates. Now you can find recipes for butter mochi that suggest adding sweetened bean paste (koshian or tsubushian), clearly a Japanese addition; others suggest adding ube (purple yam paste) or black beans or cheese (Filipino additions) and yet others chocolate in the form of cocoa powder (a haole addition).[5]

Perhaps what will finally bring mochi to widespread popularity in the West, though, is not the Filipino-Japanese-Hawaiian butter mochi, but mochi ice cream, not a Hawaii invention but a West Coast one, I am led to believe. In the 1990s mochi ice cream took Hawaii by storm. Bite-sized pieces of ice cream are covered with a thin skin of mochi. It retains its elasticity even though frozen and it insulates the ice cream. Which is better? Green tea ice cream covered with plain mochi or vanilla ice cream covered with espresso mochi? It's impossible to decide, so it's best to take both.

A SELECTION OF SWEET RICE FLOUR CONFECTIONS[6] TO BE HAD IN HAWAII

Mochi (Japanese). Sweet (glutinous) rice confections, sometimes called cakes, sweetened only slightly if at all. Served on auspicious occasions but available through the year in many different shapes, sometimes with fillings (red bean paste, for example), sometimes lightly flavored, and often colored rose or pale green.

Dango (Japanese). Boiled or steamed dumplings of sweet (glutinous) rice flour. One variety is called chichidango.

Manju (Japanese). Not a glutinous rice flour confection at all, but a cookie-sized wheat flour pastry usually stuffed with an (sweetened bean paste). Included here because manju are so often sold packaged with mochi.

Nantu (Okinawan). The Okinawan name for mochi.

Butter mochi (Local). A cake made with glutinous rice flour, sugar, coconut milk, butter, and eggs and served in brownie-sized squares. Usually cooked at home and rarely available commercially.

Bibingka (Filipino). A cake similar to butter mochi made with glutinous rice flour and coconut milk.

Cascaron (Filipino). Golf-ball-sized balls of glutinous rice flour mixed with sugar and coconut, deep-fried and served skewered on a stick.

Gau for Chinese New Year

See also the recipe for gau (p. 122).

MOCHI

(Sweet Rice Flour Confection)

Mochi can be made from scratch by steaming chalky grains of sweet rice and then pounding them. To make it at home, it is much, much easier to use ready-prepared sweet rice flour (mochiko), though the texture is different and, to many aficionados, inferior.

1 cup mochiko (sweet rice flour)
¼ teaspoon salt
1 tablespoon sugar (optional)
½ cup water
Potato starch or cornstarch

Put water in a large steamer and begin to heat. Stir together the sweet rice flour, salt, sugar (if using), and water and knead lightly to produce a soft dough. Place dampened cheesecloth or a clean tea towel over the steamer tray. Spread a ½-inch-thick layer of dough over the cloth. Place the tray in the steamer, cover, and steam for 20 minutes. Remove the tray, allow to cool for a couple of minutes, and then tip the mochi onto a cutting board. As soon as it is cool enough to handle, knead for a minute or two until it is smooth and shiny. Shape into an 8-inch roll and cut into eight pieces. Dust with the starch to prevent the mochi from sticking and place the pieces on a tray. They will sag and flatten into the traditional doorknob shape. Serve fresh the same day. Otherwise, freeze and defrost briefly in the microwave.

Yield: Eight pieces of mochi

Notes: (1) There are many recipes that suggest making the mochi in a covered microwave dish using medium power for about 8 minutes. I have tried this but found it difficult to avoid getting tough spots. (2) Mochi can be eaten out of hand. It can be grilled or pan-fried until puffed and golden. Leftover mochi, which becomes rock hard, can be cut into small pieces and deep-fried in 350 degree oil until crisp. Serve any of these as a snack with soy sauce.

DANGO

(Dainty Dumplings of Sweet Rice Flour)

½ cup mochiko (sweet rice flour)
1 teaspoon sugar
Water to make a soft dough

Form the dough into pea-sized dumplings. If desired, color half the dough pink with a drop of food coloring. Drop the dumplings into boiling water. As soon as they rise to the surface, scoop out and chill.

Yield: Enough for making an mitsumame (Japanese shave ice dessert) for six

. . .

BUTTER MOCHI

(Sweet Rice Flour and Coconut Cake)

1 pound (3 cups) mochiko (sweet rice flour)
2½ cups sugar
2 teaspoons baking powder
Two 12-ounce cans coconut milk
5 eggs
4 ounces melted butter
1 teaspoon vanilla

Preheat the oven to 350 degrees. Mix the dry ingredients in one bowl, the wet ingredients in another; combine both mixtures and pour into a 9 by 13 inch cake pan. Bake for 1½ hours. Cut into brownie-sized squares to serve.

Yield: Twenty-four servings

BIBINGKA

(Filipino Sweet Rice Flour and Coconut Confection)

This is a modern, quick version of bibingka worked out in Hawaii.[7]

5 cups mochiko (sweet rice flour)
3 cups brown sugar
1 teaspoon baking soda
2½ cups water
12-ounce can coconut milk
Banana leaves (optional)

Preheat the oven to 350 degrees. Prepare a 9 by 13 inch cake pan by lining with banana leaves wilted by immersion in boiling water, or by greasing. Mix mochiko, brown sugar, baking soda, water, and coconut milk in a large mixing bowl. Pour into pan and bake for 1 hour. Cut into brownie-sized squares to serve.

Yield: Twenty-four servings

MALASADAS AND ANDAGI: DOUGHNUTS FROM TWO ENDS OF THE EARTH

The Punahou School Carnival, so it is said, is the most ambitious high school fund-raiser in the United States. True or not, the February Carnival is an Island institution. Founded in 1841 for the children of missionaries and other haoles, Punahou proudly claims to be the oldest private school west of the Rockies.[1] It has now swelled to admit 3,000 children of every ethnic group, it boasts a lavish campus just a couple of miles from Waikiki, and it enjoys an endowment of millions.

Notwithstanding, the fund-raising continues; every year parents, staff, and students labor to produce a carnival yet more spectacular (and profitable) than the one before. Police patrol parking for blocks around; the campus is packed with alumni greeting old friends; to get from one spot to another is a matter of sharp elbows and brute force. There are rides, but rides on Oahu get a little stale because the same equipment goes from one fair or carnival to the next. Thus there are also annual themes and white elephant sales and book sales and plant sales and fruit sales with pineapples donated by Dole, and the famous homemade mango chutney that always sells out the first day.

As always in Hawaii, one of the biggest attractions is the row of food stalls selling snacks. And because Punahou is no longer just a haole school, these snacks come from all the different groups in the Islands. Especially famous are *malasadas:* Portuguese doughnuts.[2] The volunteers expect to fry and sell 85,000 malasadas in just 2 days.[3] Ladies stand above hot woks a yard in diameter full of spheres turning from white to gold in the hot fat. They roll the fresh malasadas in sugar and hand them to the customers who have been waiting patiently in line. The doughnuts are sugary and slightly crisp on the outside, unusually soft on the inside. They make addictive eating.

Portuguese immigrants from the Azores, Portuguese islands in the mid-Atlantic, brought the recipe for malasadas to Hawaii with them in the late nineteenth century.[4] What distinguishes the malasada from the everyday yeast doughnut is the eggy dough—about one egg to every cup of flour—and the use of milk or cream. In Hawaii, evaporated milk often stands in for fresh milk in this recipe as it does in so many others: evaporated milk was a boon in the days before refrigeration. Sometimes mashed potato is used in the dough, sometimes the malasadas are rolled in honey as well as in sugar, and often a touch of vanilla or nutmeg is added. Originally, malasadas, like similar doughnuts across Europe, rich with eggs and milk and sugar, were a treat to be eaten on Shrove Tuesday, the day before Lenten fasting began.

Several bakeries specialize in malasadas. On Oahu, the best known is Leonard's on Kapahulu Avenue on the edge of Waikiki. It is an old-fashioned plain-Jane bakery, but a steady string of cars pulls up to purchase the malasadas, "cooked fresh all day," individually for about 40 cents, or by the half dozen or dozen or even more. No longer are they reserved for a pre-Lent indulgence, nor are they even consumed in especially large numbers then. A trip to Leonard's one Shrove Tuesday morning showed no more than the usual steady stream of customers.

But malasadas are not the only doughnuts in Hawaii. At the Okinawan festival in late August, you will come across *andagi*, the Okinawan doughnut, from another isolated little group of islands, this time islands lying between Japan and China. After watching the moving presentation of the banners of the forty or so Okinawan associations in Hawaii, the crowd wanders over to the food stalls, here offering different Okinawan specialties, such as pig's-feet soup and pork wrapped in kelp. Once again, the doughnut booth is one of the most popular. Shaping the andagi is an art, and stall holders vary from artists —both men and women—to rank novices. These are not yeast doughnuts, as malasadas are, but cake doughnuts leavened with baking powder. The dough of flour, milk, sugar, eggs, and baking powder is soft, softer, say, than a choux pastry dough, and scarcely holds together when scooped out of the plastic-lined tin drum in which it has been mixed. I watch in admiration as one of the cooks picks up a handful of this dough in his left hand. Making a fist, he squeezes slightly and from the crevice between his thumb and forefinger emerges a round ball of yellow dough. With the forefinger of his right hand, he slides this off the fist and drops it into a wok of boiling oil. But of course the squeezing works both ways, and by now a shaggy mass of the dough is about to fall from the bottom of his fist, so with a quick flick of the wrist he throws this back up into his opening palm and within seconds repeats the process so that another ball of dough falls into the oil. Soon the balls turn from pale gold to a rich brown and are scooped out with metal skimmers to be sold by the dozen to the line of waiting people. As the young man works away with some level of dexterity, his girlfriend proudly asks the onlookers, "Can you believe it? He only started today, and he's a mainland boy too!"

Deep-frying a batch of Portuguese malasadas

Deep-frying a batch of Okinawan andagi

Many years ago, according to Okinawan legend, a handsome young samurai stole the heart of a beautiful young maiden.[5] So beautiful was she that the king himself wanted to win her heart, but all his efforts were rebuffed. When he learned that this was because she had eyes only for the samurai, he called the young man into his presence. For certain charges, he was to be banished to an impoverished outlying island. The man told his family of the fate he was to suffer for crimes he had not committed and his mother determined to help him. When he went to board the boat, she begged his guards to allow her to make him a parting gift of andagi. On reaching the island and biting into the andagi, he discovered that concealed in each ball of dough was a golden coin. Thus he was able to save himself from the worst privations of life on the island. Not the happy ending that we often expect of fairy tales perhaps, but the story does suggest how much Okinawans valued the andagi and still do. In Hawaii, they, together with the Okinawan sweet potato, are the symbol of Okinawan food.

But what is the origin of the Okinawan andagi? They seem distinct from the Japanese and Chinese traditions that were the two formative influences on Okinawan cooking. And there is the little matter of the baking powder, something not invented until the middle of the nineteenth century. If it were not for their place in Okinawan legend, one might be tempted to link them to American cake doughnuts introduced after World War II. Or does their origin go back to the earlier stages of European contact? The Portuguese are said to have introduced tempura to Japan. Could they have introduced deep-fried doughnuts to Okinawa, the yeast being subsequently abandoned for baking powder? Is it possible that the Portuguese doughnut has gone both west and east around the world to become the malasada and the andagi of Hawaii?

MALASADAS

(Portuguese Doughnuts)

Malasadas are surprisingly foolproof to make and because the dough can be refrigerated, they can be prepared well in advance of frying.

½ **teaspoon sugar**
½ **package active dry yeast**
¼ **cup warm water**
2 **cups flour**
¼ **cup sugar**
Pinch of salt
1 **tablespoon butter, melted**
2 **eggs**
⅓ **cup evaporated milk or cream**
⅓ **cup water**
Oil for deep frying

Mix sugar with yeast and warm water. Let it prove for 5 minutes. Sift the dry ingredients together. Stir in the melted butter. Beat eggs, evaporated milk, and water together and add to the flour mixture. Add yeast and mix well until you have a sticky dough. Cover and let dough rise until doubled, 1–2 hours. Punch down the dough. Let it rise a second time, about another hour. Heat oil in deep fryer to 375 degrees. Dip fingertips in oil or softened butter and pinch off golf-ball-sized pieces of dough. Drop in hot oil and cook until brown on one side; roll over and cook until brown on the other side. Drain on paper towels and roll in sugar. These do not keep and should be served immediately while still warm.

Yield: Two dozen

Note: After the dough has risen the first time, it can be refrigerated overnight. Take it out a couple of hours before frying to allow for the second rising. If you have a microwave, you can bring the dough to room temperature in the microwave, cutting the time needed to just 1 hour.

. ■ .

ANDAGI

(Okinawan Doughnuts)

Closer to cake doughnuts than to yeast doughnuts, andagi have a crisp exterior and a dry, sandy interior.

3 cups flour
1 cup sugar
4½ teaspoons baking powder
½ teaspoon salt
3 eggs, slightly beaten
1 cup milk
Oil for deep-frying

Heat oil in a deep fryer to 375 degrees. Sift the dry ingredients together. Combine eggs and milk. Add to dry ingredients. Mix thoroughly. Drop by the teaspoonful into the hot oil and fry until golden brown. Drain on paper towels and serve warm.

Yield: Three dozen

"FOOD IS NOT A RACIAL PROBLEM"

Home Economics and Hawaii's Food

When and how did the different ethnic cuisines of Hawaii become transformed into a new kind of food, Local Food? Locals reminisce about how, as plantation workers, they or their parents or grandparents sat down in the sugar or pineapple fields at lunch and shared the contents of their lunch pails. There is surely something to this. Tastes that overlapped between different ethnic groups would have made the sharing the easier: Chinese, Japanese, Koreans, and Filipinos all eat rice; Hawaiians share with the Japanese a taste for seaweed and for raw fish; Filipinos as much as Portuguese enjoy meat and fish cooked in a sour sauce.

Appealing as it is, though, the shared lunch pail story is far from the whole story. A wide range of other forces were at work. Many parents, for example, encouraged their children to learn to eat American food. Daniel Inouye, senior U.S. senator from Hawaii, recalls that when he was growing up in the 1930s, "When we ate chicken or beef, we used knives and forks. When we ate *sukiyaki* or *tempura*, we used chopsticks."[1] The plantation store, with its beef, its cans of meat, milk and fruit, and its crackers, exposed immigrants to new foods, as did advertising and time spent as a maid or cook in a kamaaina household.[2] During the 1920s and 1930s, some families began to give their children milk to drink, and at the Japanese holidays of New Year and Obon, children were treated to bottled soft drinks.[3]

World War II accelerated these changes. The men who signed up for the military encountered mainstream American food in the training camps and rations of the U. S. Armed Forces. Generous rations these for the best-fed army in the history of the world— soldiers in basic training received a staggering 5,000 calories a day —but scarcely the typical foods of Hawaii.[4] The Japanese-American

Cultivating the family vegetable garden on the plantation, an activity encouraged by the University of Hawaii Extension Service, 1950s (HSA)

volunteers went to the South, to Camp Shelby, Mississippi, for training and may well have encountered the partitioned plate lunch there for the first time.[5] During the war years, the Japanese-American soldiers longed for their soy sauce and rice. Quartermasters in the 100th Battalion foraged in the Italian countryside to find a rice substitute, returning with vermicelli.[6]

Meanwhile, things were changing back in Hawaii as well.[7] Although half of the Japanese who had come to Hawaii had already left for Japan or for the mainland, the war drove home to those who remained that there was no going back to Japan. Many Chinese and Japanese found that there was only enough rice for one meal a day; the nine-course Chinese dinner for celebrations disappeared to be replaced by American meals or Hawaiian luaus. At first, the Japanese hoarded whatever foods they could find, driving up prices for soy sauce, monosodium glutamate, and certain kinds of dried fish and seaweed. As these supplies were exhausted, and as they felt pressure to act like Americans, they turned increasingly to American dishes eaten on large plates with knives and forks. They had no squid or mochi for New Year's Day. The Chinese missed their firecrackers and substituted mainland pine nuts for their traditional watermelon seeds.

Caroline Edwards, the supervisor of home economics education for the Territory, was put in charge of designing ways to feed the population in an emergency. She pulled together a committee of eight assistants, mainly school cafeteria managers and home economics teachers. To judge by their names, at least one was Chinese and two were Japanese. Their aim was to "prepare and

A model plantation home kitchen in the 1930s (HSA)

serve *tasty* substantial meals—an emergency meal does more than keep the body alive—it helps to revive discouraged souls and BUILDS MORALE."[8] The master menu suggested that at dinner (one of the two meals to be served to adults) there be a meat, fish, soup, or dried pea or bean dish, a starchy dish such as potatoes or brown rice, enriched breadstuff and butter, cooked vegetable, tea or coffee, fruit and pudding if possible, to be served to crowds of 900 at a time in school cafeterias. With the possible exception of pork chop suey and miso soup made with milk, suggested by Marjorie Wong of Central Intermediate School, there was nary a reference to the food of most of the population.

The home economists' impact on the diet shows up even more clearly in the textbook Caroline Edwards had published a few years earlier, in 1938, her *Guidebook for Homemaking in Hawaii.* "FOOD IS NOT A RACIAL PROBLEM," she declared, capitalizing her words for emphasis, "BUT A PROBLEM DEALING WITH THE HEALTH NEEDS OF THE HUMAN BODY UNDER ACTUAL PRESENT CONDITIONS OF LIVING."[9] The very fact that she felt it necessary to say this, of course, gave the lie to her words. By the 1920s and 1930s, Hawaii's ruling haole elite worried that the majority of the territory's population scarcely corresponded to the stereotype of the Anglo-Saxon American citizen.[10] The Americanization movement moved into high gear, and one of its aspects was food: introducing immigrants to American foodways was thought to be both a symbol of assimilation and a move toward more modern, scientific, and healthy habits. The Hawaii Agricultural Experiment Station began to study ethnic foods.[11] The public education system from grade school to university which, because haoles had their own private schools and went to East Coast mainland colleges for higher education, catered primarily to nonhaoles, played a key role. The school lunch program offered the chance to teach children American eating habits.[12] In the curriculum, home economics offered prime opportunities to teach the American way of life.

Home economics—now the brunt of derisive jokes—was booming in the United States, providing women with a toehold in higher education.[13] Columbia Teacher's College aimed for leadership, turning out teachers and dieticians for schools, for government service, and for the rapidly mechanizing food industry. The land-grant university in the Territory of Hawaii, way off in the middle of the Pacific, like land-grant universities across the country, recruited graduates from Columbia.

The frontispiece of Edwards' *Guidebook for Homemaking* displays an aerial photograph supplied by the Hawaiian Sugar Planters' Association: a trim plantation village half hidden by trees, neat church at one end, neat manager's house at the other, surrounded by flat fields of cane, the mountains towering over all. The caption reads, "On the strength of our home depends the strength

THE HOME ECONOMISTS ARRIVE

Caroline Edwards was not alone. From East Coast schools, home economists had arrived in Hawaii in force. In 1922, Carey Dunlap Miller, of Irish and Swiss ancestry, stepped off the S.S. *Wilhelmina,* clutching a cage with eight white rats for her experiments.[14] She had just finished her master's degree at Columbia. For the next 23 years, she headed the Home Economics Department at the University of Hawaii, increasing the number of majors graduated each year from 1 to 160. A year or two later, her friend, Ada B. Erwin, established the Home Economics Department at Punahou, Hawaii's premier private school. In 1926, the Hawaiian Electric Company, mindful of the electric ovens that so few people knew how to use, hired Miriam Jackson. And in 1930, Katherine Bazore, born in the Middle West, but another Columbia graduate, joined the University of Hawaii faculty: "In my alphabet," she said, "'H' stands for Home Economics, Hawaii, Honolulu, and Happiness."[15]

These women, and others like them, found an immigrant population that had few of the Italians or the Jews or the Eastern and Central Europeans who crowded into the cities of the East Coast and the Middle West. Undeterred by the unfamiliar foods they encountered, they taught the women who staffed the school cafeterias, the classrooms, and the extension service. They poured out an astonishing quantity of research: among other things, they established the nutritive values of Hawaiian and other locally grown tropical food; they recorded the local Japanese diet; they established basal metabolic rates for Pacific Island peoples; they analyzed the vitamin content of local fruits; and they wrote the first books on the ethnic foods of the Islands and on the fruits of the Islands.[16] Their students who staffed the extension services and other home economists who worked for the utility companies wrote many of the most successful Local cookbooks.[17]

of our country." Many of Caroline Edwards' students would have come from towns, but the plantation economy still dominated the way people thought about the nonhaole population, and it was students from villages such as this, destined at best to work as servants in a haole household, that she seems to have had in mind.

"Hawaii has thousands of fine young Americans whose parents are not American citizens," went on Caroline Edwards. She admonished her young readers: "Show [your parents] that American education teaches proper ways of living so that you may get the most out of life. . . . In the land where your parents were born, children were probably taught that they must never question anything their parents wished them to do. In Hawaii, the aim of education is to prepare children to think out for themselves and to act with intelligence. Keeping this great difference in mind, try not to oppose your parents, but help them to see things as you learn to see them in school."[18] One parent, as if in sad response, reported: "I don't say much to my children. I know that they know and understand about America better than I. My children tell their mother what foods are good for one's health. They say we must eat more vegetables and fruits and less rice. They learn this in school—American school. I mean, I believe that their teachers are better informed along this line. So I do not interfere or ignore their suggestions. I believe that the children should obey their teachers."[19]

What things learned in school were parents to see? They were to see and learn from their daughters' home projects. That might mean accepting floor rugs made from burlap sacks, or curtains and bedspreads. It might mean getting accustomed to upholstered packing box furniture with ruffled skirts (a big change for a Japanese household).

Many of the projects centered on food. Daughters learned how to make ovens out of empty cracker cans. These could be used to bake cakes and homemade meatloaf. Daughters learned that milk was the perfect food and encouraged their families to consume some every day, perhaps in the form of a custard baked in that useful cracker-can oven. Believing that milling rice removed many of the nutrients, Caroline Edwards urged the use of brown rice, or at least of rice bran from the rice mills still operating in Hawaii, to thicken soups and stews.

To demonstrate to her students the importance of a good breakfast, Caroline Edwards turned to examples.[20] Carefully choosing names to indicate ethnic origin, she awarded high marks to Yoshiko, Kam How Wong, Cecelia (whose parents came from Portugal), and Pualani (the little Hawaiian). In Yoshiko's family, there was miso soup, daikon, rice, tea for the grown-ups, cocoa for Yoshiko, and papaya with lime from the yard; in Kam How Wong's there was winter melon soup (left over from the night before), dried shrimp

with soy sauce, green onion, rice, tea for the grown-ups, and cereal and cocoa for the children; in Cecelia's, cornmeal, sweet bread, egg and salmon patties, and coffee for the grown-ups, and milk for Cecelia; and in Pualani's poi, dried fish with a little limu and some rock salt, dried, jerked meat for Pualani's father, a policeman, and pineapple juice for Pualani.

Equally carefully avoiding names that betrayed ethnic origins, Caroline Edwards held up the sorry cases of Mary, who had learned that a steady diet of rice was not enough for her health and had substituted big pilot crackers, with the result that her arms were pitifully thin, and Sammy, who called himself smart but was really rather stupid, who ate rice and macaroni and poi.

Caroline Edwards and the other home economists had no way of knowing that adults of non-European extraction—and hence virtually all their pupils' parents—lack the enzyme to digest milk. This was not discovered until the 1970s.[21] Ovens and milk did become part of daily life in Hawaii (though Locals consume quantities of lactose tablets to help digest the milk).[22] But the brown rice campaign got nowhere; white rice was one of the luxuries that immigrants had been promised in Hawaii and white rice it has remained to this day.

Part Two

ETHNIC FOOD

THE IMMIGRANTS

Ngai k'iou gnia
Li k'oi ho
Fei saa fui li
(I beg of you after you depart to come back soon—Chinese folk song)

Yokohama deru tokya yo
Namida de deta ga
(When I left Yokohama I cried as I sailed out—Japanese folk song)

Longe da minha terra
E aqui sem consolacao
(Far from my land and here without consolation—Portuguese folk song)[1]

"Oh look," said the well-dressed woman behind me. "An old zinc food safe. And one of those bushes that grew berries we used for coffee." It was a festival at the Waipahu Cultural Center, a reconstructed plantation village strung out below the chimney and looming walls of one of the few sugar mills still working on Oahu in the mid-1990s. In the village are reconstructed buildings, ranging from a native Hawaiian straw house, through plantation houses of various decades decorated in the style of the different groups, to the dispensary and union hall of the pre-World War II period. I was in the Puerto Rican house and before long half a dozen Puerto Ricans were reminiscing about the old days on the plantation, about work in the kitchen, about the plants they had grown and the food they had eaten, and about how the young today did not know what real work was.

This conversation revealed how food was one consolation for immigrant workers far from their lands. So did everything else about the festival: the stalls selling the foods of the different ethnic groups, the cookbooks on sale in the museum, the Chinese communal kitchen with its kitchen god and enormous

wok, the Portuguese bread oven, the reconstruction of the foods offered at a Korean first birthday party, and the restored vegetable gardens. But most of all it was the conversations.[2] Grannies were showing their children what it was like on the plantation, old friends were greeting one another, teenagers were gazing at the cramped frame houses, and all were talking about food.

In the mid-nineteenth century, it was sugar that seemed to hold the future of Hawaii. There was not enough money to be made selling Hawaiian sea salt, the sweet-smelling sandalwood that fetched such prices in China was exhausted, and the whalers were no longer wintering and restocking in Hawaii as Americans turned to petroleum for their lamps. Sugar meant plantations and mills, and plantations and mills meant workers prepared to work long hours in the heat and the dust.[3] The plantation owners, many of them the children and grandchildren of the missionaries, needed labor.

Finding labor was not so easy. The Hawaiians had been devastated by the new diseases the haoles had brought with them and demoralized by the disintegration of their own culture. By the 1850s, they had dwindled to no more than about 70,000 and showed understandably little enthusiasm for the backbreaking work of the plantations.[4] Haoles the planters did not want, not unless they were mechanics.[5] It seemed inappropriate for haoles to toil in the fields as common laborers and, besides, many haoles had jumped ship and were not to be trusted. Consequently, any haole who wanted menial work on the plantation was required to "ship," that is, to sign up as for work on a ship and to agree to carry out any tasks assigned him day or night for a certain number of months for a set amount of pay. Few did so.

Thus for workers, as for all their other supplies, the plantation owners turned to Honolulu's mercantile houses, called factors—Theo. H. Davies and Company, Castle and Cooke, H. Hackfeld and Company, Alexander and

Baldwin, and C. Brewer and Company. The factors began a search that was to last for the next couple of generations. Depending on which parts of the world were so ravaged by wars and famines that their peoples would set off for distant islands to work, depending on which of these peoples were allowed in under U. S. immigration laws after Hawaii became a Territory in 1900, and depending on the plantation owner's desire to mix ethnic groups to control wages and unrest on plantations, the mercantile houses enlisted labor. In the late 1880s, Theo. H. Davies and Company wrote to a plantation manager, laconically acknowledging his order for "tobacco, portuguese laborers. We have ordered 20 men for you. lumber, 7 ft. iron bar, wool mattress, olive oil."[6]

In the early 1850s, the factors recruited Cantonese Chinese, battered by the violence of the Opium War and the devastating Taiping Rebellion, as well as by local struggles for fertile land and the perennial famines and floods. In the 1880s, they turned to poverty-stricken small tenant farmers and fishermen from the southwestern prefectures of Japan, who preferred scraping together

Details of a memorial to those who created Hawaii's sugar industry, erected on Kauai by the Hawaii Sugar Planters' Association

Above left: Puerto Rican, Japanese, and Portuguese

Above right: Hawaiian

Below left: Filipino

Below right: Haole and Chinese

PART 2: ETHNIC FOOD

their $100 passage to Honolulu to moving to the cities of their home country. In the 1880s, too, the factors brought the Portuguese, tossing for six long months on ships from Madeira and the Azores, tormented by the *soldados ingleses* (the red-coats or bed bugs), to escape the devastation in their own islands following the failure of the vineyards. In the early 1900s, after the Spanish-American War of 1898, Puerto Rican families fed up with war and with hurricanes were brought to Hawaii. In the same years, seven thousand Koreans arrived before the Yi emperor stopped emigration, horrified by accounts of his subjects' exploitation on the hemp plantations of Mexico. Then, too, there were the Okinawans from the Ryukyu Islands, part of Japan politically, but culturally distinct. The last major group to be signed up were Filipino men, recruited when Chinese and Japanese immigration was banned by the Oriental Exclusion Act.

After days crammed into the hold of a ship making its way across the hot Pacific, the immigrants sailed into Honolulu harbor, backed by mountains that, stripped by the earlier search for sandalwood, "loomed high, rugged, treeless, barren, black and dreary, out of the sea."[7] The immigrants were quarantined on flat, hot Sand Island until they walked the long narrow footbridge into the city of Honolulu itself. From there it was on to the plantations, to dusty, blazing fields, scratchy sugarcane, and the muddy water of the irrigation ditches, to serve out their contracts in the plantation camp or village, the company town of the Pacific.

Homesick, and hungry after laboring all day under the hot sun, the plantation workers were determined to go on eating what they were used to. Familiar foods were often hard to come by, especially at first. The plantation managers were not anxious to supply the rice that so many immigrant groups wanted, and prices for imported foodstuffs were high. In spite of Hawaii's range of climates, immigrants could not always get their seeds to grow. Although the Japanese succeeded in making tofu and the Koreans kim chee (pickled cabbage), sake brewing, as well as the manufacture of miso (fermented soy bean paste) and soy sauce, required cold temperatures and had traditionally been done in winter.[8]

Even so, in time the immigrants managed to obtain most of their customary ingredients. In some cases, their governments negotiated part of the diet as a condition for allowing emigration: in 1884, for example, the Japanese government stipulated that white rice be available for no more than 5 cents a pound.[9] Before long, the Chinese were growing it themselves.[10] Along with the workers came entrepreneurs who imported and peddled groceries. The immigrants themselves brought (or smuggled) seeds for their favorite vegetables; vining Japanese pumpkins quickly covered the shacks that the first Japanese immigrants constructed, for example. By the 1930s, vegetable men made the rounds of the plantation camps, their trucks packed with everything the housewife

Left: **A promotional photograph for statehood showing a Japanese farmer in traditional tabi (foot covering) raising vegetables for overseas markets, 1950s (HSA)**

Right: **Woman and child returning home after selling fruit, 1920s (HSA)**

needed to prepare a meal, including vegetables, meat, sashimi, bread, fishcake, and canned goods.[11]

Over time, ethnic foods in Hawaii took on their own character: in part, as fossilized food from the home countries; in part, as adaptations to customs in Hawaii. Thus Doreen Fernandez, a leading authority on Filipino food, told me that the recipes compiled by the Filipino Women's League for the cookbook they put together in 1975, *Hawaii Filipina's Favorite Recipes*, reminded her of the Filipino cooking of several decades earlier, and a Japanese acquaintance, who had been sent back by her parents to be raised in Japan, told me how strange she found what passed for Japanese food in Hawaii when she returned after World War II. "Too sweet," she said, wrinkling her nose. "And all messed up too," by which she meant that instead of being served in individual bowls it was all piled up on a single plate. Not that she was entirely averse to the latter: far fewer dishes to do.

In the last few decades, South Pacific Islanders, particularly Samoans, and Southeast Asians have added new ethnic cuisines. The upsurge in ethnic pride has led, as well, to back influence by the "authentic" food from the homelands of many of the immigrant groups. What follows are encounters with those of Hawaii's ethnic foods that are most visible in the public realm and that have contributed most to the evolution of Local Food.[12]

The following recipes are for some of the vegetables brought in by the immigrants and now produced commercially in the Islands.

Daikon

This elegant vegetable, carrot-shaped but twice the size and pearly white, is often called the Asian radish or turnip. Grocery stores sell Korean, Chinese, and Japanese varieties: the first about 8 inches long, cone-shaped with a green coloration at the top; the second a similar size and shape but white all over; and the third about 8 inches long but more cylindrical than conical. It takes experience to detect the difference in flavor. Daikon has a clean, fresh taste and can be eaten cooked or raw.

TAKUWAN

(Pickled Daikon)

This is a *tsukemono* (pickle) that is a necessary part of any Japanese meal. In Hawaii, the pickle is readily available in grocery stores. But it is very easy to make and a good addition wherever pickles are used, not just in Japanese meals.

½ cup sugar
¾ cup water
3 tablespoons salt
3 tablespoons vinegar
Chopped red chili pepper (optional)
2 daikon, peeled and cut in chunks the size of a fingertip

Heat the sugar, water, salt, and vinegar until the sugar and salt are dissolved. Allow to cool. Place the daikon in a glass jar and add the cooled solution and chili pepper. The solution will not quite cover the daikon at first. Seal and refrigerate. After a few hours, the daikon will render a certain amount of liquid and the pieces will be completely covered. The pickle is ready for eating after 2 days.

Yield: 1–2 quarts depending on the size of the daikon

Note: The takuwan sold in grocery stores is colored yellow; if you want to emulate this, just add a couple of drops of yellow coloring.

KOREAN DAIKON SALAD

An excellent salad with any main dish full-bodied enough to benefit from this spicy accompaniment.

1 daikon
1 tablespoon salt
1 tablespoon rice vinegar
1 tablespoon soy sauce
1 clove garlic, minced
1 inch fresh ginger, peeled and minced
2 teaspoons sugar
2 teaspoons toasted sesame seeds
Kochu jang or hot sauce to taste
Green onions, cut in rings or diagonals, to garnish

Cut the daikon into long, thin shreds by hand or in the food processor. Place in a large bowl, sprinkle with salt and allow to sit for 10 minutes. Squeeze gently to get rid of excess moisture. Mix the remaining ingredients (except green onions) and toss with the shredded daikon. Adjust seasoning and place in a clean bowl. Garnish with green onions. Serve as a salad.

Yield: Four to six servings

■ ■ ■

Ginger

Almost all the fresh ginger to be found in American supermarkets comes from Hawaii. Tender young baby ginger begins arriving in the summer; the peak for mature ginger is just after the New Year. Gleaming, silvery brown hands of ginger are available in all Hawaii markets. Many of the ethnic groups in Hawaii—Chinese, Japanese, Koreans, Southeast Asians—use copious quantities of ginger, but there is no one ginger dish that is especially associated with the Islands.

PICKLED YOUNG GINGER

(Beni Shoga)

This pickle of young ginger, thin slivers of rose pink, makes a good garnish for sushi and adapts well as a side dish to Western menus. It is essential to use the young ginger, which comes into Hawaii markets in the summer.

2 cups young ginger root, sliced paper thin
½ cup sugar
¾ cup rice vinegar
1 teaspoon salt
Touch of red coloring

Place ginger slices in saucepan, cover with water, and bring to the boil for a couple of minutes. Drain. Heat sugar, rice vinegar, and salt together until sugar and salt are dissolved. Add the coloring and pour the solution over ginger. Place in a glass jar and refrigerate. The pickle will be ready in 2–3 days.

Yield: 2 cups

. . .

Lotus Root

The lotus grows in muddy ponds and yet produces beautiful flowers, making it a sacred plant to Buddhists, who used it as a symbol of what could be achieved from unprepossessing beginnings. But it is the stem, not the flower, that is eaten. It looks like a series of chubby links of a pale beige sausage. When you tap the links, they sound hollow. You discover why when you peel and slice the links and come across a delicate lacy interior. To preserve the color, blanch in acidulated water. Lotus root stays crisp even when cooked.

DEEP-FRIED LOTUS ROOT

1 medium lotus root
Oil for deep-frying
Salt

Peel and slice the lotus root into ¼-inch slices. Deep-fry in hot oil at 375 degrees until golden and crisp. Serve with salt.

Yield: Four to six servings

STUFFED LOTUS ROOT

2–3 lotus roots
1 pound ground pork
½ cup soy sauce
¼ cup green onion, chopped
¼ cup sugar
1 tablespoon garlic, finely chopped
½ teaspoon black pepper
½ cup flour
1 egg, slightly beaten with ⅛ cup water
Oil for frying

Peel and slice the lotus roots in ⅜-inch slices. Mix the pork, soy sauce, green onion, sugar, garlic, and pepper. Pat into the holes in the slices. Dredge the pieces with flour and dip into the egg wash. Heat oil in a deep pan to about 375 degrees (or until a piece of green onion sizzles when you drop it in the oil). Slide in a batch of lotus root slices, allowing plenty of room, and fry until lightly brown. Drain on paper towels and repeat until all slices are cooked. Serve with hot dipping sauce.

Yield: Six servings

. . .

HOT DIPPING SAUCE

1 tablespoon vinegar
2 tablespoons soy sauce
1 teaspoon sugar
1 teaspoon sesame oil
1 teaspoon Tabasco sauce
Salt
1 teaspoon kochu jang sauce, optional

Mix all ingredients together and serve in a small dish.

Watercress

Hawaii's watercress is a taller and leggier variety than that found in mainland and European markets, and its stems are thicker. Large, dark green, fresh, and appetizing bunches are readily available in Hawaii. They weigh about a pound apiece, equivalent to several bunches on the mainland or in Europe.

WATERCRESS SHITASHI

(Wilted Watercress Salad with a Soy Sauce–Sesame Dressing)

Slightly sweet and salty, and topped by sesame seeds, this is a most agreeable salad.

- 1 bunch watercress (about 1 pound), cut into 1¼-inch lengths
- 1 tablespoon sesame seeds, lightly toasted to bring out the aroma
- 1 tablespoon sugar
- 2 tablespoons soy sauce
- 1 tablespoon mirin

Dip the watercress in boiling water and drain immediately. When cool, squeeze out excess water. Mix sesame seeds, sugar, soy sauce, and mirin in a bowl, adjusting quantities to taste. Add the watercress and toss. Serve at room temperature.

Yield: Four servings

• • •

STIR-FRIED WATERCRESS

This quickly prepared vegetable dish goes as well with American and European dishes as it does with Asian.[13]

- 1 bunch watercress, washed and drained
- 1 tablespoon oil
- 1 clove garlic, crushed
- 1 pinch salt

Cut watercress into 3- to 4-inch lengths. Heat frying pan. Add oil, and then stir the garlic in the oil until fragrant. Add the watercress and salt and stir-fry until just wilted.

Yield: Four servings

THE SUMIDA WATERCRESS FARM

Many Japanese in Hawaii became farmers. One such was the Sumida family.[14] The continued existence of the Sumida Farm is a classic tale of David and Goliath, the little guy (the three generations of the Sumida family who have worked the land) against the big guys (the powerful land-owner, the Bishop Estate and the Pearlridge Shopping Center). The farm occupies the few acres of bottom land in a tight valley: across one end runs a tacky suburban strip; the two other sides making up the triangle are occupied by concrete parking lots, enclosed malls, family restaurants, and a huge Sears. You can see the farm from all sides, but getting to it involves threading through the service entrances to the warehouses of this commercial district.

Defiantly situated in the middle is the gleaming green patch of land, neatly laid out in irrigated plots fringed with banana trees around which flit white butterflies. Filipino workers with straw hats to shade them against the sun cut the watercress. But the small size of the patch should not deceive; more than half of Hawaii's watercress comes from this 10-acre farm. That might mean nothing in many parts of the world, but in Hawaii people eat a lot of watercress, and big bundles of the crisp, green vegetable are piled up in all the grocery stores.

ROAST PIG BY THE GRAVE: THE CHINESE AND CHING MING

A family visiting Manoa Valley Chinese cemetery at Ching Ming

In mid-April it is already hot by midmorning at the Chinese Cemetery in the upper part of Manoa Valley. Cars stream up the valley, past the university campus, past the neatly kept middle-class frame houses, into the upper reaches below the forested cliffs of the Koolau Mountains. There the Mercedes sports cars and the pickup trucks, the rusting Chevys and the shiny new Volvos jostle for parking. Families clamber out, clad in Hawaii's weekend garb: grannies bent with age wear the beige or brown polyester slacks and silky overshirts with muted flower patterns typical of their generation; mothers sport tailored shorts, the weekend versions of dress for success; their husbands have on blue jeans and polo shirts and fancy running shoes; the kids dance around in T-shirts, shorts, and rubber thongs. Between them they struggle with huge garbage bags, brown grocery sacks, straw beach mats, squeaky plastic coolers, shiny arrangements of red gladioli, chicken wire, and golf umbrellas. They make their way into the graveyard and up the hill between the tightly packed gravestones, the green slopes of the Koolaus on three sides. This is the Chinese festival of Ching Ming, the Chinese equivalent of Memorial Day. In 1989, the Lin Yee Chung (the Manoa Chinese Cemetery) Association celebrated its 100th anniversary.[1]

Standing under the banyan tree in the cemetery, I can see down Manoa Valley to the high-rises of Waikiki and the ocean glittering blue beyond. Closer at hand is the tomb of Lum Ching, the geomancer who chose this spot for a cemetery in 1851. Then the valley floor was covered with taro patches, and the departed ancestors would have been able to see that there was food aplenty for their descendants. The taro patches have gone, but the site remains haunting as each family group clusters to remember its ancestors. Alongside the grave, joss sticks are pushed into the dirt, still soft from the winter rains. On top of the gravestone, paper money is

Left: Roast pig for the ancestors at Ching Ming

Right: Rice, roast pork, oranges, and rice cakes for Ching Ming

held down by a pebble together with a wire with red and gold petals, all surrounded by a flower lei. The red gladioli go on the grave itself.

But the centerpiece is the food. It is taken out of the squeaky plastic coolers and meticulously laid out on the ground or on a low, folding picnic table. There is a prescribed arrangement, but in practice this appears to vary with family size, income, and devotion. Most impressive is the roast suckling pig. While the family readies everything, the pig is shielded from the sun by plastic tablecloths or sheets, which make it look disconcertingly like a body ready for burial. After the observances begin, though, the sheet is whipped off and the long brown pig lies there, its skin shiny in the 80 degree heat, its ears slightly burned at the tips.

A rough and ready order emerges from the chaos. Liquor is poured into a plastic cup and added to the offerings. Each member of the family comes forward in turn to offer three quick bows at the grave. One of the older children sets off a string of firecrackers, their sounds echoing back from the surrounding mountains; the youngest child, scared, whimpers. The plastic garbage bag is turned upside down and paper money showers out; each adult picks up a handful to burn, prudently tossing it into the erect coil of chicken wire. The smell of gunpowder and burning paper and hot pig and plumeria merges, and the mountains blur in the drifts of smoke. The older generation, who made their obeisances first, rest on the beach mats, sheltering from the sun under the beach umbrellas.

Soon it is all over and done with, and the family packs up and departs. They take most of the food, including the pig, and set off for their favorite restaurant for the family feast that follows. All that remains is a charred circle in the turf; a plastic plate with pork turning greasy in the heat, buns, rice, and liquor; and, on top of the gravestone, some fading bougainvillea blossoms held in place by a used golf ball.[2]

EDIBLE PLANTS BELIEVED TO HAVE BEEN INTRODUCED BY THE CHINESE[3]

Bamboo *(Nandina domestica)*
Calamondin *(Citrus mitis)*
Chinese cabbage *(Brassica ke-tsai)*
Ginger *(Zingiber officinale).* Both the Chinese and the Japanese introduced varieties of ginger. The Chinese is taller, has larger leaves and rhizomes, and is less pungent than the Japanese.
Jesuit nut *(Trapa bicornis)*
Jujube or Chinese date *(Zizyphus jujuba)*
Kumquat *(Fortunella japonica)*
Longan or dragon's eye *(Euphoria longana)*
Loquat *(Eriobotrya japonica)*
Lotus *(Nelubium nuciferum)*
Lychee *(Litchi chinensis)*
Persimmon *(Diospyros kaki)*
Snow pea *(Pisum sativum saccharatum)*
Star anise *(Illicium verum)*
Star fruit *(Averrhoa carambola)*
Winter melon or *dung-kwa (Benincasa hispida)*

Left: Crystallized fruits and vegetables for Chinese New Year

Right: An altar in a Chinese bakery decorated for Chinese New Year

The Chinese began arriving in Hawaii soon after the haoles, many of them on the ships returning from delivering sandalwood to China.[5] It was they, it is said, who were the first to make sugar. Quite a number of them married Hawaiian women, and some dishes taken to be typically Hawaiian (chicken long rice) reflect this. Many more came later as plantation workers, as priests, as teachers, as merchants, or as farmers. Most were from Canton, and Chinese food in Hawaii still bears the marks: Cantonese favorites such as char siu, kau yuk, and winter melon soup remain popular.

From the start, the Chinese insisted on their own foods, protesting if they were expected to eat poi instead of rice, and supplementing their stipulated rations by growing vegetable gardens.[6] Single men on the plantations appointed one of the group to be their cook and to bring them hot meals in the fields. The Chinese set up truck farms, developed the rice industry, took over much of the taro growing from the Hawaiians, sold poi, and peddled vegetables and novelties. Soon there was a Chinese retail variety store in every plantation camp, and the manapua men became a feature of the Hawaii scene. In 1882, the oldest surviving restaurant in Honolulu, Wo Fat in Chinatown, opened its doors.[7] By 1896, the Chinese owned 118 general merchandise stores and 35 groceries, clustered in Chinatown.[8]

As might be expected of a people with such a forceful culinary heritage, the Chinese have remained loyal to their foods: in the 1980s most Hawaii Chinese still preferred their own food to that of any other ethnic group.[9] They ate out frequently, more than eight times a month on average. Chopsticks were still used, although sometimes knives and forks were laid on the tables beside chopsticks.

Indeed, it was the strength of the Chinese tradition, along with the Japanese, that has made modern Hawaii a society as happy to use chopsticks as to use a knife and fork, the only state in the Union where this is true. Chinese restaurants abound in the Islands, and Chinese food was the second most favored cuisine of other ethnic groups in Hawaii.[10] Chinese foodstuffs are available in the chain grocery stores, and Chinatown, although now largely taken over by Southeast Asians and Filipinos, still has Chinese groceries, butchers, noodle shops, and bakeries. Local Chinese cookbooks, for reasons that do not spring immediately to mind, are all individually authored, not community projects as are the cookbooks of many other ethnic groups.[11]

HAM-TURKEY JOOK

(Ham, Turkey, and Rice Soup)

Originally, jook was a simple rice gruel, often eaten for breakfast. Like so many traditional recipes, it has become more elaborate as incomes have risen and food tastes have changed. Now some version of turkey jook is a favored way of using up the Thanksgiving turkey, and not just among the Chinese. "After Thanksgiving, practically everyone I know makes jook," declared Wilfred Muramoto of the Hawaii Government Employees Association.[12]

3 cups rice, well washed
3 ham hocks
1 turkey carcass, broken into pieces
1 cup raw peanuts, skinned
Garnish: Lettuce; salted, preserved cabbage; Chinese
**   parsley; and green onion, all finely sliced**

Combine rice, ham hocks, turkey carcass, and peanuts in a large pot, add about a gallon of water, bring to a boil, and cover. Simmer for a couple of hours until the rice has disintegrated and the meat is falling off the bone. Remove the bones (and any bits of meat clinging to them) from the soup. Chop the meat into small pieces and return to the pot. Add salt to taste. Ladle into large soup bowls and sprinkle some of the garnish on each bowl.

Yield: 1 gallon, enough for eight meal-sized servings

CHAR SIU

(Chinese Roast Pork)

In the shops of Chinatown, glistening red strips of char siu hang from hooks, next to the red-brown roast duck and the golden roast chickens, all ready to be taken home. Essential in Island cooking, slivers of this slightly sweet, slightly spicy roast pork are used to top saimin, add to stir-fries or noodle dishes, or to stuff manapua. Char siu is also delicious sliced and served as an appetizer or in sandwiches. In Hawaii grocery stores, you can buy meat ready marinated for char siu, colored a slightly alarming vermilion. It is easy enough to make yourself if you prefer.

Recipes for char siu abound, many of them suggesting a simple marinade in hoisin sauce. This version, adapted from Sia (*Chinese Cookbook*), is less sweet than many in Hawaii. You can also decide whether or not you want to add the typical red coloring. It does give the meat a nice tinge around the edges when you slice it but adds nothing to the flavor. Traditionally, the meat is hung from racks in the oven, but a thin wire rack on a baking sheet makes a satisfactory substitute.

> **2 pounds boneless pork, preferably loin**
> **⅔ cup soy sauce**
> **2 tablespoons sherry**
> **3 tablespoons honey**
> **½ teaspoon salt**
> **4 cloves garlic, finely chopped**
> **2 tablespoons ginger, finely chopped**
> **Large pinch five-spice powder**
> **½ tablespoon red food coloring (optional)**

Trim any fat off the meat. Cut it into strips about 2 inches wide, 1 inch thick, and 6 inches long, making sure the grain runs the length of the strip. You should have about four strips. Mix the remaining ingredients in a shallow, nonreactive pan and place the strips of pork in this marinade. Leave for about 3 hours at room temperature, or 6 hours in the refrigerator. Heat the oven to 400 degrees. Place a thin rack (the kind used for cooling cake) on a baking sheet. Spray with nonstick oven spray. Lay the pork strips on top. Place in oven and roast 15 minutes, baste, and roast for another 20 minutes at 375 degrees. Allow to cool and cut into strips or slivers to serve.

Note: This pork freezes beautifully and is good to have in reserve for a quick meal.

KAU YUK

(Red Pot Roast of Pork)

One of the first Chinese dishes to appear in Hawaii cookbooks, kau yuk's popularity, I suspect, may be due to the affiliations that developed between the Hawaiians and the Chinese early in the nineteenth century. Pork was a favorite of both groups, and both were accustomed to taro.[13] Although Hawaiian and Chinese taro have different properties, in this dish they can be used interchangeably. Because it is a complicated recipe, it is worth making in quantity. Soft and almost gelatinous in texture, it is deeply flavored and a little goes a long way.

3 pounds lean belly of pork with skin on
1 slice ginger root, grated
1½ tablespoons soy sauce
1½ tablespoons sugar
1 tablespoon bourbon or whiskey
¼ teaspoon five-spice powder
2 cloves garlic, minced
3½ tablespoons red bean curd *(nam yoy)* plus a teaspoon
** of juice**
Salt to taste
1 pound Chinese taro, sliced (optional)

Place the pork in a pan, cover with water, simmer for an hour, rinse, and pat dry. Place pork skin side up in broiling pan and broil until skin is light brown and slightly puffed. Remove and place skin-side down in water until the skin is soft enough to cut. Dry, and slice into strips 1½ inches by ½ inch. Mix the ginger, soy sauce, sugar, bourbon, five-spice powder, garlic, and red bean curd. Marinate the pork in this mixture for half an hour. Arrange the pork skin side out in a bowl just large enough to hold it. Slip slices of taro between the pieces of pork and pour any remaining marinade over the mixture. Place bowl in a steamer and steam for a couple of hours until pork is almost meltingly tender. Invert bowl onto serving dish. Serve with rice.

Yield: Twelve servings

GAU

(Chinese New Year Cake)

This is the dark brown glutinous substance that so mystified me when I first arrived in Hawaii and it was identified as "just like mochi" (see p. 1). In Chinatown at New Year, stores display gau prominently, and very handsome they are too. Red paper surrounds a dense sticky cake of sweetened mochi rice. Its brown, shiny surface is scattered with sesame seeds, symbolizing many children, and in the center is a red date (jujube). Like so many Asian foods, gau is laden with symbolism.[14] The round shape stands for family unity, the sticky mochi rice for cohesiveness, the sugar for the sweetness of life, the sesame seeds for the desire for the family to multiply, the red date for good luck, and even the word for the pudding itself rhymes with the word for high. This recipe is Chinese, yes, but with distinct Local character. The use of glutinous rice flour is traditional, but the name, mochi flour, is Japanese. Brown sugar is a substitute for a preserve or jam of jujubes. And the ti leaves are quintessentially Hawaiian.

> **2 cups water**
> **1¾ cups dark brown sugar**
> **1 pound mochi flour**
> **2 tablespoons oil**
> **1 red Chinese date (jujube)**
> **Sesame seeds**
> **Ti leaves**

Stir together the water and brown sugar and heat until dissolved. When cool, add mochi flour and oil and mix well. Line an appropriately sized dish (4 inches in diameter by 3 inches deep) with oiled ti leaves and fill with mixture. Steam for 3 hours. Turn the confection out of the pan. Press date on top and sprinkle with sesame seeds. You will have a glossy dark brown pudding-cake nestled in the now-brown ti leaves with a glowing red date and a scattering of white sesame seeds on top. Wrap a piece of red paper around it if you wish. Slice into thin wedges and serve at room temperature. (Gau can be refrigerated but after a couple of days, reheat it in the microwave before serving to restore the texture.) A slice makes a delicious, chewy morsel with a cup of tea.

CRYSTALLIZED GINGER

Packages of crystallized fruits appear in Chinatown stores in time for Chinese New Year. In a shiny cellophane box nestle neat piles of candied coconut, carrot medallions, kumquats, melon, lotus root, water chestnuts, and coconut. They make an enticing display. On two corners are the brown candies, the lacy pattern of the lotus root contrasting with the wrinkled little kumquats; on opposite corners are white triangles of coconut and white strips of coconut. In the middle are disks of water chestnuts and cubes of melon, both of them white, and orange carrot medallions. Shopping for these in Chinatown, I fell into conversation with a well-to-do Chinese lady. She agreed with the assistant that these were indeed a necessity for every Chinese household for New Year's Day, but said that she herself did not eat them. Why not? They were too sweet for her taste. She preferred to put them in tea and have the heavy sugar coating float off and sweeten the tea.

In Hawaii, you can find fresh, tender crystallized ginger in Chinatown and in crack seed stores.

1 pound ginger
1½ cups sugar

Soak the ginger in water overnight. Drain, cover with fresh water, simmer for 10 minutes, and allow to cool. Strain. Peel the ginger and cut it into thin slices (⅛ inch). Cover with water and bring to a boil. Simmer until tender. If you prefer your crystallized ginger mild, change the water once or twice. If you like it hot, use just one water. Drain. Mix the sugar with 1½ cups of water and heat until dissolved. Add the ginger, bring to a boil, and simmer for 10 minutes. Allow to cool for 1 hour. Then simmer again until almost all the liquid is absorbed, about 30 minutes. Remove from heat and stir for a few minutes. Then remove the pieces of ginger and place on wax paper to cool and harden. Roll the ginger in granulated sugar and place in a sealed jar. It will keep indefinitely.

Note: Do not discard the water in which you simmer the ginger. Save it to add to lemonade or limeade for a brisk and cooling drink.

(ELEBRATING JAPANESE NEW YEAR IN HAWAII

A display of mochi for Japanese New Year

PLANTS THOUGHT TO HAVE BEEN INTRODUCED BY THE JAPANESE

Araimo, dasheen, or Japanese
taro *(Colocasia esculenta)*
Butterbur *(Petasites
japonica)*
Daikon *(Raphanus sativus
longipinnatus)*
Gobo or burdock *(Arctium
lappa)*
Shiso or beefsteak plant
(Perilla frutescens)

In late December, elegant displays begin appearing in store windows, on bank counters, in dentists' reception areas, and on the tombs in Japanese cemeteries. Two shiny white doorknob-shaped objects, mochi (unsweetened cakes of pounded glutinous rice), one slightly larger than the other, are placed on brightly printed paper; on top is balanced a tangerine, its stem and leaf still attached; and between the paper and the pile a fern can just be seen. The stickiness of the mochi signifies family togetherness at the change of the year.

One of the very first things the Japanese did when they began arriving on the plantations was to negotiate a holiday on New Year's Day, one of the major events of their calendar. Now, a hundred years later, full-page advertisements for traditional foods appear; grocery store aisles are piled with these specialties, the newspapers carefully chart the price of sashimi, and everyone prays for a bountiful catch of tuna. Mochi plays the same central role that turkey does for an American Thanksgiving or plum pudding for an English Christmas. The newspapers carry photos, friends ask one another "Did you pound mochi?," and department stores put on exhibitions for those who lack the time, space, or energy to make their own.

Traditional mochi making is worth seeing. Two men, armed with long mallets somewhat similar to croquet mallets, stand on either side of a narrow vertical cylindrical tub, about 2½ feet tall. Into the hollow at the top a third man tips a pile of steaming hot rice. The first man raises the mallet over his head as if he were going to chop firewood with an ax and brings it down hard onto the rice. As he does so, the second man raises his mallet, so that the pounding is nearly continuous. The third man dodges backward and forward, first dipping his hand into a bucket of cold water so that it will neither stick nor burn in contact with the hot rice and then flipping the rice over so that it gets thoroughly pounded. From time to time, he shakes in a little water. After about

5–10 minutes, the rice is a glutinous mass. It is cut into chunks, formed into flat cakes, and allowed to dry. The texture of mochi made this way is supposed to be superb.

There are alternatives, though they are much less colorful. The rice can be ground in a food processor. There is a gadget, somewhat resembling a sausage-maker, imported from Japan for cutting mochi. There is even a machine, about the size and price of an automatic bread-maker, that does all the work for you. Every New Year these automatic mochi makers sell out. Or easiest yet, you can buy your mochi ready-made from a grocery store or one of the specialty mochi stores in Honolulu.

Meanwhile, other customs continue to be observed, albeit many of them (like the mochi) in modified form. Housewives still clean the house from top to bottom in anticipation of New Year. They still put *kadomatsu* outside their front door, though this is no longer a live tree, picked in the forest, and mounted on a bamboo stump as it once was in the Japanese countryside, nor is it the bundle of ironwood that at first substituted in Hawaii. Instead it is purchased at Safeway, an elegant combination of cut bamboo and pine branches often shipped in from the United States mainland. Because no cooking could be done for the first 3 days of the New Year, wives once prepared food in advance—stacked lacquer boxes, with appetizers such as black beans and fishcake in the top layer, broiled or grilled food in the second, and foods cooked in broth in the third. Now things are much simpler, as families adjust to American schedules. The last meal eaten in the old year is soba (buckwheat noodles), the long strands symbolizing good luck that will continue into the New Year. By 10 o'clock, like everyone else in Honolulu Japanese families can hear the firecrackers, the

A PLANTATION VENDOR

Sanshichi Ozaki describes his beginning in business:

I arrived December 1891 with four or five hundred yen worth of Japanese foodstuffs and notions. I paid $1.50 a month for a room which I used for my living quarters and rented a chicken coop for 75¢ a month to store my merchandise. I carried my wares on my back and made the rounds of the various plantations on foot. It was not until after I was in business for three years that I began to show a profit.[1]

An offering of nuts, fruit, mochi, and liquor on a Japanese grave

sound escalating until the deafening 15 minutes following midnight, with the air thick with the smell of explosives.

Next morning begins with a bowl of ozoni soup. As in Japan, this includes sticky cakes of mochi; but whereas in Japan the soup is either clear or miso (fermented soybean paste)-based depending on the region, in Hawaii the broth may be of any kind and apart from the greens called *mizuna* or *mizoni*, it can be loaded up with all the things that Locals like to eat, such as roast pork, char siu, or fishcake, turning it into a real meal. Then it is off to the Shinto shrine—a beautiful wooden building constructed without nails and with characteristic barrel shapes supported by crossbeams on the roof. In Japan, the whole family from frail old men to restless babies would have been dressed up in their best clothes; in Hawaii, they wear T-shirts and slippers (thongs). They pass through the massive doorposts of the sacred gate under the heavy rope from which strips of white paper dangle. In Japan, the families would rinse their mouths with water scooped from the well with a communal wooden ladle; in hygienic America, they wash their hands and wipe them with a paper towel. Then they walk up the steps into the building where the priest stands wearing his angular formal headdress and holding a long wand tipped with paper strips. They sip a little sake to cleanse themselves, purchase a paper fortune or two, check their luck, and tie it to the tree in the precincts of the shrine. Finally where Japanese families used to hold all-day open houses for friends, neighbors, and family, now they usually restrict themselves to lunch or dinner. The number of dishes, as well as the number of items in each dish, must be an odd number (but not nine). Some kind of red fish—in Hawaii usually a red snapper—is served; red is a lucky color. Herring roe in soy sauce ensures a large family. Fishcake signifies health, fertility, happiness, wealth, and luck. One sweetened black bean is eaten for each year of life. In Hawaii, the table is also likely to include turkey, ham, fried noodles, macaroni and potato salad, shrimp rolls, sushi, sweet potato with chestnut, *nishime* (Japanese vegetable stew), and, above all, sashimi.

I read descriptions of the customs. I listen to friends and students describe their own experiences. I attend lectures at the community colleges or at the Academy of Art.[2] But still I have no sense of the stretch between the ideal that is described and the actual that is lived. I am sure that there must be a tension similar to the tension between the idealized Christmas of the glossy magazines and the actual messy events that people experience. But I cannot probe its boundaries in the way that I can with my own tradition. All I can do is report the form without the creative tension, as so many earlier immigrants to Hawaii have had to report the customs of the different groups they met there. What is clear is how such traditions combine strength and flexibility. In Hawaii, every aspect of the traditional observance has been modified, but the vigor with which it is celebrated, the role in holding families and communities together, is as sticky as the mochi at the center of the festivities.

When the Japanese, mostly farmers and fishermen from the southern prefectures, began arriving in Hawaii in the 1880s, conditions were trying.[3] They built their own thatched houses, with a floor of packed earth, a raised section for eating and sleeping, and a separate kitchen shed with a clay stove. A decade later they had established Japanese language schools, planted their familiar vegetables, and begun sending for their "picture brides." Men still far outnumbered women, so few cooked for themselves, instead paying the wives of other workers to fix their meals. Typically they had rice, miso, and daikon for breakfast; cold rice, beans, and vegetable stew for lunch; and rice, beef stew, dried fish, and pickled daikon for dinner. Years later, in 1974, 90-year-old Tomonosuke Takahashi recalled, "One of the married women packed lunch for me in a stack of round metal containers about five inches in diameter. On one layer she packed rice and *ume* (pickled plum). In another she usually had *nimame* (cooked beans) and *nishime* (vegetables cooked in soy sauce). Occasionally there was fish. She also provided a bottle of tea."[4]

Rice was provided under the terms of the contract, and the immigrants probably consumed less sweet potato and millet than they had in Japan. Plantation stores learned to stock *somen* (noodles), *kamaboko* (fishcake), miso, soy sauce, and daikon. At the same time, the Japanese began to add sweet bread (Portuguese), roast pork (Chinese), and poi (Hawaiian) to their diet. They also began to purchase American goods—bread, oatmeal, macaroni, crackers, pork and beans, canned fruit, fish and meat, mayonnaise, jam, cocoa and coffee, baking powder, yeast, and butter.

World War II marked a turning point in Japanese food habits in Hawaii.[5] Social pressure, service in the military, and the unavailability of key ingredients led to a more Westernized diet. By the 1980s, most Hawaii Japanese were eating a Western breakfast with coffee. For three-quarters, the most prestigious food to order in a restaurant was steak and lobster, many used forks as well as chopsticks, and most would have a Western wedding cake, white icing and all.

WESTERN WORLD'S
1ST SAKE BREWERY

TAJIRO SUMIDA'S SAKE

On 8 February 1885, when the first group of Japanese contract laborers stepped off their ship, they were cheered to see that King Kalakaua had provided ten barrels of sake for the victors in a dockside sumo tournament.[6] But they were soon disappointed; for years after, sake was either an exorbitant price or absolutely unobtainable (because of a temperance movement led by a Japanese priest and backed up by Japanese wives). In September 1908, an immigrant from Hiroshima, Tajiro Sumida, decided that by manufacturing in Honolulu he could get the price down from $2.25 to $1.50 a gallon, and, with a group of investors, he established a company to make sake. It was not a runaway success. In the Tropics, sake soon spoiled. Desperate, Sumida turned to technology. He refrigerated the fermentation area to replicate the winter conditions of sake brewing in Japan and imported lactic acid to safeguard the fermentation. That did the trick. Just 5 years later, his company was producing 17,750 casks a year. By 1920, when Prohibition closed the brewery, Sumida was the most successful Japanese businessman in Hawaii. In 1933, after repeal, he started up again. At the outbreak of World War II, Hawaii was producing 1,500,000 gallons a year from a number of sake factories and had a sizable export business to the mainland.

Sumida and the Hawaii Japanese are said to have developed many of the innovations now used in Japan: refrigeration, stainless-steel equipment, methods of brewing sake year-round, and techniques for brewing sake from California rice.

Even so, Japanese food traditions have remained strong, as New Year customs show. In the 1980s, all Hawaii Japanese continued to eat rice at least once a day. Japanese restaurants can be found all over Hawaii. Supermarket shelves are well stocked with Japanese preserved goods and favored fresh fruits and vegetables such as persimmons, daikon, chrysanthemum leaves, and araimo. There are two Japanese department stores that offer a wide range of cooking equipment and foodstuffs as well as festivals celebrating the regional foods of Japan. Many Japanese foodstuffs (sake, soy sauce, noodles, for example) are manufactured in the Islands. Since the 1970s, Buddhist temples and Japanese cultural associations, as well as individuals, have produced a range of cookbooks.[7] Prefectural associations (kenjinkai) hold annual picnics. The influx of Japanese tourists reinforces the demand for traditional restaurants and foodstuffs.

OZONI (OR ZONI) SOUP

Recipes vary widely for this soup; originally it was a simple broth with greens and mochi. Now it is often much more elaborate, the chicken breasts, for example, being a recent addition.

2 chicken breasts, sliced thin
6 cups of water or dashi
Soy sauce and salt to taste
Selection of a couple of vegetables (taro [the Japanese kind], spinach, mizuna, daikon, dried mushrooms, greens)
6–12 mochi, depending on size

Simmer the chicken in the water or dashi, adding the vegetables so that they will be ready at the same time as the chicken. Add seasonings. Toast or boil the mochi until it is soft. Arrange the chicken, vegetables, and mochi in individual soup bowls and ladle the broth over them.

Yield: Serves four

Note: For New Year the vegetables are traditionally carved into appropriate symbolic shapes.

MISO SOUP

(Japanese Broth)

This is a very simple soup, often served for breakfast or with a Japanese meal. Quick and tasty as it is, it is well worth knowing.

6 cups water
1 package dashi-no-moto
½ cup miso
Salt to taste
Green onions for garnish

Bring the water to a boil and add the other ingredients to taste. Serve garnished with green onion sliced into thin rings.

Yield: Serves four to six

Note: If you want a heartier soup, add a selection of the following: cubed tofu, beaten eggs, chopped vegetables, or noodles.

• ■ •

NIMAME

(Japanese Bean Pot)

The Japanese equivalent of Boston baked beans.

3 cups dried beans (kidney, lima, etc.)
3 cups sugar
Salt to taste

Rinse the beans and soak overnight in cold water. Drain, add fresh water to cover, and simmer for an hour or so until beans are tender. Add sugar and salt. Cook for another hour. Allow to cool. Drain off liquid and boil it down in another saucepan until thick and syrupy. Pour back over beans. Serve hot or cold as a side dish.

Yield: Six to eight servings

NISHIME

(Japanese Vegetable Stew)

The Japanese, like most ethnic groups on the plantations, depended on a vegetable stew that, with a little meat or tofu, could feed a hungry family. Marlene Hirata recalled the preparation.

> A vegetable peddler would come through our camp carrying a variety of ethnic vegetables in two large bamboo baskets which were balanced on two ends of a long pole hung over one shoulder. He was quick and agile with a rhythmic gait to his fast walk as he carried his heavy load. He would call out in Japanese, "Yasai, yasai irimasen ka?" (Vegetables, do you want any vegetables?).
>
> Many times my mother would make nishime with the vegetables she bought from the peddler; it was one of my father's favorite dishes. For the pork that was needed for this dish, my mom would send me to Mrs. Goya's truck . . . Mr. Goya raised the pigs and his wife sold the pork from her truck, which was refrigerated with ice.[8]

2 strips *nishime konbu* (dried kelp)
4 pieces dried shiitake mushrooms (soaked, washed, and cut into 1-inch pieces)
1 pound lean pork
1 tablespoon oil
1½ cups water
3 *aburage* (fried bean curds), cut to bite size
3 *konnyaku* (prepared yam paste), sliced to bite size
⅓ cup soy sauce
⅓ cup sugar
¼ cup sake
1 package dashi-no-moto
1 cup bamboo shoots, cut to bite size
1 cup carrots, cut to bite size
1 cup daikon, cut to bite size
1 cup gobo, cut to bite size
2 cups *araimo* (Japanese taro), cut to bite size

Soak konbu and mushrooms in water until soft. Wash the konbu and cut it down the center lengthwise, if it is more than 2 inches wide.

Tie into knots 2 inches apart; cut between the knots. Fry the pork in oil until it turns light brown. Add water, konbu, mushrooms, aburage, and konnyaku. Cover and cook for 15 minutes. Add soy sauce, sugar, sake, and dashi-no-moto and cook for 5 minutes. Add bamboo shoots, carrots, daikon, and gobo and cook for 15 minutes. Add araimo and cook for about 15 minutes more until the araimo is soft but not mushy. Serve with rice.

Yield: Serves six

SWEET POTATOES AND OKINAWAN SAMURAI

MATTHEW PERRY: OKINAWAN FOOD CRITIC

When Matthew Perry visited Okinawa in 1853–1854, he was very taken with the food.

On each table were dishes to the number of some twenty, of various sizes and shapes, and the exact basis of some of which no American knoweth to this day; possibly it was pig. Of the dishes, however, which were familiar to western apprehension there were sliced boiled eggs, which had been dyed crimson, fish made into rolls and boiled in fat, pieces of cold baked fish, slices of hog's liver, sugar candy, cucumbers, mustard, salted radish tops, and fragments of lean pork, fried. Cups of tea were first handed round; these were followed by very small cups of sakee, which had the taste of French liqueur. Small bamboo sticks, sharpened at one end, and which some of the guests mistook for toothpicks, were furnished, to be used as forks in taking balls of meat and dough from the soup, which made the first course. Soup consisted also

Once a year the Okinawa Center, located in the old plantation town of Waipahu in central Oahu, hosts a contest for the best sweet potato recipes. In Okinawa (or Ryukyu as the islands were called in Japanese) the sweet potato was a serious matter.[1] It was introduced there in 1605 by Noguni Sokan. As purser on one of the tributary trade ships to China, he had come across the tuber that the Chinese called *fan-shu* (barbarian potato). Noguni brought samples of the tuber back with him, and the Magistrate of Agriculture encouraged farmers to plant it. It grows readily in the subtropical climate of Okinawa and it soon spread across the islands.

The sweet potato was a godsend. The low-growing, vining plant survived the typhoons that destroyed so many other crops as they swept over the low-lying islands leaving widespread starvation in their wake. Perhaps as a result of the new source of food the population appears to have surged upward. The Okinawans called the sweet potato *han-shu* (a corruption of the Chinese name) or *to-nmu* (Chinese potato). They, in turn, introduced it to Japan, where it became established in the provinces of Nagasaki and Satsuma in time to save them from some of the worst ravages of the famine of 1733. Noguni was a hero. In 1751, a stone monument recording his deeds was erected; in 1789, his descendants were elevated to samurai status; and nearly a couple of centuries later, the Okinawan Industrial Association established yet another monument to the hero of the sweet potato.

Many varieties of sweet potato are grown in Okinawa, the original apparently being a golden yellow color. But in Hawaii an Okinawan sweet potato is a purple sweet potato. Innocent on the outside, it is a glorious purple when you cut it open. From sweet potato to samurai makes quite a story.

You can read about the sweet potato, and about much else Okinawan, in *Okinawan Cookery and Culture*. This excellent compilation, the only existing English-language Okinawan cookbook, was published in 1975 by the Oki-

Pig's-feet soup for sale at
the Okinawan festival

nawan Women's Association of Hawaii, the Hui o Laulima (which means—in Hawaiian, not Okinawan, this being Hawaii—a club or association to give a helping hand). In it, Dr. Mitsugu Sakihara of the University of Hawaii described the history and cuisine of the Okinawan Islands.

A thousand miles from Tokyo and not much less from Hong Kong, the Okinawan Islands developed a style of cooking quite distinct from that of either China or Japan, though influenced by each of them. From the fifteenth century on, the Okinawans had to pay tribute to the Chinese. Whenever a new king ascended the throne, the Chinese sent an investiture mission to the islands. This mission, which might have had as many as four or five hundred members who stayed 6 months or even longer, had to be well entertained, so the Okinawan court dispatched cooks to China to learn the art of Chinese cooking. Then in the early seventeenth century, Okinawa was subjugated by the Japanese, becoming a subfiefdom of the Tokugawa shogunate and intensifying contacts that had existed for centuries. Japanese cookery became one of twelve skills government officials had to master. The Okinawans claim that their many pork and chicken dishes and their fondness for rich sauces reflect the influ-ence of the Chinese, and the care they take in arranging their foods, that of the Japanese.

the next seven courses of the twelve, whereof the repast consisted. The other four were gingerbread, salad made of bean sprouts and young onion tops, a basket of what appeared to be some dark red fruit, but proved to be artificial balls composed of a thin dough rind covering a sugary pulp, and a delicious mixture compounded of beaten eggs and a slender white root with an aromatic taste.

In conclusion, Perry pronounced the dishes "savory and very good; much more so than those presented by Chinese cookery."[2]

KING'S SWEET BREAD

Entrepreneurs in Hawaii do not confine themselves to their own ethnic foods. In 1950, Robert Taira set up in business in Hilo.[3] His parents had come to Hawaii from Okinawa early in the century, and he had grown up on Wailea Plantation on the Big Island, one of a family of nine children. During World War II, he traveled as an interpreter in the U.S. Army. After the war, he went to bakers' school. He had already learned some techniques from his sisters, who enjoyed baking, unusual at a time when most Japanese families did not own cookbooks. Even his father apparently encouraged him.

Taira developed a recipe for Portuguese (Hawaiian) sweet bread and, with an investment of less than $500, began making it commercially. The bread was a success; bakeries and coffee shops followed in Honolulu, then plants in California and South Carolina, all managed by members of the family. By the mid-1980s the company was apparently grossing $20,000,000 a year.

Apart from pork, chicken, sweet potato, rice, and noodles, the Okinawans relied on fish, on seafood and seaweed, on soy beans and soy bean products, and on a variety of cabbages and squashes. Desserts tended to be of the mochi variety, called nantu by the Okinawans, though in Hawaii the Okinawan doughnut, the andagi, is the sweet everyone associates with the Okinawans.

Unlike the Japanese, the Okinawans ate a lot of pork.[4] In the old days, families killed a pig each winter, salting some parts in crocks (ranged with the other crocks for lard, salt, miso, and water, which are all now collectors' items), wrapping other parts in straw and hanging them from the rafters, and melting down the fattier parts for lard. *Okinawan Cookery and Culture* is full of pork recipes. Sauteed blood, for example, consists of blood sauteed in a skillet until the color changes, mixed with cooked pork belly, mushrooms, fishcake, sliced daikon, and miso. A salad of pig's ears and skin cut from the pig's face, includes boiled ears and skin salted for a day, mixed with cucumbers and bean sprouts, and seasoned with a vinegar dressing.

Okinawans seem agreed that, in Hawaii, their dishes are tastier and sweeter than in their homeland.[5] Most ingredients are readily available in grocery stores. There is no Okinawan restaurant, but one place to try Okinawan food is the annual Okinawan Festival held in September each year. It is worth going, too, for the dances, the music, and the parade of the forty different Okinawan civic groups in the Islands.

SWEET POTATO TEMPURA

Where are the recipes for the sweet potato? For all the sweet potato's fame, there are none in *Okinawan Cookery and Culture*. Sweet potatoes were food for the poor, eaten when rice was unavailable or too expensive. They are, however, often made into tempura, and this used to be sold by lunch wagons. Tempura can be made from many kinds of fish and vegetables: shrimp, squid, small fish, nori, shiso leaves, green peppers, onion, small okra, green beans, lotus root, bamboo shoots, and ogo. Mixed tempura are delicious.

2 sweet potatoes, peeled and cut into julienne strips

Tempura batter:
½ cup flour
½ cup cornstarch
1 egg
½ teaspoon salt
½ cup cold water
Oil for deep-frying

Stir batter ingredients together. Do not overstir; the batter should be lumpy. Heat oil for deep-frying to 375 degrees. Dip sweet potato strips briefly into batter (it does not matter if a few stick together). Fry until light golden brown and drain on paper towels. Serve with soy sauce or a tempura dipping sauce.

Yield: Serves four

. . .

TEMPURA DIPPING SAUCE

¼ cup mirin
¼ cup soy sauce
1 cup dashi
1 tablespoon sugar

Mix ingredients and serve in small individual bowls.

Yield: 1½ cups

Note: Grated daikon is frequently added.

OKINAWAN PIG'S-FEET SOUP

This classic dish merits five recipes in *Okinawan Cookery and Culture* and is one of the few Okinawan dishes that has made it into the plate lunch and family restaurants of Hawaii; it is regularly on the menu at the upmarket plate lunch chain, Zippy's.

It is also the traditional Okinawan New Year's Day dish. One of my students told me, screwing up her face in disgust, that she wouldn't touch it. Luckily, she continued, her auntie is Japanese so she can pick the ozoni soup instead. What about her children, I ask? Will she make pig's-feet soup for them? She shuffles and says that her dad is learning to make it from his grandmother. He loves it and perhaps it's not so bad—it's supposed to taste like chicken soup. Her dad is right; it is good.

1 long cut pig's foot
4–5 cups water
½ inch ginger
2 strips konbu (dried kelp)
1 daikon
2 tablespoons soy sauce
1½ teaspoons dashi-no-moto

Broil pig's foot until slightly browned. Wash and scrape the skin with knife under running water. Simmer for 3 hours with water and ginger until tender. Cool overnight and remove any fat. Wash the konbu, tie it in a string of loose knots, and cut between the knots. Cut daikon into 1-inch pieces. Add to soup together with the dashi-no-moto and simmer for another 30 to 40 minutes. Check seasoning and serve in large bowls.

Yield: Four servings

• ▪ •

GLAZED PORK

(Rafute)

Prepared this way, pork kept without refrigeration in the steamy Okinawan islands. Reheated, it could be stretched with vegetables and tofu. The half dozen or so recipes in *Okinawan Cookery and Culture* make the basics clear. Belly of pork is singed over hot coals to remove any remaining hair; the singed parts are scraped off. Then the pork is simmered with the addition of some combination of ginger, sugar, garlic, soy sauce, red coloring, dashi, and the Okinawan liquor *awamori* until it is soft and glazed. All the contributors insist on the importance of the liquor, which they claim prevents the pork from becoming hard when reheated.

> **1½ pounds pork belly or butt with skin on**
> **½ cup awamori (whiskey or sake can be substituted)**
> **½ cup soy sauce**
> **1 inch ginger, peeled and crushed**
> **¾ cup sugar**

Broil any pork skin until singed. Rinse under running water, scraping off any brown areas. Cut into 1½-inch cubes. Place skin side down in a shallow pot, add remaining ingredients and simmer (adding stock or water if necessary) for a couple of hours until the pork is meltingly soft. This can be eaten as it is with rice or added to vegetable and tofu dishes.

Yield: 1½ pounds pork, which will serve six to eight depending on how it is used.

. . .

KONBU MAKI

(Pork Wrapped with Konbu)

Another very popular dish of pieces of pork wrapped in konbu, tied with strips of dried gourd, and simmered in a savory sauce.

> **3 pieces konbu (dried kelp)**
> **½ pound pork butt**
> **1 medium gobo, cut into strips**
> **1 or 2 carrots, cut into strips**
> **1 package *kampyo* (dried gourd) or substitute string**
>   **or toothpicks**

Sauce:

> **1 slice ginger, ½ inch by 1 inch**
> **1 cup chicken broth**
> **3 tablespoons sugar**
> **½ teaspoon salt**
> **¼ cup soy sauce**

Wash the konbu thoroughly in cold water. Gently squeeze out any excess water. Cut each piece into lengths of 6 or 7 inches, 2½ inches wide. Cut the pork into strips, ½ inch by ½ inch by 2½ inches. Make gobo and carrot strips the same size. On one end of each length of konbu place one strip each of pork, gobo, and carrot, roll up and tie with kampyo (or use string or a toothpick if you cannot find kampyo). Place the rolls in a saucepan, cover with the sauce ingredients, and simmer about 1½ hours until the meat and konbu are soft and there is just a little rich sauce left. Serve with rice.

Yield: Four servings with other side dishes

Note: This can also be made with chicken.

· ■ ·

CHANPURU

(Tofu-Vegetable Stir-Fry)

Chanpuru is a one-dish meal. It consists of tofu broken up in a skillet (not cut with a knife), stir-fried until golden brown, seasoned generously with salt, and mixed with one or more vegetables—bean sprouts, bitter melon, cabbage, chives, grated green papaya, daikon, or carrots. Pork, sausage, ham, or fish can also be added.

2 tablespoons oil
1 block tofu
2 teaspoons salt
2 green onions, sliced
Prepared vegetables roughly twice the volume of the tofu

Heat the oil in a pan. Break the tofu into bite-sized pieces and brown, sprinkling with salt, in pan. Add green onions and vegetables and stir for a few seconds. Serve immediately.

A related dish is made with *okara*, the residue left from making tofu, to which meat, fish, root vegetables, or greens may be added to produce a stew that is kept moist by the addition of pork stock.

Yield: Four servings

SWEETENED TARO

(Taumu Ringaku)

This dish shows off the nutty flavor of taro and the slightly bitter orange peel cuts the sweetness. Use Japanese araimo, not Hawaiian taro.

1 pound cooked araimo (Japanese taro), peeled
1 cup sugar
2 tablespoons oil
3 tablespoons mirin
½ teaspoon salt
1 tablespoon orange peel, cut in fine slivers
1 tablespoon toasted white sesame seeds

Cut the taro in ¾-inch cubes. Place in a pan, barely cover with water, and add sugar, oil, mirin, and salt. Bring to a boil and cook until the taro is tender. Evaporate the liquid until the cubes are glazed. Turn into a serving dish, sprinkle with orange peel and sesame seeds and serve at room temperature.

Yield: Four servings

PIDGIN, PORK, AND THE PORTUGUESE

And if there had been more of the world
They would have reached it.[1]

Eating dinner on the lanai of my high-rise apartment, I can look across Pauoa Valley to the flat-topped and long-dormant volcano Punchbowl. Inside the crater is the National Memorial Cemetery of the Pacific, where Americans who died in the Pacific during and since World War II lie buried. Outside, the upper slopes are green and uninhabited. The lower slopes, though, are packed with neat frame houses. Among them is a modest white church, looking like the church in a child's wooden toy village, a small rectangular building with a sloping roof. This is the Church of the Holy Ghost, one of the main Portuguese churches in Honolulu. It is a humble immigrants' church, constructed by the Portuguese who settled on the slopes of Punchbowl when they left the plantations. They scratched away the raw lava, built neat houses, and planted vegetable gardens famous for their good order.[2]

What I am eating is one of Hawaii's Portuguese dishes, vinha d'alhos, pronounced (and sometimes written) vina dosh, short for carne de vinha d'alhos, literally meat in wine and garlic, actually pork pickled in wine or vinegar and garlic. It is a poignant reminder of the great Portuguese diaspora. As a student in the swinging London of the 1960s, on the prowl for cheap but tasty food, one of my favorites was the pork vindaloo to be found in every Indian restaurant. These two dishes, the pork vindaloo in an Indian restaurant in London and the pickled pork on my lanai half a world away in Hawaii, are the culinary traces of the scattering of the Portuguese around the world.

Portuguese pickled pork crops up not just in Hawaii, and London, and India, but on Cape Cod and in Malacca and in Trinidad too, wherever the Portuguese settled. In the fifteenth century, with centuries of experience of fishing voyages behind them, and with the careful plotting and funding of Prince Henry the Navigator, Portuguese sailors began venturing farther and farther

PART 2: ETHNIC FOOD

from their shores on the extreme west of Europe. By 1419, they had stumbled across the island that we now call Madeira, a couple of decades later they had reached the Azores, and by 1500 they were established in Brazil. All the while they were pushing down the coast of Africa, around the Cape of Good Hope, and across the Indian Ocean to establish an enclave in Goa on the western coast of India. A quarter of a century later, Magellan called in on the Philippines as he circumnavigated the globe. The Portuguese gained toeholds in Malacca on the coast of Malaysia, and in Macao just off the south of China, and traded with the Japanese at the port of Nagasaki. I marvel at the physical courage and determination of these voyagers. I marvel even more at the way, encouraged by their government, they married local girls, and traded far from home and in such alien tongues. Some linguists even suspect that pidgins worldwide are shaped by these first encounters between the Portuguese and the peoples they traded with. No wonder their great sixteenth-century poet, Luis Vaz de Camoes, claimed that if there had been more of the world they would have found it.

It was the lucrative spice trade the Portuguese were after, and, against all the odds, they succeeded in wresting it from the Arabs. They sailed, carrying spices (and plants too), back and forth between the Old World and the New. From the Americas they took hot chili peppers to West Africa, India, Southeast Asia, and even parts of China. Sweet potatoes and various squashes went along with them. Cinnamon, nutmeg, and black pepper they traded in the opposite direction.

Centuries later in the early 1800s the first Portuguese reached the Hawaiian Islands on ships trading out of the Portuguese colony of Macao.[3] Others, who had settled in New England, came around Cape Horn on the whaling ships. It was one of these early migrants who suggested that the Portuguese of the Azores and Madeira, reeling from the loss of their wine-growing industry to the blight that was plaguing the vines, would make good plantation workers. Already by 1855, 40,000 of them had left for the great plantations of the West Indies.[4] So from the islands that they had discovered in the Atlantic centuries before, the Portuguese came to islands even more remote, bringing their wives and children with them. Between 1878 and 1888 alone, 11,000 Portuguese arrived in the Islands, finding the topography and climate very similar to those of their homeland. By 1915, there were 20,000 Portuguese in Hawaii, as many as there were in Funchal, the capital of Madeira.

Wherever they settled, the Portuguese introduced their favorite foods, including vinha d'alhos. Perhaps originally a specialty of Madeira,[5] in each new settlement the Portuguese used locally available souring agents and spices. In India, pork, beef, or duck is soured with tamarind and spiced with ginger, coriander, cumin, and large amounts of chili pepper.[6] In Malacca, Chinese five-spice powder is used.[7] In the West Indies, the pork is soured with lime and lemon juice before being deep-fried and served with hard-boiled eggs.[8]

In Hawaii, pork, beef, fish, or turkey is soured with vinegar and spiced with chilies. In a similar manner, caldo verde, a Portuguese soup made with kale in Portugal, is made with kale and spices in India, taro leaves in the West Indies, and kale and sausage in Hawaii.

Musing, I look back at the streets of Punchbowl. Once there would have been fornos—the traditional Portuguese beehive bread oven—in at least some of the yards.[10] These were substantial affairs, nearly 6 feet high with walls that were 6 inches thick. The night before baking, the wife put a little leaven and a grated potato into a quart jar, added water and Hawaiian salt, and left the jar overnight well wrapped up against drafts. The next morning, she mixed the liquid with flour, kneaded the dough until it was elastic, lit the oven with firewood gathered from the hillsides, punched down the risen dough, kneaded it again, shaped it into loaves, and baked them twelve at a time. On special occasions—religious celebrations, weddings, baptisms, and birthdays—expensive spices, eggs, and sugar were added to make pao doce (sweet bread) and malasadas (doughnuts). Nowadays, the Hawaii Portuguese are famous for their sweet bread and malasadas, but a good plain Portuguese loaf is not to be had, at least not in the stores. Nor, apart from the church and street names such as Funchal, Lusitana, Azores, Madeira, and San Antonio is there anything to suggest that once Punchbowl was a Portuguese neighborhood.

Portuguese food in Hawaii has a much lower profile than Chinese or Japanese food. No grocery stores cater especially to the Portuguese, perhaps because most Portuguese ingredients—sausage and salt cod and beans and kale—are readily available in the chain stores. Though there are a few ethnic cookbooks, Portuguese festivals (for example, the Festival of the Holy Ghost, which Punchbowl church celebrates annually) are much more private than many of Hawaii's other celebrations.[11] Nor are there any Portuguese restaurants (though bakeries specializing in Portuguese items are quite common).

Although the cuisine as a whole remains largely unknown, certain specific foods have become popular: Portuguese sausage and rice is a standby for breakfast, and Portuguese bean soup for lunch. Sweet bread and malasadas are universally loved.

Delving deeper however, it becomes clear that the Portuguese had left their mark on the foods of Hawaii's ethnic groups long before they arrived in the Islands. It was from the Portuguese that the Koreans got their hot chili pepper, and the Chinese and the Japanese and the Filipinos got their sweet potatoes. It was from the Portuguese that the Japanese learned to make tempura and sponge (castera) cakes, that the Okinawans probably learned to make andagi and perhaps even rafute. It was the Portuguese who took bibingka between the Philippines and Goa, and it has been suggested that the Portuguese gave the Hawaiians the idea for lomilomi salmon. There was not so much of the world that the Portuguese didn't reach.

PORTUGUESE PORK MARINATED IN VINEGAR AND GARLIC

(Vinha d'Alhos)

Doubtless developed to preserve pork in warm climates, vinha d'alhos is an undemanding dish to prepare because the proportions can be varied to taste. Its crisp texture and tangy flavor make it very appealing.

2 pounds pork butt, cut into 1-inch cubes
⅔ cup white vinegar
¼ cup water
2 small red chili peppers, chopped (or 1 teaspoon of crushed red pepper flakes)
6 cloves garlic
1 teaspoon salt
Green onions, sliced, for garnish

Marinate meat with all the other ingredients in a nonreactive covered dish for 2 days. Place in a nonstick casserole or deep frying pan and simmer for 15–20 minutes until nearly tender. Then rapidly boil off the liquid. There should now be a little rendered fat in the pan. Fry the pork in this until the cubes are lightly browned and crisp. Place in serving dish and garnish with green onion rings. Serve with rice and a vegetable that is juicy or creamy to offset the crisp, slightly sour pork.

Yield: Four servings

Note: The amount of vinegar, chili peppers, and garlic can be adjusted to taste. A sprinkling of ground cumin, cloves, and allspice is added to the marinade in many households, lending an interesting spiciness to the finished dish. The Portuguese in Hawaii treat turkey, fish, and beef the same way.

. . .

PORTUGUESE BEAN SOUP

This favorite, derived from a one-dish peasant meal, crops up in almost every Island cookbook. The essential ingredients are ham or ham hock, beans, and a selection of vegetables. It makes an excellent main meal served with bread or cornbread and a salad.

> **1 ham hock**
> **Olive oil to coat pan**
> **1 good-sized onion, chopped**
> **2–3 cloves garlic**
> **2 celery stalks cut into dice**
> **1 carrot cut into dice**
> **1 cup navy beans or kidney beans, soaked overnight**
> **3 tomatoes, skinned and chopped (or substitute canned tomatoes)**
> **Dried red chili pepper, deseeded**
> **1 potato cut into dice**
> **Salt and pepper to taste**
> **3 tablespoons chopped parsley**

Take two pots (the soup can be cooked in one, but using two allows you to control how much of the salty ham stock you use). In one, place the ham hock, cover with water, and simmer until tender, about 2 hours. Remove the hock, skin, and cut the meat into small cubes. Reserve the stock. Meanwhile, in the other pan, saute the onion, garlic, celery, and carrot in olive oil until soft; then add the beans, tomatoes, chili pepper, and sufficient water to cover. Simmer until nearly done (1 hour). Then add the potato. After 5 minutes, add the cubed meat and enough of the stock to create a good flavor. Adjust the seasoning with salt and pepper. Simmer for another few minutes until the potato is cooked, add the parsley and serve.

Yield: Four servings

Note: Like many soups, this tastes better if made a day or two ahead. Macaroni is often added with the potato, which makes a very filling soup. Chunks of Portuguese sausage can also be added with the cubed meat.

· · ·

PORTUGUESE SAUSAGE

(Linguica)

Everyone in Hawaii eats Portuguese sausage, but it is very rare to see a recipe. From the start, it appears to have been made commercially (unlike blood sausage, which was made at home). This recipe is adapted from one that Madeline Nelson submitted to the Centennial Celebration Cook Book Committee of the Immaculate Conception Church in Lihue, Kauai, in 1984.

  2 pounds pork, about ⅔ lean to ⅓ fat
  ¼ cup water
  1 tablespoon vinegar
  8 cloves garlic, finely chopped
  2 dried red chili peppers, finely chopped, and deseeded
  1 teaspoon salt
  ½ teaspoon pepper
  Pinch of paprika

Chop half the pork into ¼-inch pieces and grind the remainder coarsely in a food processor. Combine in a bowl with the remaining ingredients. Refrigerate for 2 days, turning occasionally. Form into small patties and fry until brown.

Yield: 2 pounds sausage

· · ·

PICKLED ONIONS

  6–7 small to medium onions, peeled
  3 cloves garlic
  2 tablespoons salt
  3 dried red chili peppers
  3 cups vinegar
  1 cup water

Take an empty quart glass jar. Cut the onions in quarters lengthwise. Place ⅓ of the onions in the jar; add ⅓ salt, 1 clove garlic, and 1 chili pepper. Repeat twice. Fill the jar with water and vinegar and cover with a noncorroding top. It will be ready after a week.

Note: If you like a mild pickled onion, use Maui onions and Japanese rice vinegar.

. . .

HAWAIIAN SWEET BREAD
(Pao Doce)

The evaporated milk is typical of Local recipes, dating from a time when fresh milk was hard to preserve in the absence of refrigeration, but light cream can be substituted. A delicious bread for breakfast or coffee.

½ **cup mixed water and milk, warmed**
1½ **packages dry yeast**
½ **teaspoon sugar**
About 1 cup evaporated milk or light cream
5 tablespoons butter
Large pinch nutmeg
1 cup sugar
1 teaspoon grated lemon peel
4 cups bread flour
4 eggs, lightly beaten, plus 1 egg beaten for glaze
1 teaspoon salt

Mix milk, water, yeast, and sugar. Allow to stand until the mixture bubbles. In a saucepan, warm the evaporated milk. Add the butter, nutmeg, sugar, and grated lemon peel. Stir until the butter is melted. Place the flour in a large mixing bowl, add the eggs, yeast mixture, salt, and enough evaporated milk or cream to make a soft dough. Knead for about 15 minutes. Allow the loaf to rise until double in size. Punch down and allow to rise again. Form into a round loaf and allow to rise. Brush top with a mixture of beaten egg mixed with 1 tablespoon of water. Bake at 325 degrees for about 50 minutes.

Yield: One 1½ pound loaf

TRACKING DOWN THE KAMIAS: FILIPINO VEGETABLES IN HAWAII

It's nearly 8 o'clock and the sun has been up about an hour on this Saturday morning in January. The biggest and best of the People's Open Markets is about to start. The streets for several blocks around its location in Kalihi—an old neighborhood just a few blocks from downtown, home to low-income housing, recent immigrants, and storefront restaurants—are jammed with cars searching out the few parking spaces. Some 30 vans are lined up on either side of a wide cul-de-sac. In front of each van is a wooden trestle table loaded with vegetables, flowers, fish, eggs, or pastries. The jostling shoppers eye the produce but don't touch. The mere movement of a hand is sharply reprimanded. The rules are strict.

A horn sounds, and the still life springs into movement. Shoppers grab the plastic bags of vegetables, and the sellers scramble for change. No leisurely comparison shopping here, no bargaining, no gossip, no people watching. This is serious shopping, hard work, grabbing products that would be much costlier in the grocery stores if they were available at all. In just over half an hour's time the vendors will be packing up their tables and heading on to their next location some miles distant.

Carrying a large shopping basket, and stuffing $20 in change in the pocket of my shorts, I head into the melee. Right at the entrance to the cul-de-sac, I am distracted by a pickup truck. It advertises only two products: snails and *paltat* (catfish). The snails are in a big plastic bucket on the tailgate, soaking in water and ranging in size from a hefty 1½ inches in diameter to little babies only a third that size. For a moment I am tempted with visions of garlic butter. The catfish are even more exciting. The man standing on the flatbed hoists half a dozen at a time out of a cooler and flops them from his net into the aquarium tank. Live, of

Banana flower and marungay

JOSE MAGPIONG SMUGGLES MARUNGAY

In 1992, *Honolulu Magazine* ran a column whimsically titled "Fruitless Quest."[1] The author had been visited by his friend, Rama, who wanted neither beaches, nor bikinis, nor rum drinks with little umbrellas, but something he had seen on the drive from the airport: "a long, beanlike fruit that we used to eat when I was a boy growing up in India."

They did not manage to find it. But Rama was right that such fruits—known as drumsticks in English—are available in Hawaii and had he known it he could have bought them in the Open Markets. They are the pods of the marungay tree, which can be found in the back alleys of Chinatown and in the gardens of older neighborhoods such as Pauoa and Kalihi. (In English, it is called the horseradish tree because the roots purportedly taste like horse-

course. Shoppers here are discriminating, and lively fish command a premium. But today I am after vegetables, not snails or fish.

I shoulder my way quickly to the end of the cul-de-sac, eyeing the stalls on either side for particularly interesting vegetables. As a haole, I tower over most of the other shoppers—Filipinos, Southeast Asians, a few Chinese and Japanese —so that I can see the stalls and the lists of prices tacked on the sides of the vans with relative ease. Not that this helps all that much; most of the names on the lists mean nothing to me, and the vegetables on the trestle tables are largely unfamiliar.

The babble of voices around me is incomprehensible, most of them presumably speaking Ilocano or Tagalog, with a sprinkling of other Southeast Asian languages and a good dash of pidgin. But all the stall holders speak English or can make a good try at it, so there's no real difficulty. There are babies in strollers, ladies with their hair twisted up in combs, grannies wearing petal-covered hats, young men wearing T-shirts with messages that say "Practice safe sex. Go —— yourself," and older folk whose T-shirts, perhaps in reaction to those of the youth, proclaim that if they had known how nice grandchildren were, they would have had them first.

The stalls offer an intriguing variety of items. One booth sells nothing but eggs packed a dozen to a cardboard layer. They are carried away as fast as the vendor can take the money, the cardboard cartons with a string around them flopping over the customers' arms. I am tempted to cry out that the eggs are about to fall, though in fact they never do. The van that advertises live blue crabs, food stamps accepted, always draws a line; the vendors pick up the wriggling creatures with gloved hands, and people cart them off in large brown paper sacks. The flower lady has a large selection of orchids and carnations and chrysanthemums, though the red gingers and anthuriums are particularly popular; red signifies good luck in much of Asia, so they are a good choice for family graves. Spread out on the Filipino bakery table are doughnuts, yeast-raised sweet breads, and rice confections wrapped in banana leaves.

But the big attraction are the vegetables and fruits. The Filipinos have to rank as some of the world's greatest vegetable eaters, and only a few of their favorite vegetables show up in the supermarkets. So they grow their own— their vegetable gardens are famous in Hawaii—or they come here to the Open Market. Some stalls have just one or two items: Williams and apple bananas; fresh glistening pink ginger and okra; vine-ripened tomatoes, a rarity in Hawaii and one good reason for coming to the market. One stall advertises whole taro at $1.25 a piece. In fact, it's not *quite* whole taro, only the bulbous corm and the long purple stems without the leaves. These are popular and above the crowd you can see the purple shoots sticking up out of shopping baskets and above their owners' head. Another stall specializes in the many kinds of leafy vegetables that the Filipinos use so extensively in their soups and stews: sweet potato leaves, jicama leaves, bitter melon leaves, and marungay leaves curl over the edge of the table. On top are the root vegetables: the chop suey yams (jicama), creamy and bulbous; the sweet potatoes in numerous varieties; the mountain yams; the smaller Japanese version of taro; long, white daikon radishes. There are marble-sized green kalamansi limes (calamondins), football-sized yellow pomelos, warty limes, and golden tangerines; felty brown tamarind pods, spiky pineapples, silky orange cheese fruit (mamey), and richly purple banana flowers. Squash are available in profusion: sleek green squash, dark green cucumbers, long purple Japanese eggplants and round Southeast Asian ones the size of marbles, besides the loofah whose ridged shape somehow suggests science fiction nightmares, and fat round Japanese squash. There are snaky long beans, pretty furled wing beans, plump pods of soy beans, and the efficient-looking hyacinth beans (*Lablab pupurus*), and fat bunches of ong choy (swamp cabbage).

The less-harried stall holders struggle to answer my questions, hazarding explanations they hope will satisfy me. "What are these?" I ask, pointing to some bright green, shiny things packed into a plastic bag. They look like half-sized jelly beans with diminutive stems. "Turnip seeds" is the answer, presumably meaning daikon seeds, turnip being a common name for daikon. Everyone is kindly. A lady with a wide smile that reveals her golden teeth exclaims, "You buy that! You know how cook?" as I struggle with a 5-foot stem of taro. Of course I don't want to admit that I really haven't a clue, so I say yes but request her recipe all the same. She tells me to cut it in chunks and stew it with onions and coconut milk. It sounds pretty good. But then I have yet to find anything

radish. This has always puzzled me. Were the British in India perhaps so desperate for horseradish with their beef that they caused whole trees to be uprooted? Or did they use the roots of seedlings?) In any case, the tree runs to 30 feet high or more, has sprays of rounded leaves no bigger than a thumbnail, and, in season, these grooved pods the diameter of a pencil and twice as long.

In Hawaii it is the Filipinos who enjoy both the beans and the leaves of the marungay tree.[2] An early Filipino immigrant, Jose Magpiong, fearing that there would be no marungay trees in the distant islands of Hawaii, prudently collected some seeds before he left his homeland. Knowing that his clothes would be sterilized in an oven during a stopover in Hong Kong, he chose to tuck his seeds away in his guitar. When he arrived in Hawaii in 1909, he planted the very first tree, reputedly the ancestor of all the trees to be found in the Islands today.

Marungay pods on the tree

cooked with onions and coconut milk that doesn't taste good. I am even flattered to be recognized. "My white lady," says the elderly gentlemen who sells some of the best tomatoes in Hawaii, directing his assistant to give me a few extra to bring my load up to 5 pounds.

For a year or so, I was at a loss to identify these vegetables. I was not even sure which ethnic group used most of them, although I suspected the Filipinos. But Local Filipinos take them for granted. The excellent cookbooks that I now know to be published in the Philippines were not to be had in Hawaii. Filipino cookbooks written for a U. S. mainland market ignore vegetables unobtainable there, and that means just about everything in Hawaii's Open Markets. Cookbooks published in Hawaii were equally silent. Then one lucky day in a second-hand bookstore, I came across the *Manila Cook Book,* a book of Gertrude Stewart's newspaper columns published by the Manila *Evening News* in 1958.[3] Mrs. Stewart, it seemed, had grown up in Guam, the granddaughter of German emigrants and the daughter of an American marine. In those days, Guam was way off the beaten track and the family had perforce to use local tropical foods. Later the family moved to Manila, where she met and married her Scottish husband. Interned during the war, she relied on her knowledge of local foods to make life more bearable.

Mrs. Stewart's entirely admirable aim was to make the American community in the Philippines less dependent on scarce and expensive canned goods and more aware of the riches of cheap and readily available tropical ingredients. Bless her. She included a set of drawings of tropical vegetables so that at last I was able to match labels and the plants of mung beans and hyacinth beans, squash greens and sweet potato greens, *alugbati* and *kolitis, petsay* and the swamp cabbage even though I remain puzzled about what to do with many of them. She even gave, where possible, their English or Spanish translations.

Although she included almost no Filipino recipes, she suggested lots of ways of adapting Filipino vegetables to American cooking. To be sure, this was the cooking of the 1950s, with more cream-cheese fillings and cream sauces than are now fashionable. But she was clearly a fine and inventive cook with an imaginative flair for adapting new foods to Western cooking.

Even so, Mrs. Stewart was not unfailingly helpful. I came across a stall with a few plastic baggies full of objects that looked very similar to gherkins or small cucumbers, but just a tad too green and tender. The stall holder had almost sold out of her produce so she had time to answer questions. They were kamias, she said; they were "sour, for soup." Other customers arrived, and grateful for the information I handed over a dollar and left with a bag of thirty or so kamias, whatever they might be.

Preparing vegetables for sale (HSA)

Back home, I sliced the fruit to reveal star-shaped seeds. I nibbled on an experimental slice. They were indeed sour: a clean refreshing taste, less bitter than a citrus, less complex than tamarind. Mrs. Stewart made no mention of it, but after some searching, I found a recipe for a sour soup that called for souring it with kamias. How was not explained.

When my Filipina friend arrived the following week, I tentatively produced a mildewing package of kamias. "Kamias," she exclaimed, clearly surprised that I would have it in my refrigerator. "I always use that for cooking fish. You know, of course," she continued, "that kamias has more vitamin C than lemon or tamarind?" Confessing that I didn't, I urged her to tell me more. "Why, you use it for whitening your fingernails," she explained. "And moreover, it makes wonderful pickles just like little cucumbers. Just prick it all over with a needle, squeeze out the juices, and add salt and vinegar. It lasts a long time."

What is the plant like? According to my friend, it is a perennial that grows about 6 feet high, flowers all year long, and has fruit from soil level to the top of the plant. The more mature the fruit, the more sour it is. I travel around Hawaii with my eyes skinned for kamias plants, but I haven't yet seen one. But in the markets I have seen lots more kamias, or "pias" as it is sometimes called. And I have tried making pickled kamias, which do indeed keep well, are intensely sour, and are rather softer than an American pickle, as the texture of the fruit itself would suggest.

Having completed this detective work, I was leafing through Charlotte Knox's elegant illustrations in *Fruit: A Connoisseur's Guide and Cookbook* by Alan Davidson.[4] Sure enough, there was a drawing of a cluster of kamias fruits, identified in the text as belonging to a tree native to Malaysia and usually named by some cognate of its Malaysian name *belimbing asam* (*asam* for sour). It is apparently widely used in Malaysia, Indonesia, and the Philippines for pickles (that fits), in curries, and stewed as a vegetable. The fruit is apparently also extensively grown in Zanzibar, the West Indies, and Central America. And so I learned that checking a university library will probably produce a book by a scholar that identifies unfamiliar fruits and vegetables.[5] Since at least the beginning of the nineteenth century, the tropical world has been scouted by botanists in search of economically valuable products, and the results of their efforts are tucked away on library shelves. Of course, the problem of relating botany and market, botany and recipe remains.

I should have been delighted to identify the kamias, but I had mixed feelings. The world suddenly seemed a little smaller. It brought something of the disappointment that explorers must have felt when they realized that there were no new lands left to explore. My forays to the market became just that bit less exciting. Now I have to be satisfied with proselytizing about the possibilities of kamias.

Between 1910 and 1946, 126,000 Filipinos came to Hawaii to work on the plantations.[6] In the 1930s, 90% of them were Ilocanos from the northern part of the Philippines. Because they were the last group to arrive on the plantations, they were assigned the most menial jobs. The immigration laws did not permit them to bring families, and so the men lived in barracks. In the 1980s, the Filipinos were the only immigrant group to prefer other foods to their own.[7] Now they have opened a handful of restaurants, a number of grocery stores and bakeries, and they dominate the entrancing People's Open Markets. Although Filipino recipes crop up in a number of community cookbooks, there is but one cookbook devoted to Hawaii Filipino food.[8] Perhaps for these reasons Filipino food has not yet made it outside the Filipino community in Hawaii.[9]

This is too bad because the Philippines possesses a rich and complex creole food of its own. Settled by Malays, trading for generations with the Chinese, ruled by the Spanish for 300 years and by the Americans for over half a century, Filipinos have a cuisine to be proud of.[10] Apart from vegetables, they rely heavily on rice, fish, pork, and chicken. Many foods have a sour taste, and many are seasoned by *patis*, their thin fish sauce similar to many other Southeast Asian fish sauces, or *bagoong*, a thicker fish sauce. Filipinos also make a great variety of sweets, some of them deriving from the sweet rice flour–coconut tradition of Southeast Asia, others from the wheat flour–sugar traditions of the Spanish.

In 1965, the immigration laws were changed and families were allowed to enter, so, with any luck, in a few years Filipino food will be fully accepted. It has too many delicious dishes to continue unappreciated.

SINIGANG

(Sour Fish Soup)

A Filipino classic, this soup is so basic to the cuisine that Knorr manufactures both a soup mix and stock cubes. Asian stores sell these, but the flavor is better if homemade. The most common souring agent is tamarind, and tamarind extract, too, can be found in Asian stores. You can also use kamias, or even lemon or lime, though the flavor will be different. This soup is adaptable, quick and simple to make, and adapts well to microwave cooking.

4 cups water
2 unripe tamarind pods or 3–4 kamias
½ cup onion, sliced
2 cloves garlic, finely chopped
2 tomatoes, halved
1 inch ginger, peeled and cut in chunks
8 ounces firm white fish or shrimp
1 cup marungay leaves or watercress
Salt and patis (fish sauce) to taste

Wash the tamarind pods (which will be furry brown on the outside and pale green inside) or the kamias, place in a saucepan, cover with 2 cups of the water, and simmer for 20 minutes or so until tender. Meanwhile, place onion, garlic, tomatoes, and ginger (which prevents the fish from tasting fishy) in a second saucepan and cover with the remaining 2 cups of water. Simmer for 20 minutes or so until tender. Mash the tomatoes against the side of the pan to extract the flesh; scoop out and discard the tomato skin and the chunks of ginger. Take the first pan off the heat, mash the tamarind pods or kamias against the side to extract the juices, and then scoop out the flesh. The remaining liquid will taste quite sour. Then add the fish or shrimp and the greens to the saucepan of vegetables. Heat until fish is just cooked through. As you do so, add soured tamarind liquid, salt, patis, and water to make about six cups, adjusting the seasoning to taste.

Yield: Four servings

Note: Traditionally, water from washing rice was used to thicken the soup very slightly. A teaspoon of cornstarch mixed with water and added in the final stages of cooking will give the same effect. But this should not be a thick soup.

PINACBET

(Filipino Mixed Vegetables)

The ingredients in this Ilocano dish can be varied, as they can in all vegetable stews, though bitter melon, eggplant, and okra are musts. Bitter melon is bitter, a flavor I happen to love; with the increasing popularity of bitter vegetables such as endive and radicchio, it may become a favored vegetable. If you are hesitant, pinacbet is a good place to try bitter melon because the bitter flavor is muted in the medley of vegetables. The bagoong (fish sauce) is typically Filipino. Soy sauce can be substituted—the result will hardly be Filipino, but still tasty.

> **3 or 4 eggplants, preferably the long Japanese kind, cut into strips about 1 inch long and ¼ inch on the side**
> **½ pound okra, wiped and the caps cut off**
> **2 bitter melons, cut into strips about 1 inch long and ¼ inch on the side**
> **2–3 tomatoes, cut in segments**
> **6 long beans or green beans, cut into 1-inch lengths**
> **1 medium onion, halved and sliced**
> **1½ inches of fresh ginger, peeled and crushed**
> **1 tablespoon bagoong or soy sauce**
> **Salt to taste**

Layer all the ingredients in a shallow pan, preferably one that can be brought to the table. Add water almost to cover, loosely cover the pan, and simmer for about 20 to 25 minutes until the vegetables are tender. Shake occasionally to ensure that all the vegetables are evenly cooked but do not stir. The dish should be almost solid, but not dry. Serve with rice.

Yield: Serves four to six as a side dish

Note: With the addition of ½ pound pork cut in shreds, and a side dish of rice this makes a satisfying meal.

PORK ADOBO

(Filipino Pork in Vinegar and Soy Sauce)

This rich stew of tender pork in a slightly sour soy sauce is reminiscent of Portuguese vinha d'alhos and just as tasty.

2 pounds lean pork cut into 1-inch cubes
1 teaspoon ground black pepper
3–4 crushed bay leaves
¼ cup vinegar
1 clove garlic, crushed
Salt to taste
¼ cup soy sauce

Combine pork, pepper, bay leaves, vinegar, garlic, and salt in a saucepan and simmer for half an hour. Add the soy sauce and continue to cook until the pork is tender, about another half hour to an hour. A small amount of slightly thickened sauce should surround the meat. Serve with rice.

Yield: Four servings

Note: Pork spareribs cut into 1-inch chunks or chicken pieces also make good adobo. If desired, the sauce can be lightly thickened with cornstarch.

· · ·

LUMPIA

(Filipino Egg Rolls)

Lumpia is the Filipino version of an egg roll, part of the Chinese legacy in the Philippines. Ground or chopped fillings are rolled in a thin wrapper rather similar to a crepe. They can be eaten without further ado or gently fried until golden. Lumpia's origin may be Chinese, but the texture of the wrapper, much thinner and crisper than an egg roll, and the fillings are distinctly Filipino. In Hawaii, lumpia is a favorite fast food at carnivals and fairs.

To fill the rolls:

Lumpia wrappers are tricky to make and are usually purchased in Asian stores in cardboard boxes about 1 foot square and ½ inch thick. Their texture is quite different from egg roll wrappers, more like thin crepes, and indeed crepes can be substituted if necessary. Take the lumpia wrappers out of the package and cover with a damp towel so that they do not dry out. Carefully peel off the first wrapper and place the shiny side down. Spoon a tablespoon of filling across one end of the wrapper. Begin to roll up, pressing in the filling with your curved fingers. As soon as you have completed a half turn, fold in the two sides of the wrapper and continue to roll. You should end up with a tight cigar-shaped object. Rub a little water on the end of the wrapper to seal. Continue until you have used up all the filling. With a vegetable filling these rolls can be served just as they are. To fry the rolls, heat ½ inch of oil gently in a frying pan. It should not be too hot or the rolls will brown too quickly. Cook the rolls a few at a time, turning to brown them evenly until they are crisp and a light golden color. These are good just as they are, but if you wish you can serve a sweet-sour dipping sauce with them.

Pork filling:
1 tablespoon cooking oil
2 cloves garlic, finely chopped
1 onion, finely chopped
1 pound pork, ground
Salt, pepper, and soy sauce to taste
1 cup carrots, finely diced
1 cup bean sprouts

Heat the oil in a frying pan and saute the garlic and onion. Add the pork and stir until it turns color. Add the seasonings and the carrots and simmer until the carrots are tender. Stir in the bean sprouts. Allow the mixture to cool before stuffing the lumpia.

Beef and raisin filling:

A Filipina acquaintance gave me this recipe, which is apparently not common in the Philippines. However, it is well worth trying. It makes an excellent party dish as it can be cooked several hours in advance and the rolls will stay crisp.
1 pound ground beef
2–3 cloves garlic, chopped
2 ounces raisins, soaked
2 hard-boiled eggs, chopped
2–3 ounces frozen green peas
Salt to taste

Place the beef in a pan, add the garlic and a little water, and simmer gently until the beef turns color. Allow the mixture to cool and add the raisins, eggs, peas, and salt to taste. Then proceed to fill and fry the wrappers. Serve the golden cylinders arranged on a bed of shredded greens on a large platter.

Yield: Twenty-four lumpia

. . .

LUMPIA SAUCE

Add 2 or 3 finely minced garlic cloves to ¼ cup of vinegar and ¼ cup soy sauce. Season to taste with salt, sugar, and hot sauce.

. . .

BITSU-BITSU

(Sweet Potato Scones)

Chewy-crunchy in texture, this is a delicious and unusual confection. The grated sweet potato will seem dry at first but when the sugar and flour are added it gives off enough liquid to make the mixture hold together.

2 cups peeled and grated sweet potato
¼ cup flour
¼ cup sugar
Oil for frying

Mix together the sweet potato, flour, and sugar. Form into patties about 2 inches in diameter and ½ inch thick. Heat oil in a frying pan or griddle and fry gently for about 5 minutes on each side until golden brown. Serve with tea or cocoa as a sweet.

Yield: Six servings

THE LONG ARM OF EMPIRE

Canned Goods in Chinatown

Hawaii, like other tropical lands, was sucked into world commerce in the nineteenth century, sending off sugar and canned pineapple to the mainland United States and Europe, receiving in return canned foods. They are still coming, not just SPAM and crackers, but all kinds of processed foods. A stroll around the groceries of Chinatown drives home how much the Tropics use these products from the temperate lands. Just consider:

Longevity Brand Full Cream Sweetened Condensed Milk. The label, its legend in Chinese and Vietnamese, shows an elderly Chinese mandarin with flowing robes and a droopy moustache who appears to be carrying gau. Sun Hing Foods of California distributes this under license from the Cooperative Condensfabriek of Holland.

Ribena Concentrated Blackcurrant Juice Drink (By Appointment to Her Majesty the Queen), dark purple, almost black in a tall, handsome bottle with a gold cap, and Lucozade Glucose Drink, in a tall, clear bottle covered with crinkly yellow cellophane. How well I remember them both. My parents heartily disapproved of Lucozade, which they regarded, with some justice, as expensive sugar water, but they just as heartily endorsed blackcurrant juice with its high vitamin C content. Both drinks are made by Beechams, best known in Britain as the maker of Beechams' Pills, an all-purpose remedy for every conceivable ill.

Knorr Instant Chicken Flavor Bouillon in the familiar green and yellow packaging, but in huge cans labeled in Chinese characters, the flavor adjusted to Asian taste. This is produced by Knorr Products of Thayngen, Switzerland.

Horlicks Malted Food Drink Mix (interesting name when you think about it). Korean roasted barley tea and other cereal-thickened hot drinks had seemed strange to me until I realized that the major ingredients of Horlicks are wheat flour and malted barley with milk products and sugar added.

Ovaltine, a real polyglot. Ovaltine is essentially Horlicks with a little cocoa

and sugar. It comes in a bright orange can, labeled in both Chinese characters and English, proclaiming that since 1932, "Ovaltine has been recognized as the food beverage of the Olympic Games and other famous sports events." Ovaltine is manufactured in Great Britain but distributed from Minneapolis.

Quaker Instant Oats in a can, not cardboard, from Spuiboulevard, in Dordrecht, Holland.

Rowntrees Fruit Gums and Pastilles made in Great Britain by an old Quaker company. They are distributed by Nestlés of Switzerland.

Bird's Custard Powder. This colored, sugared cornstarch, to be mixed with milk to make an imitation egg custard, was an early convenience food, available from the 1840s. My father inveighed against it on the rare occasions when my mother dared make use of it. We would have real egg custard, real cream, or nothing at all. But someone is buying it in Chinatown, Honolulu, Hawaii.

Libby, McNeill & Libby's Cooked Corned Beef, which has been enjoyed in Hawaii for more than a hundred years. The handsome black, red, and yellow tapered can announces that this brand of corned beef received the highest awards at the International Health Exposition in London in 1884, the World's Columbian Exhibition in Chicago in 1893, the Panama Pacific International Exposition in 1915, not to mention being inspected and passed by the Argentine Secretariat of Agriculture, Livestock and Fishery established in 1930. It is a product of Argentina, but distributed by the Libby Division of the Carnation Company of Glendale, California.

Part Three

KAMAAINA

FOOD

HAWAII'S CROP PARADE: THE VEGETABLE RESOURCES OF THE TROPICS

Abaca, acacia, akala, alcohol, alfafa, algaroba, allspice, angleton grass, apple, apricot, arrowhead, arrowroot, artichoke, asparagus, Australian bluegrass, avocado, and awa.

(Plants beginning with "a" tried out as commercial crops in Hawaii)[2]

MANINI DON MARIN

In the early 1790s, the Spaniard Francisco de Paula Marin, usually given the honorific title of "Don," arrived in Hawaii. He seems to have been born in Spain in 1774 (4 years before Cook first set eyes on Hawaii), served in the Spanish Naval Service in the colony at Nootka Sound in Alaska, deserted, and somehow ended up in Hawaii. Apart from voyages to the South Seas, China, and California, he remained in the Islands for the rest of his life. He rollicked with Hawaiian monarchy, all the while conscious that he was in the Islands on their sufferance, and fathered at least twenty-three children by three or more women.[1]

Marin kept a sharp eye open for plants to grow in Hawaii and is popularly credited with an impressive array

The island of Oahu boasts no less than six botanic gardens. Four are run by the City: Foster Botanic, Wahiawa, Hoomaluhia, and Koko Head; one is run by the University of Hawaii, the Lyon Arboretum; and yet another is a commercial operation, Waimea Falls Park. Surely, I puzzled, that is a lot of botanical gardens for an island that at its greatest extent measures no more than 50 by 30 miles.

My fog cleared as I realized that the plantation owners of Hawaii had established many (not all) of these gardens as research stations. They were designed not as green refuges for an urban public but as laboratories to experiment with plants for farms and ranches and plantations, part of the great worldwide campaign waged by Europeans and Americans in the nineteenth century to exploit the plants of the tropical world.[3] Unlike most other tropical lands, the Hawaiian Islands were unusually short of economically valuable plants because they are so young geologically and because they are barricaded by thousands of miles of ocean. Only the sweet-smelling sandalwood commanded a ready market and that was quickly exhausted. Thus Hawaii was a net importer, not exporter of plant species, trying out plants from all over the world.

From the start, the haoles who came to Hawaii brought plants with them. In the 1790s, Captain George Vancouver of the British Navy left cuttings from grape vines, orange plants, and the seeds of various other fruits and vegetables that he had picked up in California. Shortly thereafter a migrant Spaniard, by the name of Don Marin, made a career out of growing and selling or bartering plants, some of which had been introduced before him, some of which he had introduced himself.[4] Most of the plants were from the Tropics, but some came from temperate zones and grew on the cooler mountain slopes. By 1836, when the *Sandwich Island Gazette*[5] listed what Hawaii had to offer for sale, it was largely the products of plants and animals imported since Contact: hides and goat skins, tobacco, beans, castor beans, cotton, sugar, molasses, coffee, indigo, sweetmeats, corn, beef, and pork. Only arrowroot, tapa, wood, paint oil from the kukui nut, and moss for mattresses were native.

In the middle of the nineteenth century, Honolulu was still a frontier town, its streets narrow and winding, its houses thrown up of rough coral slabs or of frame construction, whatever had come to hand. Hawaiian peddlers roamed the streets with poles over their shoulders supporting calabashes of poi. The Chinese had set up small businesses and restaurants. Sailors stayed for the winter, taking their pleasure after the rigors of whaling in the North Pacific. The Hawaiian monarchy had acquired a taste for imported food, for palaces, for ships, and for overseas education, and the haoles who now owned or leased land were looking for ways of making money. The answer was agriculture, plantation agriculture. With this in mind, the Royal Hawaiian Agricultural Society was founded in the 1850s to promote agriculture in the Islands. For the next century and a half, plantation agriculture dominated every aspect of life in Hawaii. Sugar and pineapple joined the sugar, coffee, tea, and chocolate grown in other parts of the Tropics for consumption in temperate latitudes.

The search for markets eventually contributed to the overthrow of the Hawaiian monarchy. The search for products demanded the creation of a medley of institutions dedicated to agricultural research. In 1895, the Hawaiian Sugar Planters' Association founded an experiment station, followed a few years later by a Pineapple Research Institute. In 1901 the federal government established what came to be called the Hawaii Experiment Station. A College of Agriculture and Mechanical Arts was founded in 1907, transmuting into the University of Hawaii a decade later. Soon agricultural research at the university was integrated with that at the Hawaii Experiment Station. The Hawaiian Sugar Planters' Association sent its scientists around the world, to India, to Burma, to Malaysia, to the Philippines, and to the Amazon Basin, to collect seeds and saplings. By the early 1930s, the extension movement was well under way, with farm advisors and home demonstration agents in every county. David Crawford, for years president of the University of Hawaii, summed up these labors in his book, *Hawaii's Crop Parade*, which he published in 1937. There, page after page, he listed in alphabetical order the major commercial crops that had been tried in Hawaii. Almost all of them had failed, for lack of space, for lack of appropriate climate, for lack of mechanization, for lack of market, for lack of pesticides. All that human ingenuity, all that capital invested, and all those failures.

Under a *Monodora myristica* tree in Foster Botanic Gardens on Vineyard

of introductions. Whether or not he should be is in question. What is not questioned is that he gardened, he preserved meat, he made butter and cheese, and he planted a vineyard, its location just east of Honolulu memorialized by the name Vineyard Street. With these supplies, he kept a kind of open mess for ships' captains who called in to pick up sandalwood or to replenish supplies for whaling in arctic waters.

Marin's fortunes declined in the 1820s. He did not get on with the stern New England missionaries, who frowned on his lifestyle and envied his skill with plants. Possibly because he was reluctant to help them garden, he was nicknamed "Manini." This was probably a play on words by the Hawaiians— manini is a small reef fish. Today, plant nurseries advertise *manienie*, known elsewhere as Bermuda grass; you can eat a manini mango; and to call someone manini is to accuse them of stinginess.

INTRODUCED PLANTS

In the 1820s when the missionaries arrived, the following plants had been introduced:

- Beans
- Bermuda grass
- Cabbage
- Castor beans
- Cherimoya
- Coffee
- Cotton
- Figs
- Grapes—probably the Isabella grape from Madeira
- Mangoes—probably from Mexico
- Watermelon
- Peppers of various kinds
- Pineapple
- Potatoes
- Tobacco
- Tomatoes
- Wheat

Street (named for Don Marin's vineyard) close to downtown Honolulu is a bronze plaque that tells the story in another way. It reads:

> This tree is a living memorial to Harold Lloyd Lyon, first director of the Foster Botanical Garden. It was imported as No. 9670 representing at his death on May 15, 1957 the number of new plants he had introduced into Hawaii from other parts of the world.

BEEFING UP HAWAII

Rolling grassy hills, post and wire fences, wild flowers on the verges, over-hanging eucalyptus, sleek Herefords grazing, and honest-to-goodness cow-boys with feather hatbands; not, perhaps, what most people would expect of tropical islands in the Pacific but typical of some of the most beautiful drives in the northern part of the Big Island and in Upcountry Maui. Only a fraction of Hawaii's land is suitable for agriculture. Huge stretches, particularly on the dry leeward sides, cannot be cultivated; they are too short of water and have too little soil covering the rough volcanic rock. Instead cowboys, many of them native Hawaiians, work on huge ranches. The story of cattle in Hawaii goes back to the first years of European contact.

In 1793, Captain George Vancouver sailed H.M.S. *Discovery* into Kawaihae harbor on the Big Island and altered forever the diet of the Hawaiians, for with him he brought six cows, a bull, four ewes, and two rams.[1] It was a tense time. Just 14 years earlier, Vancouver had been with Captain Cook when he was clubbed to death under the cliffs at Kealakekua Bay a few miles to the south.[2] In the meantime, Kamehameha I, making good use of British firearms, had conquered all the islands except Kauai. If the British were to be able to use the Sandwich Islands (as Cook had called them) to reprovision their Navy, they had to get on good terms with Kamehameha. The animals to be presented to him as gifts served a double purpose.

For some time, Kamehameha was nowhere to be found and the Hawaiians themselves seemed indifferent to the strange new beasts. In any case, the animals were in sorry shape, having had little water for days and no green forage for weeks as the little vessel plowed its way slowly across the vast Pacific Ocean. In Kawaihae, a chief came

In the 1930s cattle on the Big Island were herded out to ships to be transported to other Hawaiian islands (HSA).

JOHN PALMER PARKER

The Parker Ranch covers most of the northern end of the Big Island. It is one of the largest, if not the largest, ranches in private hands in the United States.[3] It was founded by John Palmer Parker, one of the first haoles to settle in the Islands. He came from a respectable family involved in the whaling business in Newtown, Massachusetts, went to sea, and jumped ship in Hawaii in 1809 when he was 19 years old.

The Hawaiians were understandably wary of the riffraff from around the world who wanted to live in their islands, but Parker learned Hawaiian and wangled a job as manager of one of the royal fishponds. He left the Islands for a while, sailing to China with a ship from New England, but persuaded the Hawaiians to take him back and then started a small truck farm. He married into the Hawaiian royal family and within a few years was fully occupied hunting and slaughtering the wild cattle and getting their meat, hides, and tallow to market. He took his pay in cattle and embarked on a breeding and improvement program. In 1845, when the Hawaiian government began legalizing private ownership of land, John Parker was ready; he filed his claim immediately and was granted 2 acres in 1847. From that small beginning, the ranch grew to 640 acres in 1850 and to some 227,000 acres carrying 50,000 head of cattle and 800 horses in the late twentieth century.

out to greet Vancouver with six hogs and a selection of vegetables. In return, Vancouver handed over a ram, two ewes, and a ewe lamb, somewhat to the displeasure of the chief, who would have much preferred firearms and who gave not a hoot that an individual called King George of England had said that there should be no trade in them. For the next week or so, Vancouver sailed down the coast, his cattle getting weaker and weaker, trying to find someone who could take him to Kamehameha. Finally, when the bull and one of the cows could no longer stand, he persuaded one of Kamehameha's close relatives to take them ashore. Kamehameha apparently was intrigued. A couple of days later he himself came out to the ship with a mighty retinue of canoes and presented the visitor with fine feathered helmets and some ninety pigs.

Kamehameha oversaw landing the animals. Vancouver's account does not elaborate, but hoisting five cows, two ewes, and a ram, even in weakened condition, into canoes lined with paddlers must have been quite a game. The cows, after all, were Texas longhorns. But some of the cows dropped calves, and Vancouver brought more cattle on a return visit the following year. He persuaded the king to agree that the cattle would be taboo—*kapu* in Hawaiian— for 10 years, until they had had time to multiply, and that death would be the penalty for anyone injuring or killing the animals. Only the king was to be allowed to take male animals for his own table. Vancouver wrung out one more concession: women, as well as men, were to be allowed to eat the meat. Kamehameha accepted on condition that it was not from the same animal.

On the slopes of the volcanoes that make up the Big Island, the cattle multiplied prodigiously.[4] Within 20 years they had become a pest, trampling crops, destroying taro patches, and, on occasion, attacking the people themselves. At that point, the Hawaiian monarchy, in want of cash to buy the various European goods that they enjoyed, thought of the cattle. New England whalers were beginning to winter in the Islands and they would pay for meat.

Cowboys were hired from California, cowboys of the then-typical California mix of American Indian, Mexican, and Spanish heritage, whom the Hawaiians called *paniolos* (from *Espagnols*).[5] The paniolos broke the horses that by this time were also running wild over the mountains, and they tanned leather, constructed saddles, and wove lariats. That done, they began hunting the wild cattle on horseback. They roped and tamed steers to drag wagons of beef from the interior to the coastlines where the merchant ships and whalers were waiting.

Thus began the long history of ranching in the Hawaiian Islands. Not only did the Hawaiians take to life on the ranch, they also took to beef. So, too, did the successive immigrant groups who came to work on the plantations. When they first arrived, the Chinese and Japanese subsisted largely on the vegetable dishes and rice familiar from their homelands. In Canton, the Chinese had

eaten little or no beef and in the southern prefectures of Japan, the farmers and fishermen had depended on fish and beans for most of their protein. Besides, Buddhism frowned on the eating of meat. Many plantations had ranches attached, and beef must have made its way into the plantation stores. By the beginning of the twentieth century, beef stew was a regular part of the diet for plantation workers. By the time the Chinese and Japanese left the plantations, however, they each had their favored beef dishes. In Hawaii, fund-raising cookbooks put out by Buddhist temples are full of meat recipes.

PIPIKAULA[6]

(Dried Beef)

Dried beef has been popular in Hawaii for a century and a half. It can be bought in many markets or seen hanging in strips above the stove in Hawaiian restaurants. Its most popular form is as pipikaula, a term apparently derived from "pipi"—the Hawaiian pronunciation of beef

BRINGING HOME THE BEEF

It was one thing to raise beef on the Big Island. It was another to get it to market. After whaling declined, so did the demand for salt beef. The market for fresh beef was in Honolulu, a couple of hundred miles away.

The cattle were herded down to Kawaihae harbor. The steamer *Humuula* anchored offshore. Powerful carthorses herded the panicky cattle into the surf. Paniolos lashed the thrashing beasts by their heads to waiting whaleboats, six to a side. Their body buoyancy kept them afloat while a motorboat towed the whole lot out to the waiting steamer. There, slings were passed under the bellies of the cattle to hoist them on to the deck. They were roped to the rail by their horns while the steamer tossed through the night on the choppy seas between the Big Island and Honolulu.

That was how it was done until 1937, when a wharf was built at Kawaihae.[7]

—and "kaula" for rope, though whether this referred to the rope from which the meat was hung to dry or its resultant texture is not clear.[8] The Hawaiians had been drying fish for centuries so it might well have occurred to them to dry beef. Or perhaps the Hispanic cowboys brought the method with them from California, because Mexicans have their own dried beef, *cecina*. Pipikaula is often served as bacon might be served, broiled or fried until brown, with poi or rice on the side.

1½ pounds beef tenderloin
2 tablespoons salt, preferably sea salt
½ cup soy sauce
½ teaspoon sugar
1 tablespoon lemon juice

Pound the meat and cut into pieces 4 inches long, 2 inches wide, and ¾ inch thick. Sprinkle with salt, soy sauce, sugar, and lemon juice. Dry in the sun for several days, taking care to screen the meat from dust and flies (a screened box was traditionally used for beef and fish).

Yield: ¾ pound dried beef

Note: Many Hawaiians like a fattier meat for pipikaula.

. . .

BEEF JERKY

Jerky, also popular in Hawaii, is thinner than pipikaula. The thin-cut beef sold in grocery stores for teriyaki works well. Or buy any piece of lean beef, half freeze it to make cutting easier, and then with a very sharp knife cut the thinnest slices you can with the grain. If you cut against the grain, the finished product will simply crumble. Pound the slices with the end of a bottle or other blunt instrument, but do not use an indented meat pounder because it breaks up the fibers. Jerky makes a good snack with drinks or to take on a hike or picnic. Although homemade jerky is not cheap (a pound of fresh beef will yield only half a pound of jerky), it is vastly superior to store-bought jerky.

2 pounds lean beef, sliced into pieces ⅛ inch thick and as large as possible
2 tablespoons salt
Marinade (optional)

Rub the salt and marinade into the beef and allow to sit in a bowl for half an hour or so, turning from time to time so that the flavor thoroughly penetrates the meat. Then hang the beef in a dry, airy, screened place. I have used clothespins to hang the beef from strings stretched between chairs on a screened lanai or porch. For a while, the rags of graying meat look a little odd, but they smell sweet and fresh. After a day the beef will be semidry. A couple of days later, it will be thoroughly dry. Wrap it loosely to keep clean. Unless the weather is very humid, it will keep several days at room temperature. Serve jerky as it is or brown it briefly under the grill or in a heavy frying pan.

Yield: 1 pound jerky

Note: Jerky can be made using the lowest possible oven temperature overnight; it is also possible to use the defrost setting of a microwave oven if you check every couple of minutes and keep turning the meat. If you have a dehydrator, follow the instructions.

Asian marinade:

Jerky in Hawaii is commonly marinated with Asian seasonings.
- **1 inch ginger**
- **2 cloves garlic**
- **½ cup soy sauce**
- **2 tablespoons sugar**
- **1 tablespoon sesame oil**
- **1 teaspoon hot pepper sauce**

Crush the ginger and garlic in a mortar and pestle and mix with the other ingredients.

Mexican marinade (in remembrance of those first cowboys):
- **Cumin seed**
- **Lime juice**
- **Ground red chilies**
- **Oregano**

Toast the cumin seed lightly in a heavy frying pan until it smells aromatic and turns color. Grind in a mortar and mix with lime juice, chilies, and oregano.

PARKER RANCH BEEF STEW

Cowboys and other ranch employees came in from 2 o'clock in the morning to eat stew and rice at the Parker Ranch Restaurant.[9] Meat from an older cow or steer was cooked over a wood-burning stove in a 15-gallon stock pot. At the end of the day, fresh ingredients were added, and the procedure continued for as much as a week. The cook, Akona, was Chinese, and he added his own touch, the ginger. Quantities in this version are reduced to family size. Squash-like chayotes (*Sechium edule*) grow readily in Hawaii.

> **2 pounds beef short ribs cut into 2-inch pieces**
> **1 clove garlic, minced**
> **1-inch piece fresh ginger root, unpeeled**
> **1 medium onion, sliced**
> **2 medium potatoes, peeled and quartered**
> **3 chayotes, peeled and cut in half (or 6 carrots, halved)**
> **Salt to taste**

Combine the ingredients in a large pot. Add water to cover. Simmer over medium heat until the meat is tender and the potatoes have thickened the gravy (2–3 hours). Serve with rice.

Yield: Four to six servings

• ■ •

LUAU STEW

(Beef Stew with Taro Leaves)

Luau stew made use of ingredients readily available on the ranch. The taro leaves thicken the stew.

Traditionally this was eaten with poi, raw onions, limu, and chili pepper, but it is good eaten with rice and a side dish of raw onions.

> **2 pounds beef stew meat or mixed beef and pork**
> **2 tablespoons cooking oil**
> **2 chopped onions**
> **2 pounds taro leaves, previously cooked for 1 hour and**
> ** chopped (see p. 223)**
> **Salt**

In a large pot, fry the onions slowly in the oil until they turn a golden brown color but do not burn. Add the meat and turn until browned. Add water to cover. After about an hour add the taro leaves. Simmer until tender, about another hour. Add salt to taste.

Yield: Four servings

· · ·

LOCAL-STYLE OXTAIL SOUP

(Clear Oxtail Soup with Ginger and Star Anise)

This soup of Chinese origin is a favorite lunch dish in Hawaii and is worthy of wider renown. The chunks of succulent meat in the hollows of the bone, the flavorful broth, and the edge added by the ginger, Chinese parsley, and green onions make a very satisfying dish for lunch or supper with rice on the side. It also makes a good supper.

2 pounds oxtail in pieces
1½ quarts water
¾ cup shelled and skinned raw peanuts
1 clove garlic, crushed
1 slice orange peel
1 piece star anise
Small piece of ginger root finely chopped
Salt to taste
Chopped green onions and Chinese parsley (cilantro)
   to garnish

Place the oxtail in a large stock pot and add water, peanuts, garlic, orange peel, star anise, and ginger. Bring to a boil, skim off any grayish scum, and simmer for 2 to 3 hours until oxtail is tender. Place in the refrigerator overnight for the flavor to develop. Next day remove the oxtail and peanuts, strain the stock, and then reheat with the oxtail and peanuts. In Hawaii, the meat is always left on the bone, but it could be taken off if you wish. When the soup is piping hot, adjust the seasoning. To serve, put two or three pieces of oxtail and some peanuts in each of four deep oriental soup bowls and fill each with broth. Garnish with a little chopped green onion and Chinese parsley. Serve with a bowl of boiled white rice and small containers of soy sauce and grated ginger on the side. The rice is eaten with chopsticks, the soup with a ceramic Asian soup spoon.

Yield: Four servings

BEEF HEKKA (SUKIYAKI)

(Japanese Beef and Vegetable Fondue)

Judging by both early cookbooks and reports of oldtimers, this was one of the first Japanese recipes to gain general acceptance in Hawaii.[10] Versions of it may be found in almost all cookbooks in the Islands. The selection of vegetables can be varied depending on what is available.

1 pound tender beef, sliced paper thin
4 ounces mushrooms, sliced thin
1 cup bamboo shoots
1 block tofu, cut in bite-sized cubes
1 bunch green onions, cut in 1½-inch lengths
½ pound watercress, cut in ½-inch lengths
4 tablespoons sugar
½ cup soy sauce
½ cup mirin or water

Arrange the meat and vegetables on a large platter. Heat an electric frying pan or wok at the table. Add the sugar, soy sauce, and mirin and heat until sugar has dissolved. Add the beef and cook for 1 minute, add the mushrooms, bamboo shoots, and tofu and cook another minute, and then add the green onions and watercress. Let each person use chopsticks to select the items they want. Serve with rice.

Yield: Four servings

CHRISTIAN FOOD AND CHRISTIAN LIVING: THE IMPACT OF THE MISSIONARIES

On the edge of downtown Honolulu, just down from Iolani Palace, the palace of the Hawaiian monarchy, and next to Kawaiahao Church, an imposing structure of coral blocks sometimes described as Hawaii's Westminster Abbey, stands a small cluster of white frame houses, pleasantly shaded by tall trees. These are the houses of the Congregationalist missionaries who began arriving from New England in 1826.[1] On reaching the Islands after tossing and vomiting for weeks on the rough passage from Cape Horn, they had dispersed to the different islands, putting up in whatever shelter they could persuade the Hawaiians to provide. Some were granted permission to stay in this spot, not then cool with grass and trees but a hot, bare, dusty plain scattered with a few Hawaiian straw houses.[2]

The missionaries found it much more difficult to feed themselves in this strange land than had the haoles who had come before them. Their predecessors had almost all been single men who solved the problem by living with Hawaiian women. The missionaries, though, were married, a condition of their service, and the women wanted to create homes for their husbands and children. Unlike the ragtag beachcombers who had preceded them, the missionaries were not in the Islands in search of adventure, not out to make their fortune, not fleeing from unknown troubles at home, but had arrived with a high moral purpose—to save the souls of the Hawaiians. They were in the Islands to convert the natives to Christian living, eating right was part of living right, and eating right was eating good New England food.

That, at least, was the theory. In practice, climate and supplies made a New England diet impossible. Without salaries, subsisting on donations from the Board of Missionaries, a body that had no experience with the Tropics, tolerated by the Hawaiian chiefs but without any legal or economic rights, totally ignorant of tropical foods, the missionary wives found that housekeeping became a matter of catch as catch could. They were no Don Marins successfully gardening with plants already familiar to them. They were no John Palmer Parkers cheerfully adapting to Hawaiian food from the start. They were young women far from home struggling to make a life that they considered a decent moral example.

Every aspect of cooking and eating created problems. Water was a problem because many mission settlements were far from fresh water and it had to be fetched in, carried in two gourds hung from the ends of a pole balanced on the shoulders. Cooking was a problem because, at least in the early years, it had to be done on outdoor fires without even the hook that they remembered from New England. Ingredients were a problem: the Board sent out barrels of flour and dried and salt meat, but the flour arrived caked and crawling with weevils after the 6-month voyage and the salt meat, too, was on the verge of spoiling. Bodies craved fresh meat instead.

In desperation, the missionary wives, with some pangs of conscience, offered Hawaiians food and clothing in return for help with their household chores (at least until the antislavery agitation led them to offer wages as well). They sought every way of enhancing their meager rations. They began adapting to local food. Taro quickly took the place of the potato and, to a large extent, of bread as well. Green mangoes stood in for apples, luau leaves for spinach, and salt salmon for salt cod. For land to garden, and sometimes even for domestic animals, they bartered sewing and English lessons with the chiefs. For chicken, fish, Polynesian arrowroot, taro, and firewood, they paid other Hawaiians with cloth, fishhooks, needles, and scissors. Precious gifts of fresh meat sometimes turned up from other haoles, such as the sawyers near Hilo, who hunted the cattle that ran wild in the mountains and felt sorry enough for the struggling missionaries to pass along part of their surplus. Packages of food, including dried apples for the apple pies they so badly missed, arrived with the rare letters from home. They swapped their own best products: a wife who could make little cheeses exchanged these for a sister's guava jelly or marmalade. And visiting sea captains, grateful for a little hospitality on land, volunteered raisins, molasses, butter, or oil, and even wine and brandy, scorned by temperance-minded sisters, but welcomed by the rest.

Even so, the missionary diet was pretty dreary. Breakfast might consist of fried taro or a bowl of arrowroot or rice; the midday meal consisted of taro, one of the unfamiliar garden vegetables, and the everlasting salt meat, or perhaps boiled or fried fish, followed by a pudding of rice or arrowroot; supper was taro again, or possibly bread, bananas, and milk.

A missionary was not supposed to dwell on food. But a missionary wife was faced with the task of feeding her household with unfamiliar ingredients and primitive equipment, all the while pregnant or nursing. If anything happened to her, the whole family suffered. She was miles away from haole doctors. She had no modern medicines. Staying healthy was uppermost in her mind and about the only thing she could do to improve her chances of this was to eat as well as possible. In their letters and diaries, as in their lives, the missionary wives had no choice but to dwell on food.

THE WANT OF FRUIT:
STILL FELT IN HAWAII

On New Year's morning the streets of the older neighborhoods of Honolulu—Pauoa or Liliha or Kalihi—are red with the shredded paper from the thousands upon thousands of firecrackers set off the night before.[1] The trade winds have already blown away the choking smoke that clogged the valleys, and the smell of cordite has quite vanished. The neighborhoods are deserted; those who are not sleeping off the night before have gone off to the Shinto shrines to start the year on a proper footing.

Above the reddened streets, citrus fruits hang from the trees that crowd the small yards. Land in Hawaii is scarce and expensive, and lawns are a luxury only the very rich can afford. For the rest, any plot big enough for a lawn is big enough for an *ohana* zoning permit (one that allows other family members to build) so that the houses are stacked higgledy-piggledy along lanes off the main streets. Covered with peeling gray or green paint, these are small frame houses, and their design owes a good bit to the New England haoles so dominant in nineteenth-century Hawaii. On the sagging front steps are piled pair

Green mangoes (HSA)

after pair of slippers (thongs) because no one wears shoes in the house. In the small lean-to garages are stacks of old boxes, coolers, surfboards, the washer, broken-down vehicles, washing lines, and all the other detritus that can't be crammed into the tiny house that has neither an attic nor a basement. Some houses have a cut-out circular moon door superimposed on their New England–style facade or smart little red Chinese lions rampant on the handrail of the concrete balustrade, suggesting that they are occupied by Chinese families. Others have set concrete slabs in the front yards and crammed them with bouganvillea and dendrobium orchids in plastic and concrete pots, and hung weights on wires to shape the branches of the trees. Japanese, one assumes. Some of the old frame houses have been torn down to be replaced by houses of concrete blocks, spacious verandas on their second floors finished with ornate red concrete balustrades. Aha, Filipino. Yet others

present mysteries. One has the narrow area between the frame walls and the chain-link fence packed with 6-foot-high dendrobium orchids, their jointed green and white stems too thick to push through. Hanging amidst them are two dolls, not any old dolls, but fine china dolls, their dresses faded in the bright sun, their eyes open and unblinking. When the trades blow, they twist and twist in the wind.

In all these yards, there are fruit trees. On New Year's Day, golden tangerines glow against the dark green of the tree in one yard, vast lemony globes of pummelo in the next. Oranges do not do so well in Hawaii's climate, but even they fill the hand heavily and satisfyingly, green, smooth-skinned and slightly rashed, unlike their perfect and artificially ripened mainland counterparts. There are big knobbly-skinned limes and tart marble-sized calamondin limes. In February, the mangoes start to flower. The air is still cool in the early morning, the cocks crow just a mile from downtown skyscrapers, and above the yards handsome mango trees soar 50 feet over the rooftops, their blade-shaped leaves drooping down in clusters and the ends of the stems curving upward into a pyramid of small reddish or orangish flowers, giving the trees a halo of dusty color when viewed from a distance. By April, the trees are hung with unripe green mangoes, already mature enough for chutney, drooping down like ornaments on a Christmas tree. Other stems, without fruit, stick out, giving the trees an untidy, unshaven appearance.

In June, fruit falls from the passion fruit vines that twine over chain-link fences. You can push your fingernails through the leathery rind and break it open to suck out the delicious acidy, pulpy seeds inside. Sprays of rose-colored lychees dangle from striking green trees. Nothing beats a lychee straight from

Papayas, bananas, and sugarcane for sale

the tree, still warm from the sun. Mangoes are beginning to fall to the sidewalk, creating sticky messes that attract swarms of little flies. Householders sally forth with fruit pickers (bags on the end of long poles) to collect the fruit. A mango tree produces a lot of fruit. A bag of mangoes is about as welcome in Hawaii as a bag of zucchini on the mainland. Nevertheless, brown grocery bags full of mangoes are toted to the family, to friends, and to offices across the state. Those who are already overloaded with rich-smelling mangoes, leave little piles on their lava-rock garden walls—together with the equally embarrassingly overabundant avocados—in the hope that passersby will pick them up.

With all these glorious fruits, it is disappointing to find that the major grocery stores carry little in the way of tropical fruits: papayas, oranges from the Kona Coast of the Big Island, pineapples, mangoes, and apple bananas are about it. Hawaii agriculture is oriented toward mainland, not Local, markets. This is nothing new. "You feel the want of it here," complained Mark Twain, talking of fruit.[2] James Girvin, librarian of the Hawaiian Gazette Company, was of the same opinion: "For a tropical country the markets afforded very little variety of fruits. Oranges, breadfruit, ohias (mountain apples), bananas, and a few guavas, were all that was noticeable, whereas in the West Indies a hundred kinds of fruit would be offered."[3] Even so, judging by earlier cookbooks, more tropical fruits were used in the late nineteenth and early twentieth centuries than are used now.[4]

Perhaps the reason is that tropical fruits—few of them native to Hawaii in any case—were unfamiliar to most of the early immigrants.[5] Older recipes use them as substitutes, mangoes for apples, for example. Now grocery stores stock apples for the haoles and persimmons for the Japanese, a practice which continues to restrict the market for the more unfamiliar tropical fruits. The want of fruit is made worse by the persistent fruit flies that damage so many Hawaii crops, destroy the chance of exporting them, and thus discourage commercial production.

Still, with persistence tropical fruits can be found in Hawaii. Friends and acquaintances bring unusual citrus and mango varieties from their gardens. Hikes into the mountains lead to wild guavas and passion fruit. The Open Markets and Chinatown offer star apples, cheese fruit, and jackfruit. Tamarind pods can be picked up on the campus of the University of Hawaii at Manoa.

The following recipes simply suggest uses for a few of Hawaii's fruits.[6] If the traditional uses of fruit in cakes and pies and mousses seem a little heavy, there are alternatives. The Hawaii Regional Cuisine chefs are experimenting with fruit salsas and fresh chutneys for meats and fish. Older cookbooks offer recipes for drinks and ices that bear reviving. The shave ice and the crack seed of the Japanese and the Chinese suggest possibilities. The immigrants from Southeast Asia and the Philippines have long-established and still to be explored ways of preparing these fruits.

Bananas

The fictional master planter's loving description of Hawaii's bananas suggests the uses to which they were once put, many of them still worth trying.

> The banana is . . . par excellence the staple dish of the islands . . .
> Always bunches hung on the verandas for every one to help themselves
> to, but when cut up and served with cream and sugar they were preferred
> by many to strawberries. Fried in butter, or made into fritters, or boiled
> in water, or baked in their jackets, or dried and made into a fragrant
> sweet flour which can be used for many purposes, the banana is the sav-
> iour of the housekeeper. Bananas and oranges thinly sliced and in alter-
> nate layers with sugar, and well cooled before serving, was described by
> many as simply delicious.[7]

Apple (Brazilian) bananas are readily available in supermarkets and worth the additional price. Bought green they ripen rapidly. Half the size of a Williams Hybrid (the kind usually marketed commercially), they have a much clearer, sharper taste. Use them for the following recipes if you can. If not, substitute Williams Hybrid, remembering that they are twice the size.

TURRON

(Filipino Banana Fritter)

Lumpia wrappers make a delicate fritter. Take one apple banana, a little brown sugar, and two lumpia wrappers per person. Cut the banana in half lengthwise and roll in brown sugar. Place on one side of the lumpia wrapper and roll up, tucking in the sides of the wrapping as if making a parcel. Dampen the edge of the wrapper to seal. Heat about 1 inch of cooking oil in a wok or deep frying pan. Place the wrapped bananas in the oil and fry over gentle heat until golden brown. Remove, blot on paper towels, and serve immediately.

• • •

APPLE BANANA-COCONUT-TAPIOCA PUDDING

This delicious variant on an old favorite has been popularized in recent years in Hawaii by the Thais and Vietnamese. Using the microwave rather than cooking the tapioca on top of the stove eliminates the problems of sticking and burning. Small plastic cartons of brown, aromatic palm sugar can be found in Asian stores and give the dish an appealing pale coffee color and pleasant aroma. Brown sugar can be substituted. Tapiocas vary, so experiment with the cooking times. Thais like the pudding a little runny, but by varying the amount of coconut milk you can adjust the texture to your taste.

> **2½ cups water**
> **3 tablespoons palm sugar or brown sugar**
> **Pinch of salt**
> **¼ pound quick-cooking pearl tapioca**
> **¾ cup coconut milk (frozen or canned)**
> **2 apple bananas**

Pour the water into a large microwave dish and heat to boiling. Add the sugar and salt and stir until dissolved. Add the tapioca and microwave at half power for 10 minutes. Check. If the tapioca has not softened and thickened the sugar solution, continue microwaving a few minutes at a time until that happens. Remove from the microwave and stir in the coconut milk. Take four glass dishes, slice half an apple banana in the bottom of each, and pour the tapioca pudding over the fruit. Press plastic wrap over each surface to prevent hardening and allow to cool to room temperature.

Yield: Four servings

Guavas

Guavas are hard to find in Hawaii markets (although you can buy heavily sweetened guava nectar), ironic when weedy trees clamber all over the mountains dropping fruit and attracting clouds of flies. Guavas are often made into jelly, but guava cake is also popular.

GUAVA CAKE

1 cup butter
2 cups sugar
4 eggs
3 cups flour
1 teaspoon baking powder
½ teaspoon cinnamon
1 cup guava pulp (fresh or frozen concentrate)
½ cup guava juice
Red coloring to tint the cake pink (optional)

Preheat the oven to 350 degrees. Cream the butter and sugar together and add the eggs one by one, beating well. Stir the baking powder into the flour. Mix guava pulp and juice together. Add flour and liquids in alternate portions to the creamed mixture and stir to blend. Pour into a greased and floured 13 by 9 inch cake pan. Bake for 30 minutes or until top of cake springs back when lightly pressed with a finger. Frost with a butter cream frosting of 1 cup softened butter, 2½ cups powdered sugar, and sufficient milk to make a creamy consistency.

Yield: Sixteen servings

• • •

Lychees and Longans

Fresh lychees can be found in Chinatown and in some stores during their brief season in June, and very beautiful they are with their pinkish stems and rose-colored, knobbly, round-shelled fruit with green leaves still attached. They are best bought still on the stem, which keeps them fresher. To pick out the juiciest lychees, press the shell on the side opposite the stem. If it is cushiony and gives under the pressure, then you have a good one. If you feel the hard pit, then the flesh is sparse. To get to the succulent white fruit, pierce the shell with a fingernail and peel it back. The fruit can then be eaten whole and the smooth brown pit discretely discarded, or it can be pitted and halved or sliced for other uses.

Many Local cookbooks suggest stuffing with cream cheese, but to my mind the silky texture and rich flavor of the lychee is not complimented by the cloying commercial product. Fresh lychees are such a treat that they deserve to be piled up on a platter decorated with the leaves (or perhaps hung in bunches from a vertical frame such as the kind used to dry spaghetti) to be eaten after a meal. Lots of napkins or fingerbowls should be provided.

Longans come into season late in the year. In both taste and appearance they are like a lychee reduced to marble size. Their popular name, "dragon's eye," is apt indeed.

Mangoes

A wide variety of named and unnamed varieties grow in Hawaii, and their tastes can be quite dissimilar. The main season for ripe mangoes is midsummer though some are available at other times of year. They are messy fruit to handle because the firm skin covers very soft flesh, which clings to the seed. The easiest way to deal with them is to stand the mango upright and make two cuts down the wider sides parallel to the flat internal pit. Pull away these two cheeks. Cut slices or crosshatches across them. Then turn the cheek inside out and cut close to the skin with the knife. Slices or chunks then fall off to be used as you want. If you are short of mangoes, you can then tackle the small amount of flesh remaining on the mango seed. If you have an excess, you can throw the rest out.

Green mangoes have many uses for savory dishes, pickles, and chutneys. In Hawaii "common" mangoes are usually chosen for these purposes. (Developed varieties are often too turpentiny.) They are easier to deal with because the flesh is still firm and you can cut right through the seed, which is still soft, and pop it out with the knife. A green mango, peeled, with a shake of soy sauce or salt, is a common snack in the Islands and one well worth trying if you can find green mangoes.

POTATOES AND MANGO

The missionaries commonly substituted mango for apple in pie and other sweet dishes. Some of the other early haoles came from Germany, and occasionally a German recipe crops up in Hawaii cookbooks. In Germany this savory dish would have been made with pears.[8]

4 medium red boiling potatoes
4 green mangoes
Butter to garnish

Take two medium-sized saucepans and put water on to boil. Add salt. Peel the potatoes, cut in quarters, and add to one pan. Peel the mangoes, cut in quarters, remove the seeds and add to the other pan. Boil both until tender, about 20 minutes. Place in a serving dish, toss with a little butter.

Yield: Four servings

. ■ ■

MANGO SAUCE

This sauce was commonly used by kamaainas as a substitute for applesauce. It has a similar tartness but the flavor is distinctly different; it is a sauce worth knowing to serve with pork, ham, or sausages.

4 green mangoes
Sugar, cinnamon, and cloves to taste

Peel the mangoes, cut into slices, and remove the seeds. Simmer with a little water until tender, about 10 minutes. Add sugar and spices to taste. Serve warm or cold.

Yield: Six to eight servings

. ■ ■

MANGO CHUTNEY

To judge by memoirs and recipe books, mango chutney has been made in Hawaii since at least the middle of the nineteenth century. It is best made with green mangoes. For those with mango trees in Hawaii, this is a welcome way of getting a head start on the crop. Most Hawaiian recipes for mango chutney start off with instructions such as "take 50 mangoes"—which might seem extravagant on the mainland but wouldn't make a dent in the crop from a single tree in Hawaii. Chutney is a very forgiving product; a little more or less of any ingredient is not crucial.

10 green mangoes (about 5 cups)
2 cups sugar (raw sugar gives a good taste)
¾ cup white vinegar
1 tablespoon finely chopped garlic
1 tablespoon finely chopped ginger
2–3 hot red chili peppers, sliced (to taste)
½ teaspoon allspice
Pinch salt

Peel mangoes and cut in quarters through the seed, which will still be soft. Pop the seed out with the tip of a knife. Cut into pieces about 1 inch long, ½ inch wide, and ¼ inch thick. Place all the ingredients in a nonreactive saucepan and bring to a boil. Simmer until the mango has almost disintegrated and the chutney is dark brown. This will take about ½ hour to 40 minutes. Stir from time to time to prevent sticking. Cool and place in sterilized glass jars. Serve with curries or cold meats.

Yield: About 1½ quarts

• ■ •

PICKLED MANGO

Like mango chutney, pickled mango goes well with cold meats.
16 cups green mango chunks
3 cups water
3 cups brown raw sugar
2 cups vinegar
Salt to taste (about ½ cup)
2 tablespoons red food coloring (optional)

Prepare the mangoes. Mix all other ingredients and bring to a boil. Allow to cool slightly. Place the mangoes in sterilized glass jars, pour the pickling solution over the fruit, and seal.

Yield: 4 quarts

Note: Chopped fresh ginger or five-spice powder can be added for flavor.

MANGO BREAD

Mango bread is to Hawaii what zucchini bread is to the mainland, a way of using up a surplus. Nevertheless, it can be excellent. Green mangoes can be used instead of ripe mangoes and give a nice tang.

1¼ cups flour
½ cup sugar
1½ teaspoons baking powder
½ teaspoon baking soda
1 teaspoon ground cinnamon
1 teaspoon ground cloves
1 teaspoon ground nutmeg
1 egg, beaten
¼ cup vegetable oil
½ cup milk
1½ cups ripe half-inch mango cubes

Preheat oven to 350 degrees. Grease and flour a 9 by 5 inch loaf pan. Combine flour, sugar, baking powder, baking soda, and spices in a large bowl. Stir in egg, oil, and milk. Fold in the drained mango cubes. Pour the batter into the pan and bake at 350 degrees for 50 minutes, or until a toothpick comes out clean. Cool for a few minutes, remove from the pan, and allow to cool thoroughly on a wire rack.

Yield: One loaf

· · ·

MANGO MOUSSE

This recipe does not come from Hawaii though it might as well. Condensed milk is very much a part of Hawaii's culinary heritage, as it is in many parts of the tropical world. In this recipe, the acidity of the mangoes and limes thickens the condensed milk.

2 pounds ripe mangoes, peeled and sliced
1 14-ounce can condensed milk
Lime juice to taste
1 cup heavy cream, whipped

Place mangoes, condensed milk, and lime juice in a food processor and process until smooth. Fold in whipped cream. Pour into glass dishes and chill for a couple of hours. Garnish with a dendrobium orchid or a sprig of bougainvillea.

Yield: Four servings

MANGOES AND STICKY RICE

Thai restaurants in Hawaii offer this dessert when mangoes are in season. The juicy chilled mango contrasts nicely with the succulent rice.

1 cup Thai sticky rice
1 cup coconut milk
Sugar to taste
3–4 ripe mangoes, chilled

Rinse the rice in several changes of water until the water runs clear. Place the rice in a bowl, cover with water, and soak for several hours. Drain. Place a clean dishtowel in a steamer and place the sticky rice on the towel. Steam for about 45 minutes or until tender. Remove from the heat, and place the rice in a bowl. Stir in the coconut milk and sugar to taste. Using a small bowl as a mold, mound onto four plates. Peel and slice the mangoes and arrange the slices around the rice.

Yield: Four generous servings

• ■ •

MANGO COCKTAIL

An aromatic tropical drink that makes a pleasant alternative to the mai tai.

2 ripe mangoes, peeled and sliced
Ice cubes
6 jiggers rum
Sugar and lime juice to taste

Whirl all in a blender and serve in wide glasses with a dendrobium orchid blossom.

Yield: Four cocktails

Papaya

Solo papayas (papayas suitable for one person) are one of the few tropical fruits readily available in Hawaii stores. Like mangoes, papayas are often used green; in this form, their texture and flavor resemble squash.

BREAKFAST PAPAYA

Papaya for breakfast is common around the Tropics. It is important to have fully ripe papayas and to sharpen the taste with a little citrus juice. The seeds are edible and peppery and a few left in the fruit make a happy addition.

For each person, cut a papaya in half, scoop out the small black seeds, and garnish with a wedge of lime or a halved calamondin.

• • •

GREEN PAPAYA SALAD

Since the arrival of the Southeast Asians in Hawaii, green papaya salad is well on the way to becoming an Island classic. The fish sauce (Thai nam pla or Vietnamese nuoc mam or Filipino patis) enhances the taste, but soy sauce can be substituted if desired.

1 medium green papaya
1 carrot
1 clove garlic
Fresh red chili pepper (ideally the tiny Thai bird's-eye chili)
2 tablespoons fish sauce
1 lime, cut in wedges

Grate the papaya and carrot, ideally into thin shreds an inch or so long, and mound on two plates. Grind the garlic and chili pepper together in a mortar and combine with the fish sauce. Pour this dressing over the salad. Garnish with lime wedges.

Yield: Two large servings

Note: Green papaya salad can be rolled up in lettuce leaves to be eaten as a finger food. It can also be dressed up with chopped peanuts, sliced roast pork, halved boiled shrimp, or pieces of beef jerky, when it becomes an ideal light lunch.

CHICKEN TINOLA

(Chicken and Green Papaya Casserole)

This delicate Filipino dish brings out the squashlike properties of green papaya. It is important not to overcook the papaya but to ensure it stays crisp-tender.

2 tablespoons cooking oil
2 pounds chicken pieces
1 medium onion, sliced
1 slice ginger, crushed
2 medium-sized green papayas
2 cups marungay leaves (optional)
Salt to taste

Pour the cooking oil in a deep pan and saute the chicken until it turns brown. Add the onion and ginger and continue sauteing until the onion is transparent. Cover with water (use the water from washing rice if you want to thicken the sauce slightly) and simmer for about 45 minutes. Peel the papayas, scoop out the seeds, and slice. Add to chicken and cook for another few minutes until the chicken and papaya are both tender. Add the marungay leaves. Remove pot from heat. Serve immediately with hot rice.

Yield: Four servings

• • •

Roselle

Once roselle bushes (*Hibiscus sabdariffa*) were found in many gardens in Hawaii, and in the early twentieth century there were 200 acres under commercial cultivation on Maui and the Big Island.[9] Older cookbooks suggest using the calyx as a substitute for cranberries and also for a slightly bitter, refreshing, gloriously red drink.[10] Today the drink has dropped out of the Hawaiian repertoire (although roselle continues to provide the red coloring for many commercial herb teas). The drink is worth reviving if you are lucky enough to have a roselle bush in your garden. If not, you can sometimes find the dried calyxes in health food stores. They may be called "jamaica flowers," the Mexican name. A delicious and thirst-quenching drink to be taken after exercise, on a hot afternoon, or with spicy foods.

ROSELLE REFRESHER

1 cup dried roselle calyxes
Sugar to taste

Heat 4 cups water to boiling and add the roselle calyxes. Allow to steep for a few minutes until the water is burgundy-colored. Then strain and refrigerate. The infusion keeps for 4 or 5 days in the refrigerator. It is refreshing unsweetened, but you can add sugar to taste. Dilute a little if too strong for your taste.

Yield: 4 cups

. . .

Star Fruit

Star fruit come into season in May and June and again in November and December. Sometimes they appear in the grocery stores, but you are better off looking in Open Markets and in Chinatown. There are both sweet and sour varieties. The sour variety can be used with fish in the way that lemon can. The Chinese also turn it into crack seed. Star fruit makes a very pretty background addition to a tropical fruit salad, and it can be used for relish, salsa, or added to vegetables for crispness and tartness. It also makes an excellent sorbet.

Star Apple

About the size of an apple with a smooth green skin, in the hand a ripe star apple feels like a plastic bag filled with water. It is not regularly available in grocery stores, but I have found it in Chinatown in the spring. Inside is a delicately flavored, white slippery pulp with a star-shaped arrangement of black seeds in the center. Good eaten out of the skin. A few drops of lime juice bring out the flavor.

Tamarind

Handsome tamarind trees shade many streets, parks, and gardens in Hawaii, but today their pods are left to rot. This is a pity, because tamarind is an excellent souring agent and can be used for drinks and in many meat and fish dishes as it once was in Hawaii and still is in many parts of the tropical world.

In Hawaii you can buy pods in the Open Markets or collect your own. They can be found in many older parts of town, but be sure that you don't confuse them with the less bulbous, darker pods of the common shower tree. They are about the size and shape of a fava bean pod and a light brown in color. Pods can also be bought in Latin American stores, and packages of prepared pulp are available in many Asian stores. If you use the prepared pulp, follow the instructions on the package.

To make your own tamarind extract, follow these instructions:

8 large, fresh tamarind pods (about 8 ounces)
2 cups water

Pick the brittle brown shell off the tamarind pods and discard the long strings between it and the pulp and seeds. Add a little water and soak for about an hour until the pulp softens. Place the pods in a strainer over a container. Pour 1 cup of the water over the pods, mashing them with a spoon to free the pulp. A thick brown liquid will drip into the container. Repeat with the rest of the water and discard the remaining seeds. The extract can now be stored in the refrigerator for 4 or 5 days. It can be used to sour pork (as the Indians do in vindaloo, see p. 141), to make a sour soup (see p. 153), or to make an excellent tamarinade.

Yield: 2 cups tamarind extract

. ■ .

TAMARINADE

This drink was once popular in Hawaii and deserves to be so again. It makes a pleasant alternative to lemonade on a hot afternoon.

2 cups tamarind extract
½ cup sugar
2 cups water

Add sugar and water to tamarind extract and stir to dissolve. Adjust sweetness to taste and serve over ice.

Yield: 4 cups

Wi

The fruit (pronounced vee) is green when unripe, yellow when ripe, and about the size and shape of a lemon, with a perfectly smooth skin and one large rough seed. It is firm and crisp, so one can see why it is called an apple. I have found wi in Chinatown early in the year. Substituted for mango in chutney, it makes an interesting alternative.

TROPICAL FRUIT SALAD

This salad, made with ingredients readily available in Hawaii, makes a nice change from the usual fruit salad. Ingredients can be varied with the season.

1 papaya, cubed
2 mangoes, cubed
2 dozen lychees, quartered (or one large can lychees)
1 dozen guavas, flesh cooked and sieved
3 apple bananas, sliced
2 ounces crystallized ginger, finely chopped
1 jigger rum
Sugar and lime juice to taste

Place all ingredients in a glass bowl and adjust seasoning. Serve with coconut cream.

Yield: Eight to ten servings

KING SUGAR

Then on! bear on, the plough is ready,
With which to turn the waiting soil;
The torch of science now burns steady,
To light you on your chosen toil;
Then swerve not from the path before you,
But onward with unfaltering tread;
Success shall wave her banner o'er you,
And Hawaii rise as from the dead.

(Ode composed by the poet laureate of the Royal Hawaiian Agricultural
Society in 1852 when the hopes for a Hawaiian sugar industry seemed dim)[1]

Below: **Barbecuing chicken
for a fund-raiser**

Opposite: **Pushing down
burnt sugarcane before
hauling it to the mill**

When I first came to Hawaii, I wondered about the clouds of smoke that I could
see from my high-rise apartment. Why did no one else seem the least bit per-
turbed? Why were there no fire sirens? Now I share the general insouciance.
If the smoke is coming from some spot in the city of Honolulu, odds are high
that it is simply the sign of a fund-raising barbecue chicken sale. Every Saturday
in school and grocery store parking lots across the state huge racks of chicken
are grilled, billowing out clouds of smoke.

But if the smoke is off in the countryside, chances are that a
sugar company is burning cane. It is an impressive sight. Driving
through a plantation outside Lihue on Kauai, for example, I came
upon signs warning of smoke ahead. I rolled up my window,
turned on the lights, and inched forward through the darkness. It
was scarcely possible to make out the great stalks of cane standing
8 feet tall on either side of the road. The company firetrucks were
waiting in case the blaze got out of hand, but the companies are
experienced at this. No one complained about the smoke. Sugar
was still powerful.

Burning marks the end of the 2-year life of the cane, serving to get rid of the dead leaves on the stalks. After the fires died down and the stalks alone were left standing in a blackened field, huge tractors used surprisingly low-tech gates fastened to their fenders to push down the cane stalks. The egrets circled, waiting to get a good meal off the fleeing insects (I assume). Soon the cane was hauled off to the mill in monstrous trucks, bearing down the cane haul roads, stirring up clouds of red dust.

King Sugar it was called in Hawaii.[2] For more than a hundred years, sugar dominated the Hawaiian economy, was implicated in Hawaii's shift from an independent kingdom to a territory of the United States, and was the major force in creating the ethnic mix of present-day Hawaii. Hawaii's climate, with its warm temperatures and plentiful rain, at least on the windward sides of the islands, proved ideal for sugar cultivation. The Great Mahele of 1848—the dismantling of the traditional system of land ownership in Hawaii, in which all lands were owned by the king and held in trust by lesser mortals—freed up land for foreigners looking for profitable agricultural ventures. To them it seemed obvious that the most promising market was the United States. The California gold rush created an enormous demand for all food products from Hawaii, sugar among them. In the 1860s, the American Civil War reduced or destroyed the sugar-producing capabilities of the southern states. But Hawaii was still an independent kingdom and negotiating a treaty that gave favorable trade terms was slow going. During the Civil War, Washington politicians had more pressing concerns than the fate of some remote Pacific islands. It was not until 9 September 1876 that the Kingdom of Hawaii signed a reciprocity

**MARK TWAIN:
SUGAR HISTORIAN**

As early as the mid-1860s, well before the reciprocity treaty, Mark Twain marveled at the productivity of sugar, to him the surpassing wonder of the Islands, beating the beaches, the mountains, and the volcanoes. In letters intended to make his reputation with strange tales of tropical isles, he devoted pages to detailed statistics on sugar. At the Lewers Plantation on Maui, he wrote, the main building was some 200 feet long and 40 wide, painted a snowy white and powered by an overshot waterwheel. Around the mill was a plantation village with "quarters for white employes, native huts and a row of frame quarters for Chinese coolies." Hawaiian workers delivered loads of cane to the mill. Inside, the cane was washed and chopped, passed between heavy rollers to squeeze out the juice, mixed with calcium carbonate and heated to clarify it, evaporated to a syrup, boiled to thicken it, centrifuged to separate the molasses from the purer sugar, and packed for shipping to the mainland. The whole process took no more than a couple of days. "A land which produces six, eight, ten, twelve, yea even thirteen thousand pounds of sugar to the acre on unmanured soil!" he exclaimed. Worldwide, the average sugar yield per acre was something like 500 to 1,000 pounds; in Hawaii it ran to 5,000 pounds.[3]

treaty with the United States of America that, among other things, allowed Hawaii to export sugar duty free to the United States. Sugar shipments soared: 375 tons in 1850, 572 tons in 1860, 9,392 tons in 1870, 31,792 tons in 1880, 129,899 tons in 1890, and by 1920, 556,871 tons.[4] At their peak, Hawaii's plantations were the most productive and efficient in the world.

But King Sugar has been deposed. In 1991, I went out to the Wailua Sugar Mill on Oahu's North Shore. From a distance, it gleamed bronze in the sunlight, lying at the center of a web of hardened red-dirt cane haul roads stretching off into the cane fields. Coming closer, I realized that the effect was created by the thin layer of red dust that covered the mill, its ramshackle chain-link fence, its frame and metal buildings, and its corrugated iron roofs, dust that mimicked the color of the rusting metal and peeling wood beneath. The ground between the buildings was bare of plants, covered only by piles of junk and a few rusted-out cane haul trucks. The mill was still working. On the Saturday in November when I was there, wisps of gray smoke were coming out of one of the stacks and one valve was blowing out steam. Sitting on a catwalk 20 feet above the ground, knees spread apart, elbows propped on the fence in front, was a man staring into the distance, the only human figure visible in the great, decaying mill.

Hawaii's sugar was grown for export, not for local consumption. Locals eat sugar, of course, but there are few special Local recipes. Nor is there a substantial rum industry as there is in the West Indies. Even though Hawaii supplemented its earnings in the nineteenth century by catering to whalers and seafarers who called in for rest and relaxation, the missionary influence was too strong. Still, sugar has left its mark in the pervasive sweetness of Hawaii's food: sweet teriyaki sauce, sweet filling in the manapua, sugar added to all the Japanese foods. For the plantation worker with little money to spend, sugar was a cheap way to add flavor to a limited diet.

The University of Hawaii Agricultural Extension Service, though, did come up with a recipe for a syrup using coconut.[5]

COCONUT SYRUP

1 cup water, heated to boiling
3 cups fresh coconut, grated (see p. 227)
½ cup sugar
¼ teaspoon cream of tartar

Pour the boiling water over the grated fresh coconut. Strain the mixture to extract milk from the coconut. Take ¾ cup of the coconut milk and mix with the sugar and cream of tartar. Stir until the sugar is dissolved. Without stirring, cook slowly until syrup drops from the spoon—almost the jelly test. Add half of the remaining liquid and continue cooking until the syrup gives the same test. Then add the remaining liquid and cook again until the syrup drops from the spoon (224 degrees F.). Remove from heat and pour into a sterilized jar or cool and beat thoroughly. If poured directly into the jar, the syrup remains transparent, but must be stirred before using to mix the oil that rises to the top. If the syrup is beaten, it becomes thick and milk white.

JUICY PINEAPPLE FROM THE FAIR HAWAIIAN ISLES

Talk about your Boston beans or hoe-cake from the south,
Or chicken a la Maryland that melts in your mouth,
There's nothing in creation or that's in the eating line
That can compare in flavor to the "apple of the pine."

This pineapple, this pineapple, it's got me going right,
I call for it at breakfast and cry for it at night,
And every minute in between if you would win my smiles
Give me a juicy pineapple from the fair Hawaiian Isles.

("Pineapple Rag," words by James A. Dunbar and music by Alfredo Perez,
composed for Hawaiian Pineapple Day, 16 November 1916)[1]

In the early 1990s, I flew to the little island of Lanai. Situated in Maui's shadow, it gets very little rain, nothing like enough to grow sugar but just enough to grow pineapple. Its tiny airport still boasted a faded sign proclaiming it "The Pineapple Island." "You'll get dirty," friends warned. They were right. We drove through huge fields of pine, as pineapple is called locally, in an open four-wheel-drive vehicle. The plantation workers were covered head to foot, with long pants, long-sleeved shirts, hats, cloths swathed about their heads and covering their mouths, and goggles, giving them an uncanny resemblance to workers in a nuclear power plant. When I returned, I had to soak my clothes overnight before washing to get the red dirt out of them; I had to tackle my body with a nailbrush, not a wash cloth; and my handkerchiefs were soiled for days. I had not experienced such deeply ingrained dirt since trips into coal mines as a geology student. The only difference was that Lanai's dirt was red, not black.

If any fruit is popularly associated with Hawaii, it is the pineapple. Four generations of American families have grown up on cans of Dole or Del Monte

pineapple. Many of them have visited Hawaii and carried home awkward
packs of fresh pineapple (often to find them cheaper in their hometown supermarkets). Pineapple is not native to Hawaii, though. Its association with the
Islands is the result of the marketing savvy of James Dole and William Eames,
founders of the Dole and Del Monte companies, respectively.[2] Together, they
turned pineapple from the symbol of well-to-do hospitality to the convenient
can on the pantry shelf. The fruit that the nobility of eighteenth-century Europe
had instructed their gardeners to nurture in their greenhouses, that was the
very token of privilege on both sides of the Atlantic, gradually became a common cliché in a canned fruit salad.[3]

At the old cannery in Honolulu, now a shopping center, the story of the
Dole Company is repeated every few minutes. James Dole, fresh from Harvard,
set off to Hawaii to make his fortune in 1899, just after the Hawaiian Monarchy
was overthrown and the Islands annexed by the United States. Homestead land
was available for ambitious young men from the mainland if they were prepared
to pay the price to purchase or rent it. If your uncle, Sanford Ballard Dole, happened to be the first governor of the Territory, it helped smooth the way. Dole,
like William Eames, took land on the dry plateau around Wahiawa in central
Oahu.

Pineapple was not new to Hawaii. Don Marin had planted it in the early
nineteenth century.[4] Since that time there had been intermittent attempts to
turn it into a commercial crop. It had been tried in the days of the gold rush,
when almost anything could be sold in California, but too many pineapples
spoiled on the journey. It was tried again in the 1880s by a certain Captain John
Kidwell, who introduced the Smooth Cayenne variety that he had seen growing
in hothouses in England.

Dole, then, was not just a lucky lad who hit the market at the right time, but
a very canny businessman with a flair for marketing. From the start he realized

that Hawaii's population of not much more than 150,000 could not sustain large-scale pineapple production. Shipping fresh pineapple to California, even if the problem of spoilage could be solved, did not help much because pineapple came in at just the same time that peaches and pears hit the market. Canning it would have to be. Dole used his gift for raising capital to finance the import of a boiler and an engine from the Erie City Iron Works and peelers from New York. He persuaded the Hunt family (the California fruit canners) to cooperate in the tricky business of canning. Even so, the first batch of canned pineapple kept exploding, some 25% of the whole pack. In time, the problem was solved by a new machine that placed a larger cover with crimped edges on each can.

By 1906, Dole was doing so well that the American Can Company agreed to build a can-making factory in Honolulu, and Walter Dillingham's Oahu Rail and Land Company was willing to run a railway line from Wahiawa to Honolulu. Dole did not stop. He lured a certain Henry Gabriel Ginaca from the Honolulu Iron Works (which supplied the giant rival sugar companies) and set him to designing a machine to peel and core pineapples. By 1913, after a couple of failures, Ginaca succeeded in making a machine that handled thirty-five pineapples a minute. When he retired from the company, he had been issued eleven patents on his machines, which could then do 100 pineapples a minute. Large-scale commercial processing was well on its way.

There remained the problem of selling the American housewife on canned pineapple. Dole's strategy was to make pineapple to Hawaii what tobacco was to Havana. He persuaded his competitors to subscribe to a joint advertising campaign. "Hawaiian Pineapple is no more like other canned pineapple than a Baldwin apple is like a raw turnip," ran the ads. "Don't ask for pineapple alone, insist on Hawaiian pineapple."[5] With gorgeous color photos of slices of pineapple against exotic tropical backgrounds and easy to use but faintly exotic

Field of newly planted pineapple on Lanai in the 1920s (HSA)

recipes, Dole's marketing worked wonders. To this day, any dish labeled "Hawaiian" on the mainland, in Europe, in Latin America, and probably in many other parts of the world, is doused in pineapple.

By the early 1920s, Dole had made enough money to buy the island of Lanai. Within 5 years he had turned a dry island, home to fewer than 100 families and without roads, water supply, or a harbor, into a giant pineapple plantation of 20,000 acres surrounding a plantation town that housed 1,000 workers and their families. All went well until the Depression; Hawaiian pineapple then began to seem like a very expendable luxury to many mainland families. Dole had never been fully accepted by the kamaaina establishment in the Islands and when he tried to use a cheaper freight line than the well-connected Matson Company, he found himself in difficulties. In the mid-1930s, the Dole Company was reorganized; Castle and Cooke, one of the so-called Big Five companies that dominated Hawaii, took over; and Dole found himself with nothing more than an honorary position as chairman of the board.

Workers placing pineapple on a conveyer belt where they are dumped into portable bins for shipment to canneries, 1950s (HSA)

For years, pineapple was big business: acre upon acre of pineapple under a scorching sun, prickly and inaccessible, with signs prohibiting passersby from picking the forbidden fruit and lumbering machines, making their way down the red-dirt roads that traverse the fields, throwing up clouds of red dust. When the fields were ready for planting, acres of red dirt with black plastic strips laid out with military precision, piles of little pineapple heads were dumped, ready to be inserted in the plastic strips for their 2-year growth to a new pineapple. The military analogy is not a bad one. Pineapple fields are like rows of infantry, their bayonet-shaped leaves ready to repel any intruder. As Jane Grigson, author of the prize-winning *Fruit Book*, has remarked, one would have hoped that at least the symbol of hospitality would wave majestically on long stems, swaying in the tropical breeze.[6] Sad to say, the plants are squat, spiny, and, in large masses, impenetrable.

Now though, the pineapple industry is in trouble in Hawaii; pineapples can be grown much more cheaply elsewhere. The water tower in the shape of a giant pineapple that served as a Honolulu landmark for so long was torn down in 1993. Lanai has two luxury hotels and has changed its name from "The Pineapple Island" to "Your Private Island."

Kamaaina books offer a few recipes for pickled pineapple, pineapple preserve, and pineapple sherbet. In general, though, Local Hawaii cookbooks offer little in the way of pineapple recipes. Local kids do seize on ripe pineapples for a snack when hungry, smashing them to the ground and then nibbling on the juicy bits. But, by contrast with Mexico, for example, where there are a host of imaginative traditional pineapple recipes, pineapples were as foreign to most of Hawaii's population as potatoes or carrots. Such recipes as there are tend to use the same canned, crushed pineapple that you find on the mainland. During World War II, the Hawaiian Electric Company issued its own publication, the *Health for Victory Club*. Its readers were exhorted to make every day a "canless day," in part by using fresh pineapple instead of canned.[7] In short, mangoes, not pineapples, are the Local fruit of choice.

Although pineapples are available all year round, they are sweetest in summer. Growers are experimenting with varieties other than the Smooth Cayenne, staple of the canning industry because of its high acidity and stable growth pattern. One to look for is a white pineapple, sweet and luscious. For other recipes, see the index.

PINEAPPLE SHERBET

Mr. A. Marques contributed this recipe to the *Hawaiian Cook Book*, published by the Woman's Society of Central Union Church in Honolulu in 1909:

> "Take 4 pineapples, fresh and perfectly ripe: grate them and let them steep 3 hours in a syrup of sugar (good sugar boiled with water to first degree); the syrup will thus get well saturated with the perfume of the fruit. Add the juice of 2 limes, pass the whole through a sieve by stirring with a wooden spoon, so as to extract all the pulp. Throw into the freezer. Some add the whites of eggs beaten, but if the syrup is good it is generally considered useless."[8]

Sherbet is an excellent way to serve pineapple, but the quantities are large for a present-day family and the lime unnecessary unless the pineapple is particularly sweet.

½ pineapple, peeled and trimmed
Sugar syrup to taste (about ¼–½ cup sugar dissolved in
   an equal amount of water)
Mint leaves to decorate

Puree the pineapple in a food processor. Stir in the syrup to taste, remembering that when frozen it will taste less sweet. Place in a freezerproof glass bowl and freeze, turning occasionally with a metal spoon to prevent large crystals from forming. To serve, scoop into individual dishes or stemmed glasses and decorate with mint leaves.

Yield: Four servings

. . .

PINEAPPLE PRESERVE

Pineapple preserves were a kamaaina favorite; they are good with toast for breakfast.

3–4 cups fresh pineapple, peeled, trimmed, and chopped into ½-inch pieces (about 1 small pineapple)
1½ cups sugar
½ tablespoon lemon juice
½ rind of one lemon, cut into thin shreds

Combine all ingredents and cook slowly in a nonreactive saucepan for 2 hours. Pour into hot sterilized jars and seal.

Yield: 2–3 cups

. . .

PICKLED PINEAPPLE

Today we would be more likely to call this recipe, which comes from Agnes Alexander's *How to Use Hawaiian Fruit*, originally published in 1910, "pineapple salsa."

Take 1 measure vinegar, 3 measures brown sugar, a few whole cloves and pepper corns. Boil together. Add 4 measures pineapple cut into small pieces, and boil until fruit is golden yellow. If the syrup is not rich, boil down before pouring it over the fruit. If preferred, use 1 tsp cinnamon to ½ tsp cloves tied in cloth for spicing.[9]

PINEAPPLE KANTEN

Elizabeth Andoh, in *An American Taste of Japan*, reported how delighted she was to discover when she was in Hawaii that kanten, unlike Western gelatin, sets with fresh pineapple. She suggested making this dessert in pleated-foil muffin liners, which can be peeled away easily after the mixture is set.[10] Serve the inverted gels on individual plates, perhaps with a green fern leaf or purple dendrobium orchid to set off the pale yellow gel. This makes a fresh, light, and elegant ending to a meal.

> **1 stick kanten (also called agar or agar-agar) (about ⅛–¼ ounce)**
> **1 cup water**
> **¼ cup sugar**
> **1½ to 1¾ cups pureed fresh pineapple (about half a pineapple peeled and trimmed)**

Rinse the kanten stick and soak in a bowl of water for about 15 minutes to soften. In a saucepan large enough to hold all the ingredients, heat the water and sugar until the sugar has dissolved. Take the kanten from the bowl of water, squeeze gently to remove excess water, and shred into the sugar solution. Cook slowly for about 5 minutes until all the gel is dissolved. Remove from heat and add the pineapple puree. Place six muffin liners in a muffin pan for support and pour the mixture into the liners. Use a toothpick to prick any bubbles. Allow the gel to stand at room temperature until set, up to half an hour. Chill thoroughly in the refrigerator. To serve, peel off the foil liners and invert the gels onto individual serving plates.

Yield: Serves six

Note: Although it is particularly nice to be able to capture the taste of fresh pineapple this way, the method lends itself to use with other fruits. It is best, though, to choose ones with strong flavors that stand up to the chilling.

THE GRACIOUS POI SUPPER

Up a small street on the slopes of Diamond Head lies La Pietra, a mansion built in a vaguely Mediterranean or Mexican style. It now houses a girls' school, and the plants in its paved central courtyard could do with a little more attention. Even so, standing in the upper corridor, the curve of Waikiki at one's back, gazing down into the space below, it is still possible to imagine the parties that took place here in the first half of the twentieth century. For this was the home of the Walter Dillinghams, who controlled the railroads that carried the sugar from the plantations of Hawaii to the harbors, and Mrs. Walter Dillingham was famed as one of Hawaii's leading hostesses.[1]

Most of the kamaaina guests at those parties were descended from American, English, or German immigrants, many of whom had married well-born Hawaiian women.[2] Some had missionary ancestors. Many had acquired land and done well growing sugar. Others were from the great merchant houses of Honolulu, the Big Five. All intermarried, their kamaaina society circling around the triple pillars of Central Union Church, the Oahu Country Club, and the Outrigger Canoe Club.

By the late nineteenth century, the language of this group was overwhelmingly English. But when it came to food, bilingualism, not monolingualism, prevailed. At luaus and poi suppers, haole food and eating habits were abandoned. The noble Hawaiian women who had married haoles ensured that a taste for Hawaiian foods and Hawaiian ways of eating them were not lost.[3] Far from it—they became one of the most gracious parts of kamaaina cuisine. Hawaiian food—lomi salmon, limu, various kinds of poi (taro, breadfruit, sweet potato), chicken luau, and inamona relish—was eaten with enthusiasm and with the fingers. When the Hawaiian royalty entertained, they demonstrated an equal willingness to offer the most elaborate European dinners or traditional Hawaiian food.

Poi board and pounder,
corms, stalks, and poi of
the favored lehua variety

HEINRICH HACKFELD, FACTOR

By 1846, Heinrich Hackfeld had visited Honolulu three times, the last time having lost his ship in the China Sea and being taken on to Honolulu by Captain John Dominis (another famous name in the Islands).[4] Born in Germany, Hackfeld had commenced his career on the China run, stopping at Honolulu after rounding Cape Horn on his way to Canton, then the principal East Asian port.

After his 1846 visit, Hackfeld returned to Germany, purchased some $8,000 worth of goods and a ship under the Hawaiian flag, and sailed back to Honolulu in 1848. He intended to make a fortune like the Dutch in the East Indies and the British in Canton. He planned to sell groceries and dry goods to the whalers, but had the bad timing to arrive just as the

No one evokes that era and the way of life of the kamaaina elite as well as Maili Yardley, who for years wrote a column for the local newspaper as well as a number of books. She described the poi supper that was the epitome of gracious entertaining.[5] In a spacious plantation home or a great house of Honolulu, long tables were covered first with ti leaves and then with ferns. Down the center, flowers were strewed in leis, in bouquets, or in bunches tied with ti-leaf bows. Bowls of fresh fruit, watermelon, pineapple, papaya, bananas, and grapes, completed the effect. Draped over every chair, waiting for the guests, were leis, fragrant maile vines for the men and sweet carnation or ginger or tuberose for the women. A formal service was set, crystal glasses for wine and water, coconut dishes with a high polish for poi, and rich damask napkins. Silverware was used only for the fruit cocktail that preceded the main meal; thereafter fingerbowls were provided.

The guests arrived resplendent, the women in silk or brocade holokus (long dresses with trains), the men in tuxedos with silk shirts and red silk sashes tied around their waists. For each guest, relish dishes containing inamona (roasted, ground kukui nuts), red salt, green onions, chili peppers, limu, dried fish, and dried shrimp were provided. Other dishes contained lomilomi salmon and opihi. Cooked crabs were scattered the length of the table. After prayers, the hot dishes were brought in: laulau, kalua pig, chicken luau, squid luau, and mullet baked in ti leaves. While the guests ate, the music boys played soft Hawaiian melodies. After the main course, coffee was served with coconut cake, haupia, and fresh fruit. Then everyone adjourned to the lanai or the lawn to watch the hula girls in their ti-leaf skirts and leis and perhaps even join them.

Kamaaina poi suppers are events that most people in Hawaii never experienced, neither the haoles who ran the plantation stores and the engineering shops, nor the plantation workers, nor those who came later to the Islands. Like the elaborate weekends of the East Coast elite on Long Island or the dinner parties of Edwardian England, they are symbols of a vanished society.

To judge by the cookbooks, everyday fare was plain American food, with an occasional German accent: devil's food cake, brownies, Maryland crab cakes, salmon ring, spaghetti with meat sauce, tomato aspic, as well as German apple cake, cheese torte, pancakes, and fruit soups.[6] Many of the ingredients were imported. By the 1880s, grocery stores advertised the arrival of ships from the West Coast carrying not only California goods (smoked beef, salmon, potatoes, and hominy), but also German fruit syrups in bottles, French wine vinegar and chocolate, and English jams, oatmeal, bacon, and herbs in tins.[7] Some substitutions were made: local fish for cod in chowders; green mango sauce for applesauce in applesauce cake, luau (taro) leaves for spinach. Papaya was used as both a fruit and a vegetable, being either baked like a squash or fried. Taro was regularly eaten in place of potatoes or bread, and breadfruit was baked or boiled and then fried. As in the ports of the East Coast of the United States, curried dishes and chutneys found favor.

Breaking into this bilingual haole-Hawaiian theme are hints of the creole food that has since become so important in Hawaii. Chinese and Japanese cooks gradually made rice the most popular starch and added soy sauce to the diet. Every kamaaina cookbook contains Chinese (or Chinese-inspired) recipes for such dishes as boiled rice, egg flower soup (egg drop soup), egg foo young, pork and taro pot roast (kau yuk), or pork with green peppers.[8] Japanese recipes are scarcer, but fried shrimp (shrimp tempura), hekka (as sukiyaki is called in Hawaii), and saimin with meat sticks do appear.

The *Hilo Woman's Club Cook Book* reveals how nonhaole food made its way into haole society between the first edition of 1937 and the eleventh of 1974. From the start the cookbook included Island produce: fish; coconut—pies and waffles and ice cream and cakes; avocado—salads and cocktails; the banana—pies and cakes; guava—jellies, preserves, ice cream, and an interesting ketchup made with guavas instead of tomatoes; mango—preserved, pickled, and chutneyed and in pies, cakes, and ice cream; papaia [sic] baked as a vegetable, pickled and chutneyed, and in desserts; pineapples similarly; figs, ohelos, pohas and passion fruit (also called water lemon and lilikoi), and pummelo, roselle, and the soursop; taro in the inevitable taro puffs; and a couple of breadfruit recipes. The recipes, though, were European or American. The brief Chinese section (with most of the recipes submitted by haoles) included fried rice, chop suey, and Chinese chicken or duck. Japanese cooking was represented by sukiyaki and barbecued meat, contributed by James Miyake, chef of the Hilo Yacht

whaling industry was declining. In the nick of time, he was saved by the California gold rush, when the forty-niners turned to Hawaii for their provisions (raising the foreign population of the Islands from 600 in 1848 to 1,500 in 1849).

What really made Hackfeld's fortune, though, was the rise of the sugar plantations. Their owners, many of them from missionary families, had no idea about commerce, shipping, insurance, or sales, skills that Hackfeld had learned as a China hand. He became a factor, building up a fleet that plied between Bremen and Honolulu. Pretty soon, he also owned substantial plantations in his own right.

All went well until World War I, when a German-owned company became unacceptable. The financial power passed into American hands, the company's name was changed to American Factors, and his store's name to Liberty House. It remains the leading department store in Hawaii.

Club, and Mrs. Kub's broiled steak a la Japanese. By 1974, rice, Chinese, Japanese, Filipino, Greek, Italian, Korean, Portuguese, Puerto Rican, and Scottish food merited whole sections, as did tropical drinks.

TARO CAKES

Taro cakes were a favorite way for haoles to prepare taro. Perhaps they modeled this recipe on potato croquettes. Perhaps, though, it shows the influence of Chinese plantation cooks, who "had learned the art of making delicious cakes from taro, both fried and baked, and kept up the reputation of the ranch as a place where a traveller was sure of a good meal. Some of those good old Chinese cooks can be compared favorably with many of the old mammys of the south."[9]

To prepare taro, see p. 221. For taro cakes, you need cooked, riced taro. Because taro turns glutinous much more easily than potatoes, do not under any circumstances attempt to use a food processor or even a mixer. A potato ricer or food mill is ideal, extracting the slightly fibrous chunks left by the uneven cooking of the taro and turning out a fine, dry riced taro.

2 cups riced taro
¼ tablespoon baking powder
1 teaspoon sugar
Butter as needed

Mix all the ingredients except butter. Shape into rolls about 1 inch in diameter. Place on a buttered baking sheet, make a small indentation in each roll, and top with a teaspoon or so of butter. Bake in a 350 degree oven for 15–20 minutes until lightly browned. Serve as you would bread rolls, hot, with more butter.

Yield: Eight cakes

Note: The uncooked rolls can be frozen on a cookie sheet, stored in a plastic bag, and used as needed.

DEEP-FRIED TARO PUFFS

Taro puffs are tastier then potato croquettes and can be used the same way. They also make a good finger food for a party if you can arrange to cook them just ahead of time. Kamaaina recipes suggest adding a chopped Portuguese sausage if they are to be served that way.

2 cups riced taro
Salt to taste
2 rounded tablespoons flour
Water to make a soft dough

Mix all ingredients to a soft dough. Allow to rest for several hours (or overnight for a tangy, sour taste). Shape into round balls 1 to 1½ inches in diameter. Deep fry in oil at 350 degrees until light and browned.

Yield: Four servings to accompany a meal, more for hors d'oeuvres

. ■ .

POI COCKTAIL

(Milk with Poi)

Poi cocktail (so-called) is nothing more than a few heaping table-spoonfuls of poi added to a glass of cold milk. Judging by the frequency with which this recipe appears, it was a favorite with haoles in the nineteenth and early twentieth centuries. It is reputedly a great pick-me-up, which is easy to believe because poi is very digestible.[10] Doctors recommend poi for babies who cannot tolerate milk or who have upset stomachs. For those who want something a little less soothing, poi cocktail can be turned into a shake with ice cream or spiced up with a little liquor.

TARO CHIPS

Taro chips are available in stores but delicious made at home. Use Chinese taro (bun long), available in Chinatown and in Open Markets in Hawaii. The purple fibers running through the taro make the prettiest chips imaginable, like pieces of fine Japanese paper.

Heat oil in a deep-fryer to 380 degrees F. Peel the taro and slice as thinly as possible. Big chips are dramatic, but you will need a heavy knife to cut through the dense taro corm. Fry until crisp and sprinkle with salt.

. ■ .

HAWAIIAN CURRY

Hawaiian curry is one of that huge genre of curries, found in Britain, in the South's country captain, and in Japan, that make Indians tear their hair out explaining that curry powder is not an Indian ingredient and that flour is no part of a curry. In Hawaii, curry sauces—although they contain flour—usually also contain coconut cream and garlic and fresh ginger as well as curry powder. I suspect that they are adaptations of Southeast Asian curries, which rely heavily on coconut milk.

Typically a sauce was made by frying a chopped onion, a little garlic, a little ginger root and adding a tablespoon of curry powder and 4 tablespoons of flour. Into this was stirred a quart of milk, the cream of one coconut, and cooked beef or chicken. It was served with condiments such as grated coconut, chopped candied ginger, mango chutney, pickled onions, and Bombay duck.

FOOD FOR VISITORS

Once in a while we take guests to one of the luxury beachfront hotels in the tourist district of Waikiki—the Halekulani or the Royal Hawaiian or the Moana —to have a drink and watch the sunset. It is pure enchantment. The trees and grass are lush and green, carefully manicured, and with nary a brown leaf or drooping stem. Out to sea ships glide past, sliding smoothly through the water. Sitting at our table, we watch the sparrows and the doves peck around, the bronzed surfers pull in, the palms leaning toward the ocean, and the sky turning from blue to rose as the sun goes down. The flares around the bar area are lit, scarcely showing at first but becoming distinct and then suddenly bright as the sky darkens.

This is the Hawaii of dreams. No hustle, no traffic, no hurried plate lunches, no apprehensive plantation workers, no students dozing because they worked the night shift. Instead it is back to the Islands where mainland executives and Japanese honeymooners and workers who have saved for years for a dream vacation and Canadian pensioners who cannot stand the cold in their bones for another winter come to find solace. A con job? An outrage against the Hawaiian people? The best way for Hawaii to survive economically? Only time and politics will tell. Whose nightmare? Whose dream?

Dreams matter; maybe the creation of dreams is not so bad. Out to sea the sun is setting: it is now a golden disk and you can even venture to look at it for a fleeting second. If you keep looking, perhaps you will catch a glimpse of the famous green flash as the last bit of the sun leaves the horizon. It goes surprisingly fast. The distant Waianae mountain range loses its definition, changing to a mere silhouette against the glowing sky. A beautiful girl is singing hapahaole (half-haole) songs. She is a little dark and faintly exotic, and her hair is long, black, and gently waving, bound around her forehead with a fresh flower head lei tipped low over her eyebrows. Two musicians, one with a ukelele and the other with a cello, play as she sings, the darkening sky descending, her body undulating gently in time to the music. A sparrow lands on our table to pick up the crumbs. The waiters pack away the last of the portable tables from the wedding and reception on the lawn. Far out in the twilight, the surfers catch the last waves before calling it a day. My drink is deep blue, decorated with slices of fruit and purple dendrobium orchids. It is hard not to succumb to the charm, to the sense of deep peace and relaxation as the soft air sinks around me. My guests breath deeply and remark how lucky we are to be in Hawaii.

Visitors have been coming to Hawaii for well over a hundred years, first the rich on the Matson liners that plied across the Pacific, then the well-to-do on the first jets with their sleepers for the long Pacific haul, and now a mix of nationalities and classes. From the start, Hawaii had the attraction of the exotic. Early visitors were swept up into the social life of the Islands, the gracious poi suppers, the luaus. In later years, in part by happenstance, in part by conscious design, a whole class of food was created for visitors and for "Hawaiian" or "Polynesian" restaurants on the mainland and in other parts of the world.[1] It was based on the Hawaiian luau with a centerpiece of pig roasted in an underground imu; it was softened by Cantonese Chinese cuisine, wontons, and long rice; it was given a pervasive flavoring of sweet-sour aided by the pineapples of Dole and Del Monte; and it was finished off by the creation of exotic tropical drinks, particularly the mai tai.[2] The Matson Company printed special menus for their liners in exotic tropical colors, many of which are now collectors' items. Jim Dole had his employees dream up recipe after recipe for his canned and fresh pineapple (see pp. 198–199). "Trader Vic" founded a whole chain of successful restaurants with his Polynesian motif, and in the years following the gray days of World War II, they charmed the American public. My father-in-law, who served in the Pacific, went back to Hawaii time and again, drawn by the memories of the soft Islands with their opportunities for rest and recreation after the desolate atoll on which he was stationed. In the 1960s, a whole series of cookbooks appeared featuring Polynesian food, some in Hawaii and some on the mainland, and it became quite the thing to do to have a luau in Washington or Toronto.[3] Commercial luaus continue to do a booming trade night after night.

CRISPY WONTON

Crispy wontons are popularly thought of as a Chinese dish. Authentic or not, they are a fixture at parties in Hawaii. Chopped shrimp can replace part of the pork, and chopped water chestnuts make a crunchy addition.

¼ pound ground pork
2 green onions, chopped
4 sprigs Chinese parsley, chopped
1 teaspoon soy sauce
½ teaspoon salt
1 teaspoon ginger juice
2 dozen fresh wonton pi wrappers
Oil for deep-frying

Combine the filling ingredients. Place 1 teaspoon of filling in the middle of a wonton square and moisten the edges. Fold diagonally to form a triangle. Turn the base of the triangle toward you, take the two points, and twist them a little as if wringing out a cloth. Repeat until all the filling is used up. Heat the oil for deep-frying, drop the wontons in one by one so that they do not stick together, and cook for a minute or two until deep golden brown. Drain and serve warm with a dipping sauce: sweet and sour sauce or soy sauce mixed with mustard are favorites.

Yield: Two dozen

Note: Wonton pi wrappers can be obtained at noodle shops in Chinatown or in any grocery store in Hawaii.

. . .

SWEET AND SOUR DIPPING SAUCE

¾ cup sugar
¼ cup soy sauce
⅓ cup vinegar
⅔ cup water
3 tablespoons cornstarch

Mix the ingredients and stir over low heat until thickened.

Yield: 1¼ cups

CHICKEN LONG RICE

"Long rice" is the Local term for Chinese bean thread noodles. Chicken long rice is featured on all commercial luau menus. Originally it was a Chinese dish, not a Hawaiian one. This recipe is adapted from Sam Choy, who is now a mover and shaker in the Hawaii Regional Cuisine movement.[4] He grew up in the little town of Laie on Oahu and as a child helped his father prepare luaus. It is a mild recipe and depends for success on the quality of the ingredients and on the appealing slippery texture of the long rice.

- **10 shiitake mushrooms**
- **2 cups chicken stock**
- **1 pound boneless chicken breasts, skinned and cut into ½-inch cubes**
- **1 inch ginger root, crushed**
- **1 carrot, cut in thin strips**
- **1 cup celery, thinly sliced**
- **½ medium onion, thinly sliced**
- **2 ounces long rice, soaked in warm water several minutes**
- **2 green onions, cut in 1-inch lengths**

Place the mushrooms in a bowl and cover with boiling water. Leave to soak for 15 minutes or so. Simmer chicken stock, chicken cubes and ginger for 4 minutes. Drain and slice the mushrooms, throwing out the hard stem. Add the mushrooms, carrot, celery, and onion to the stock and simmer for another 4 minutes. Finally, add the long rice cut into 3-inch lengths and the green onions. Simmer another couple of minutes until the stock is absorbed and the long rice is translucent.

Yield: Six servings

· · ·

MAI TAI

(Pineapple Rum Cocktail)

Kamaaina Hawaii did not have a strong tradition of alcoholic drinks, thanks to the combination of the missionary influence and Prohibition. Insofar as there was an alcoholic drink typical of the Islands, it was *okolehao*, a word literally meaning iron bottom said to come from the old cast-iron rendering kettles that the whalers carried.[5] During Prohibition, the bootlegger arrived after dark with wooden kegs of okolehao. From these charcoal-lined kegs, the liquor was siphoned off into gallon bottles.[6] Today a little is made commercially, but it is not commonly drunk in the Islands.

The drink that is associated with the Islands, the mai tai, was designed for visitors. It is surprisingly difficult to find a recipe in cookbooks designed for the Hawaii market.

1½ ounces light rum
1½ ounces dark rum
3 ounces pineapple juice
3 ounces orange juice
3 ounces lemon juice
½ ounce orange liqueur (optional)
Orchids, paper umbrellas, pineapple sticks to garnish

Mix the ingredients together and pour over crushed ice. Garnish as desired.

Yield: Two servings

. . .

BOUGAINVILLEA CHAMPAGNE

This festive drink, which I modified from a Mexican recipe, takes advantage of the brilliant tropical fluorescent pink imparted by the bougainvillea that grows throughout the Islands.

2 tablespoons sugar
2 tablespoons water
One handful magenta bougainvillea
1 bottle of champagne, chilled

Heat the sugar and water together to make a syrup. Allow to cool. Steep the bougainvillea flowers in the syrup until it takes on an intense color. Strain the syrup into a pretty pitcher. Add the champagne and decorate with bougainvillea and mint leaves.

Part Four

IN THE
BEGINNING:
HAWAIIAN
FOOD

WHAT THE FIRST IMMIGRANTS FOUND

EDIBLE PLANTS INTRODUCED BY THE HAWAIIANS

Botanists are not sure exactly how many plants the Hawaiians introduced; it was certainly not less than twenty-seven and may have been over thirty.[1] Many of these were for food, including:

kalo taro (*Colocasia esculenta*)

ulu breadfruit (*Artocarpus altilis*)

uala sweet potato (*Ipomoea batatas*)

uhi yams (*Dioscorea* sp.)

maia banana (*Musa acuminata* hybrids)

niu coconut (*Cocos nucifera*)

ko sugarcane (*Saccharum officinarum*)

ki ti (*Cordyline fruticosa*)

ohia mountain apple (*Syzgium malaccense*)

kukui candlenut (*Aleurites moluccana*)

awa awa or kava (*Piper methysticum*)

pia Polynesian arrowroot (*Tacca leontopetaloides*)

They also brought chickens, pigs, dogs, and, inadvertently, rats.

The first immigrants found a shoreline full of fish and shellfish and limu for the taking. They found a land with lumbering, flightless birds, easy enough to catch, and nests full of tasty eggs. They found fresh water to drink, at least in parts of the Islands. So far so good. But there was not much else that was edible: a few ferns, a couple of kinds of fruit high up in the mountains. Most important, there were no edible carbohydrates.[2] Without the edible plants that the immigrants brought with them, they might have survived, but they could hardly have prospered to become the populous and vigorous people that they did.

A TASTE FOR TARO

Pause and receive thanks, O god
O Kane, O Kane-of-lifegiving water;
Here is lu'au, the first leaves of our taro;
Turn back, and eat, O god;
May my family also eat,
The pigs eat,
The dogs eat.
Grant success to me, your offspring,
In farming, in fishing, in house-building,
Until I am bent with age, blear-eyed as a rat, dried as a *hala* leaf,
And reach advanced old age;
This is the life that is yours to grant.
'Amama, the kapu is free; the prayer has gone on its way.

Hawaiian prayer for planting taro[1]

Of all the beautiful views in Hawaii, one of the most beautiful is from the
Hanalei overlook on the north shore of the island of Kauai. Off in the distance,
the sharply eroded cliffs of the Napali coast loom dark and angled. Down to the
right the ocean is banded in blues and turquoises. And at your feet the ground
falls away to a deep U-shaped valley. The producers of *South Pacific* came to this
spot in the 1950s on their way to film an island paradise. The flower children
followed Puff the Magic Dragon up this road to Hanalei in the 1960s, searching
for somewhere to live in harmony with nature. Today, passengers stand beside
their cars, entranced with the waterfalls coursing down the mountains.

What makes the scene so haunting is not just the natural beauty of the
mountains and the ocean; it is the man-made beauty of the patterned fields on
the valley floor—jade fields, brown fields, and flooded fields shining in the
light, only to be suddenly obscured by drifts of misty rain. The fields are divided

**Taro patches in Hanalei Valley,
Kauai**

by narrow grassy strips, the Hanalei River winds through them, and one narrow road bisects the valley, leading past a couple of green frame houses and a corrugated metal barn, all doll-like from this height. Raised as I was on the carefully groomed landscapes of England where the ideal vista was that of the great eighteenth-century landscape gardeners, I find the raw lava, rough vegetation, and jagged crags of much of Hawaii a bit threatening. I prefer this scene where people have maintained a stable and productive life on the land, where order prevails, and where that order is so harmonious. When one of the light drifting rains of Hawaii veils the valley so that only the occasional field shines through, it is a scene that would have delighted—in their different ways—one of the great Dutch landscape painters or a John Constable or a W. H. Turner. This landscape was created by the labor of generation upon generation, first of Hawaiians and more recently of Chinese and Japanese and Filipinos. This was one of the places, many of them now abandoned to scraggly scrub, suburban sprawl, or the green uniformity of sugarcane, where the Hawaiians grew taro, the staple of their diet.

Neither the breadfruit that the Marquesans depended on nor the baking banana that was so important to the Tahitians was to play the same role in Hawaii. Instead, the Hawaiians subsisted primarily on taro, its swollen, fleshy corm providing their daily staple.[2] Where taro originally came from is a matter of conjecture, but ethnobotanists suggest that it was first cultivated in India or in Southeast Asia.[3] From there it spread west and east: west to Africa and on to the Caribbean and Latin America with the slave trade; east to China, Japan, and the Polynesian islands, eventually ending up in its most remote location— Hawaii. And nowhere in the world did a people come to depend so heavily on taro as did the Hawaiians.

Taro did well by the Hawaiians. The small numbers of original settlers who came to the Islands, probably in the third century A.D., grew and multiplied over the centuries.[4] No one is sure how large the Hawaiian population was when Captain Cook first sighted the Islands in the 1770s; appraisals vary widely from the traditional figure of a quarter of a million to revisionist estimates of 800,000.[5] From the point of view of food production, though, even the lowest estimates are impressive. Then Hawaii was self-sufficient; nowadays, with a population of about a million, it has to import almost all its food and could not survive for more than a week or two without the container ships that plow across the Pacific into Honolulu harbor.

So it is not surprising that the Hawaiians gave taro a prominent place in their creation stories. According to

Harvesting taro in Hanalei Valley, Kauai

one version, the sky principle, Wakea, mated with the earth principle, Papa, to produce two offspring: from the body of the first, which died, sprang the taro plant; from the second came the human race. The very word for the family in Hawaiian—*ohana*—is derived from the word for the cormlets—*oha*—that branch out from the swollen subterranean stem—the corm—of the plant.

Taro entering oven for steam cooking (HSA)

Men alone could work with taro because of its moment for the society; women were prohibited from doing so. After the taro corm had been harvested, they had to deal with it quickly. Although the corm's rugged appearance and similarity to other root crops might suggest that it would keep well, in fact, the inside becomes brown, spongy, and unappetizing in just a few days. When the only way of cooking taro was to bake it in an underground oven (an *imu*) that used a good bit of firewood, it would have been important to turn it into a product that kept well. This was *paiai*, a smooth mass of pounded, cooked taro.

In the past, taro was baked in an imu until tender; in recent times, a cleaned, 5-gallon kerosene can eased the job considerably. As soon as the taro was cool, it was peeled. Then it was set on a large, slightly hollowed board about 3 feet long. The man who was to pound the poi sat with his legs straddling the board and pounded it with a stone mallet. (Sometimes two men might sit at either end of an especially large board.) From time to time, the man dipped the tips of his fingers into a bowl of water and shook them over the mass of taro, all the while constantly turning it. When the pounded taro was still solid, he stopped. This paiai kept well and was light enough to be carried to other locations.

A great deal of nonsense has been bandied about on the topic of poi. To many, poi is a bad joke, a purple mess that tastes like wallpaper paste. It's true that purple is not a color that many of us associate with food and it's true that the slightly viscous texture of poi is not familiar either. But poi is no less tasty than unsalted mashed potatoes, though its flavor is a subtle one, at least until it is slightly sour and fermented. I also suspect that the poi that is now available in the supermarket is about as typical of good poi as the bread on the shelves is of a good rye or wheat bread. Perhaps more non-Hawaiians would be converted if they had the chance to do as Isabella Abbott did as a small child in Lahaina, and sneak fingerfuls from the poi board as the taro was being pounded. Like freshly made bread, she reported, "few things are quite as enticing."[6]

In fact, poi does not have to be made of taro, though this was the overwhelming favorite. It could also be made from sweet potato, and in certain

Commercially made fresh poi (HSA)

dry areas on the leeward coasts this replaced taro poi. It was never as popular, though, in part because it fermented so rapidly. Breadfruit too could be used. In a pinch, as in World War II when taro was scarce, poi could be made by pouring boiling water over potato starch or flour.[7] This could be mixed with taro poi and was best when served sour.

Poi was served in wooden calabashes, often gorgeous hand-carved wooden bowls, some of them huge. After Western contact, earthenware crocks began to take their place, crocks called *kelemania* (Germany), presumably from their place of origin. According to the Hawaiian ethnobotanist Isabella Abbott, it was not unusual in the old days for a man to consume 5 pounds of poi at one sitting.[8] But the diet was low in fat, and by and large the Hawaiians had handsome physiques, to judge by reports of early travelers.[9]

Driving down from the Hanalei overlook, I gaze at the taro patches. The Hanalei River is diverted into an intricate system of irrigation and drainage channels, laborious to construct and laborious to maintain, which distribute water to the walled patches (paddies). This is wet-land taro. Engineering and maintaining taro patches take ingenuity and continual vigilance.[10]

In the newly planted patches in the Hanalei Valley (perhaps half an acre in size), I can see spikes of taro sticking up where slips have been pushed down into the muddy bottom of the field. The plant does not grow from seed; instead it is propagated by planting the corms or the corms and parts of the stem.

In the patches that are close to harvesting, the water is invisible, covered by a mass of handsome, heart-shaped leaves a foot or more long. Several men make their way through the muddy water, loosening the corms with wooden paddles, and bending double to pull them out of the mud. The corms weigh a couple of pounds and are swollen to a barrel-shaped protuberance. The men strip off the leaves and upper stems, and save some of the slips for the next planting. They throw the taro onto a small raft and when this is full, they drag it back to a truck waiting on the narrow wall between the patches.

Taro acreage has increased in recent years because of higher prices, though much of it is Chinese taro, not poi taro.[11] Poi is now a luxury food.[12] In the mid-1990s, when a 20-pound bag of rice went for about $6, a 2-pound ready-to-eat plastic bag of poi cost $4. Even at these prices, Island production cannot meet the demand. In 1992 there were only about 500 acres of land in taro cultivation, producing 6.7 million pounds. Grocery stores announce poi shortages, with deliveries restricted to 3 days a week; local papers track the poi shortages as they occur.

Consumers ask "Why is taro so much more expensive than rice?" The answer is that it is still planted and harvested by hand. If that were true of rice, rice prices would be sky high too. But rice is farmed in great fields by huge machines. Unless the cultivation of taro is mechanized, it is doubtful that it will ever be a major crop. Culturally significant it clearly is, but it is a rare individual who is willing to spend long hours up to the knees in mud, bent double cultivating and harvesting the plant in the hot sun. Watching the men harvest taro, I am glad that it is not my feet squelching in the mud, my back bent double, my head catching the beating sun. Captain George Vancouver had the same reaction when he visited the Islands 200 years ago. In Tahiti "groves of the lofty and umbrageous bread fruit, apple, palm and other trees" eased the life of the population. In Hawaii, "the inhabitants, whether planting, weeding, or gathering, must, during the whole of these operations, be up to their middles in mud, and exposed to the rays of the vertical sun."[13] Hard labor as well as natural advantages went into the making of Hanalei Valley.

PREPARING POI TARO

Different kinds of taro vary much more than, say, the different kinds of potatoes usually found in the supermarkets. Make sure you have the right kind. From the outside, a poi taro corm is an unprepossessing object, the length of a man's forearm, somewhat thicker, and slightly ridged. It (and all other parts of the plant too) is also a menace to the unwary because it contains calcium oxalate crystals, which can cause unpleasant inflammations. It is advisable to wear rubber gloves when handling any part of the plant.

Why, then, would anyone want to mess with taro, I asked myself? I had not realized, though, how beautiful it would be when I cut into it, its creamy white flesh flecked with threads of purple. Nor had I realized until I cooked it that Isabella Abbott was absolutely right about something you never usually see mentioned: the enticing aroma.

Peel the taro. Cut into large chunks and boil for about 40 minutes until tender and smelling of chestnuts. (Many people change the cooking water a couple of times.) Allow to cool slightly, but not completely before proceeding to turn it into poi or ricing it (see pp. 206 and 223).

SORTING OUT TARO

Taro (*Colocasia esculenta*) is a member of the arum family, cousin to anthuriums, philodendrons, diffenbachias, and calla lilies. Some botanists split taro into many species, others lump all varieties of taro into one species. Two major kinds are used for food: var. *antiquorum,* which has tough spongy corms and is popular with Hawaiians, and var. *globulifera* with much crisper corms.

The Handys, who did much of the early work on Hawaiian horticulture, reported that the Hawaiians themselves had more than three hundred different names for taro;[14] even allowing for redundancy, this suggests that Hawaiians bred their taro as carefully as Americans bred potatoes or apples. Even into the early twentieth century, taro of different kinds could be obtained, taro that made poi of different colors and different tastes, taro that was reserved for the alii (the nobility) and taro that could be eaten by anyone, and taro that was used for medicinal purposes. The leaves, the stems, and even the rare flowers that are produced were eaten, though in the old days the latter were kept for the alii.

In grocery stores in Hawaii today, you can buy four different kinds of taro: Hawaiian, Chinese, Samoan, and Japanese. It is important to distinguish them because they have quite different properties and hence quite different uses.

Hawaiian taro: A wet-land taro, almost a foot long, hairy, brown, and ridged. It makes the best poi. A special variety of Hawaiian taro is grown commercially for its leaves, luau.

Chinese taro (sometimes called bun long): A dry-land variety. This looks like Hawaiian taro except that it is only about half as long. It does not cause as much stinging or burning as Hawaiian taro and has a crispy texture when cooked that is popular with other Pacific Islanders in Hawaii. It is used for making taro chips.

Japanese taro (usually called araimo or sometimes dasheen): Much smaller and shaped rather like a turnip. It is used in a variety of stewed Japanese dishes, see p. 130.

Samoan taro: This variety is the largest of the commercially available taros, frequently as much as 5–6 inches in diameter. Smooth and light tan on the outside, it has light-colored flesh. It is imported for the use of the Samoan community.

Taro products

POI

(Pounded Taro)

To make your own poi, place cooked taro in a food processor and process with a little water until you produce a consistency that will cling to a finger. Poi sold in the market is a blend of just two varieties (not several different kinds as in the nineteenth and early twentieth centuries). It is packaged in plastic bags color coded so that customers can select the desired degree of sourness. Enticing the poi out of the plastic can be tricky; the recommended method is to pour a little water into the bag and knead for a few minutes.

. ■ .

KULOLO

(Steamed Taro and Coconut Confection)

This sweet confection of grated taro mixed with grated coconut and traditionally steamed in ti leaves in an imu, looks like a pale chocolate fudge and has a sweet nutty taste. If it was already being prepared prior to European contact it would have been forbidden to women, for whom coconut was taboo. Today kulolo wrapped in plastic wrap is available in grocery stores. Like other taro products it is not cheap: $3–4 for a piece the size of a large brownie.

. ■ .

LUAU LEAVES

(Taro Leaves)

Taro leaves can be purchased in any grocery store in Hawaii. On the mainland, they can sometimes be found in Caribbean stores under the very descriptive name "elephant leaves," since they are the size of elephant ears. They have tough veins that have to be stripped off. It is wise to use rubber gloves. Then, like every other part of the plant, they have to be cooked for 45 minutes to an hour to destroy the calcium oxalate crystals. But, like the other parts, they have that heavenly smell. Spinach can be substituted in a pinch.

In Hawaii, and also in the Caribbean, India, and Indonesia, taro leaves are used for wrapping other ingredients, in the same way that Europeans might use cabbage leaves or grape leaves. They are also chopped and added to soups and stews.

LAULAU

(Pork and Salt Fish Steamed with Taro Leaves)

Laulau is a classic of Hawaiian cookery, perhaps dating back before European contact, but now utilizing ingredients that became available only subsequently. The long cooking deals with the calcium oxalate. An almost identical dish is made in the Caribbean, where a dry-land taro called callaloo is grown.[15] It was not influence, that I can tell, but similar ingredients—seafood, salted meat or fish, and taro—that produced such similar dishes.

> **8 ti leaves**
> **½ pound salt butterfish, rinsed several times to remove excess salt**
> **¾ pound pork butt in 1-inch cubes**
> **4 boned chicken thighs**
> **1-pound package luau leaves, washed and dried**
> **1 tablespoon Hawaiian salt**

For each serving, place two ti leaves in a cross on the counter. Wrap one-fourth of the butterfish, one-fourth of the pork, and one chicken thigh, seasoned with Hawaiian salt, in three or four luau leaves and place on one of these containers-to-be. (Nowadays chopped luau leaves are often substituted for the wrapping.) Fold up the ti leaves and secure with string. Place on a steamer and steam for 3 to 4 hours. Sad to say, the leaves turn a disappointing brownish color, but the aroma when you open them is tempting. Place one on each plate, letting each individual open the package.

Yield: Four servings

THE COCONUT AND THE ARROWROOT

With graceful slanting trunks and feathery tops swaying in the breeze, coconut palms are the very essence of a tropical paradise. Mark Twain, who could be sour on occasion, may have dismissed them as colossal ragged parasols, underhung with bunches of magnified grapes, but he was the exception.[1] For most of us, coconut palms fringing a white sand beach are the stuff that dreams are made of.

I arrived in Hawaii expecting a rich repertoire of dishes using coconut. I did indeed find plenty of coconut palms. They are an essential part of the ambiance of tropical resorts, and hotel developers pay good prices for mature palms. Stories are passed around of palm rustling to keep up with the seemingly incessant demand. Rustled or not, palms are trucked to construction sites—flatbeds make their way along the narrow streets of downtown Honolulu with three or four trunks roped down, their fronds swaying out behind. At the resorts they are lashed in place until their shallow root system takes hold. No nuts are allowed to develop. A ripe coconut is hard and heavy, and a falling coconut is a peril to the unwary passerby. Coconut palms are regularly and carefully trimmed to make sure no such disasters occur.

As it turns out, Hawaii has never depended heavily on the coconut. In Southeast Asia and the South Pacific, coconuts truly were and are the staff of life, supplying not only coconut milk and sterile water, but also rope, oil, broom fibers and food containers. The Hawaiians brought coconuts with them. (Although coconuts can drift enormous distances and still grow when they reach land, Isabella Abbott argued convincingly that the Pacific currents could scarcely have carried the coconut to Hawaii.[2]) The climate in Hawaii is somewhat less than ideal for coconuts, which like 70 inches of rain a year and the warm temperatures found south of Hawaii between the tropics of Capricorn and Cancer. Consequently, Hawaii does not have a great array of coconut dishes compared with the multiple uses in South Pacific islands.[3]

Coconut palms

There, apart from the commoner uses, the sap from the palm was used to make toddy, the husk or young shoots of certain varieties was eaten, and the albumen (meat) was fermented. The Hawaiians have a few simple but pleasant ways of using coconut in fish and chicken stews and to sweeten puddings of taro, sweet potato and Polynesian arrowroot. But subsequent immigrants—New Englanders, Germans, Chinese, Japanese, and Portuguese—came from lands where coconut was unfamiliar. Only with the arrival of the Filipinos and the Southeast Asians has Hawaii had immigrants with a rich assortment of coconut recipes.

SPOON MEAT

(Young Coconut Meat)

Spoon meat is the soft meat inside a young coconut, so-called because the semitranslucent, quivering flesh can be scooped out with a spoon. In Hawaii, you can sometimes find young coconuts in Chinatown markets. Chill the coconut, slash off the top, which has yet to become completely hard (or have the vendor slash it off for you), and spoon out the meat. The light texture and delicate flavor are to be savored.

COCONUT WATER

Coconut water is so sterile that in World War II surgeons used it as an emergency substitute for glucose, dripping it directly into the arms of patients wounded in the war in the Pacific. Extract water from a coconut by piercing a couple of the eyes with a sharp instrument and letting it trickle out.

. . .

COCONUT MILK AND CREAM

If you are using the milk in a delicate dish where the flavor is all important, it is worth making your own. Crack a coconut by hammering gently around its perimeter halfway between the two ends or (in desperation) place on a hard surface and hit hard with a hammer. Use a knife to wedge the meat from the shell. There is no need to shave off the brown skin unless you wish to use grated coconut in a dessert where a snowy white appearance is important. Place the meat in a food processor with an equal amount of boiling water. Using the metal blade, process until you have a puree. Place a large sieve over a bowl, line the sieve with dampened cheesecloth (or a dampened tea towel), tip in the puree, and allow it to drip. Wring the bundle to extract the last drops. You may be able to extract a little more milk if you add a little more boiling water, but be careful not to dilute it too much. An average coconut will yield 2–3 cups. If you allow the milk to stand in the refrigerator, the cream will separate and rise to the top. Skimmed off, it can be substituted for dairy cream; it is particularly good served with tropical fruit. Canned or frozen coconut milk makes an acceptable substitute in most dishes. The milk canned in Thailand is less sweet than the milk sold frozen in Hawaii, and I prefer it for savory dishes.

. . .

SQUID LUAU

(Octopus in Coconut and Taro Leaf Sauce)

This is a Hawaiian classic, rich and creamy with taro leaves, and full of tender pieces of octopus, usually called squid in Hawaii. This recipe is adapted from one submitted by Lei Kaelemakule Lincoln Collins, musician and Hulihee Palace curator, to Kona Outdoor Circle's *Kona Kitchens*.

4 tablespoons butter
4 cups cooked, chopped luau leaves (or substitute cooked, chopped spinach)
2 cups coconut milk
2 cups squid, simmered for a couple of hours and cut into ½-inch pieces
Salt to taste

Melt the butter in a saucepan and stir in the luau leaves. Add the coconut milk, squid, and salt. Heat to just below boiling so that the milk does not curdle. Salt to taste. Serve immediately with poi or rice.

Yield: Four servings

Note: This is not a dish that keeps well because it tends to sour. Chicken can be substituted for the squid.

. ■ .

HAUPIA

(Coconut Pudding)

The Hawaiian dessert most commonly encountered by visitors is haupia. At every commercial luau, a thick and stodgy pudding of cornstarch and coconut milk is cut into squares and served on pieces of green ti leaf. This version is a long way from the original. Juliet Rice Wichman, whose family has lived in Hawaii for generations, crisply described haupia made with cornstarch as an abomination.[4] Hawaiian ethnobotanist Isabella Abbott is of the same opinion.[5] Both insist that the coconut milk should be thickened with *pia*, the Polynesian arrowroot. Better yet, it should be wrapped in ti leaves and steamed, not simply boiled in a saucepan. Occasionally in a market in Chinatown, boxes of "arrowroots," presumably Hawaiian pia, are on sale. They are big and rough and heavy, not greatly different in appearance from Hawaiian taro. From Isabella Abbott, I learned that the Hawaiians would have grated these, soaked the gratings in water, and then dried the remains to cakes of powder. However, no commercially prepared Polynesian arrowroot was to be found.

Powdered "arrowroot" is sold in health-food stores, in the spice section of supermarkets, and in Chinatown. But many different substances are marketed under the name "arrowroot," not all of them giving so stable and transparent a gel as others.[6] In England, and I would guess in the United States, most substances sold as arrowroot turn out to be manioc flour (cassava starch), which gives an inferior gel. The most highly regarded "arrowroot" is West Indian (*Maranta arundinacea*); I was able to obtain some of this, identified by its botanical name, from England. How it compares with Polynesian arrowroot (*Tacca leontopetaloides*) I was unable to ascertain, having no certified samples of the latter.

Haupia made with this West Indian arrowroot was indeed creamier, almost gelatinous, nothing like so solid and pasty, and with a clearer flavor than haupia made with cornstarch. It is worth seeking out arrowroot, with the caveat that you may not be getting what you expect.

5 tablespoons arrowroot (or 6 tablespoons cornstarch)
6 tablespoons sugar
3 cups coconut milk

Mix arrowroot and sugar in a saucepan and gradually add coconut milk, beating with a whisk to prevent lumps from forming. Heat until just simmering, continuing to stir with the whisk until the mixture thickens. Pour into a square 8-inch cake pan and chill. Cut into 2-inch-square pieces and serve on sections of ti leaf.

Yield: Sixteen servings

Note: Squares of haupia are also good served on a dessert plate with a puree of fruit, preferably tropical fruit, spooned over them.

INAMONA: A CONDIMENT TO PLEASE AN EPICURE

Madam had eaten inamona, roast kukui-nut crushed with salt and pepper, and felt certain from its richness that it would be a condiment that would please an epicure, and tried her hand at making it in different ways. After roasting the nut and discarding the shell she crushed the kernel into a paste and added salt and a taste of red pepper in the natural state. This made a healthful and appetizing condiment and her recipe for its manufacture was sought by many of the island ladies. Her husband remarked to her on one occasion that with advertising sufficient and putting it up in marketable form she might make a fortune.[1]

Behind Honolulu, the steep slopes of the Koolau Mountains climb up to meet the clouds that hang over their peaks whenever the trade winds are blowing, which is almost always. The clouds drop heavy rains along the crest and down the slopes, which, too steep for development, are clothed in bright green forest. On closer inspection, though, there are patches where the trees are a sickly pale green, looking as if they need a good shot of iron supplement. This is not so. The sickly pale green is the normal color of the *kukui* tree, the tree that produces the nuts that the fictional Madam and her Master Planter husband found so delicious and thought had such commercial potential. The kukui tree was one of the plants introduced to the Islands by the Hawaiians.[2] They used it to provide a drug, a dye for tapa cloth and for tattooing; its oily nuts served as simple candles; and the unshelled nuts could be used in leis, dramatic in their black, rounded angularity when tumbled and polished (though this is probably a post-European Contact custom).

The only culinary use of kukui in Hawaii seems to have been as the relish described by the Master Planter. Making this, even if you live in Hawaii, requires a modicum of ingenuity unless you happen to have a kukui tree in your yard. Hawaiian kukui nuts are not available in the stores or even the Open Markets, and so it requires a hike into the mountains, a kind kukui-owning friend, or a little scavenging. I was able to collect nuts that had fallen on the sidewalk in the residential suburb of Manoa. Following instructions in Local recipe books, I placed a handful in a 250 degree oven for an hour and a half. This serves two purposes: first, it makes it possible to crack the hard shells, and second, by destroying the mildly toxic substance that makes the raw kernel a powerful laxative, renders it safe to eat.

It was not the ideal experiment for an apartment, because the roasting nuts give off an acrid, sinus-blocking smell, but it worked. When I took the nuts out to the lanai and hammered them on the tiled floor, they shattered easily and the kernels fell out. I crushed the nuts in a mortar and added sea salt and chili pepper. This produced inamona, a rich paste, a more exciting condiment than, say, chopped peanuts, to serve in pinches with poke or with cooked fish.

Even so, it is rare to encounter inamona in Hawaii although a few fish markets offer it in plastic containers. Kukui nuts are by and large neglected; in the fall, they lie scattered beneath the trees in the forest and in the gardens of homes in the older neighborhoods, their green fleshy outside covering, slightly larger than a golf ball, gradually turning brown and splitting to release the rocky shells inside. A few must get picked up, because craft shops and gift stores around Hawaii sell kukui-nut leis; many of these, however, come from Taiwan.[3]

This neglect would be easier to understand if kukui were some idiosyncratic Hawaiian specialty. But kukui is simply the Hawaiian name for *Aleurites moluccana*, or the candlenut tree. Candlenuts are appreciated across Asia from India through Southeast Asia to the Philippines and they are widely used in Indonesian and Malayan cooking. They look and taste very much like the macadamia nut (*Macadamia ternifolia*).[4] The chief difference, apart from the fact that the kukui is distinctly larger, is that the kukui has a slightly bitter taste in the same way that a walnut does, adding a nice touch to savory dishes. It might be said that kukui nuts need to be roasted prior to use to cut the laxative effect, but then macadamias too are normally roasted prior to use.

The irony is that, although Hawaiian kukui nuts are not available in stores, prepared candlenut kernels, white and waxy and neatly packed in clinging plastic, are actually sold in Hawaii in Southeast Asian stores under their Indonesian name, *kemiri*. Indonesian cookbooks suggest some interesting ways of using candlenuts or kukuis in addition to inamona. I offer a couple of recipes in the spirit of Hawaii's ever-changing cuisine. Macadamias can be substituted in every instance, but to my mind are better for eating out of hand or in sweet dishes.

INAMONA

(Kukui Nut [Candlenut] Relish)

12 kukui nut kernels (or 24 macadamia nuts)
1 teaspoon salt
Ground red chili pepper

Toast the nuts in a 250 degree oven until golden. Place in a mortar and crush roughly with a pestle. The texture should not be too smooth. Add salt and red pepper to taste. Place in a small bowl and serve with poke or with simple grilled dishes.

Yield: 1/3–1/2 cup

• ■ •

KUKUI CHILI SAUCE

(Candlenut/Macadamia Nut Sauce)

This is an Indonesian-inspired recipe, a thick sauce that can be used for dipping or stirred into noodle soups. Twelve chilies will give a fiery result; start with fewer, if you wish, and work up.

6 dry red chili peppers, toasted in a pan (adjust to taste)
6 jalapeños, toasted and skinned (optional)
1 clove garlic, toasted
4 kukui nut kernels, roasted (or substitute
   6 macadamia nuts)
Pinch salt
Pinch sugar
Lime juice to taste

Pound the chilies, garlic, and kukui nuts together until you have a paste. Add salt, sugar, and enough lime juice and water to make a thick sauce.

Yield: 1/3 cup

• ■ •

CHICKEN IN KUKUI/MACADAMIA NUT SAUCE

Another Indonesian-inspired recipe, this rich dish is not for everyday but for special occasions.

½ onion
3 cloves garlic
2–3 kukui nut kernels, roasted (or 4–6 macadamia nuts)
½ teaspoon ground cumin
1 teaspoon ground coriander
3 cups coconut milk
8 chicken thighs and drumsticks
Fish sauce and salt to taste

Put the onion, garlic, and kukui nuts and a little water in a blender and reduce to a paste. Place the paste in a pan with cumin, coriander, coconut milk, and chicken and simmer for about 40 minutes until the sauce is thick and the chicken cooked. Add fish sauce and salt to taste. Serve with rice.

Yield: Serves four

Note: If fish sauce is not available, make do by substituting a couple of anchovies.

. . .

KUKUI/MACADAMIA NUT BAKED AND GRILLED FISH

This is another Indonesian-inspired dish, which can be made with mullet, snapper, or mackerel.

3 fresh red chili peppers, seeded
3 kukui nut kernels (or 6 macadamia nuts)
1 inch ginger, peeled
1 large tomato, peeled and chopped
½ teaspoon turmeric
2 tablespoons chopped mint
4 tablespoons chopped green onion
2 teaspoons salt
1 fish weighing about 2 pounds, cleaned and split down the belly

Grind the chilies, nuts, and ginger to a paste in a mortar or in the blender. Add the tomato, turmeric, mint, green onion, and salt and rub the paste all over the fish inside and out. Wrap the fish loosely in aluminum foil and leave to marinate for half an hour. Bake in a preheated 375 degree oven for 15 minutes. Unwrap the parcel, put on the grill, and grill for 5 minutes. Serve with rice.

Yield: Four servings

SALT, LIKE THE SEA, LIKE THE EARTH, LIKE HUMAN SWEAT AND TEARS

> They passed around candy before dinner; it was a regular welcome
> party. The few Hawaiian workers passed around salt. Chinese take a
> bit of sugar to remind them in times of bitter struggle of the sweetness
> of life, and Hawaiians take a few grains of salt on the tongue because
> it tastes like the sea, like the earth, like human sweat and tears.[1]

A couple of miles from the little town of Hanapepe on the south shore of Kauai
is one of Hawaii's many perfect beaches: a crescent of white sand with a rocky
point at each end, the blue sea, a couple of spear fishers diving off the reef that
cuts across the crescent, and behind the sand beach, a coconut grove where you
can camp. Its name is Salt Pond Beach. Here, Hawaiians have made salt for
generations. Off to one side of the coconut grove is a flat expanse of red earth
perhaps a couple of acres in extent, circled with sagging wire fencing, and
hand-lettered signs that warn "*Kapu*" and "Keep Out." Inside are small piles of
dirt (a couple of wheelbarrows or so) and a series of pits about the width of a
man's outstretched arms. These are the salt ponds that gave the name to Salt
Pond Beach.

Every spring, local Hawaiian families that belong to the Hui Hana Pa'akai
o Hanapepe (the Salt Association of Hanapepe) came (and still come) here to
make salt by the ancient methods.[2] The season opened in May when the marshy
waters of the rainy season receded. The ponds were cleared and a piece of iron
was used to smooth the rough clay to a leakproof finish. When that had dried
in the sun, old cans and buckets were lowered by rope into wells to haul up
brackish water and transfer it to a curing pond. After evaporating for 3–4 days,
it was carried to the shallow drying basin. After another 2 or 3 days, crystals
began to form and float to the surface; as the water evaporated, more was
poured in from the curing pond. When 3 inches of pure salt had formed, it was
harvested by pushing long-handled rakes across the basin and piling it into a
bamboo basket. Tossing the basket and rubbing the large crystals in the palms

of their hands, the workers broke the salt down, piled it in mounds, and left it to dry for a week before bagging it.

Surrounded by millions of square miles of salt water, the Hawaiians still needed usable salt. Like the Roman soldier, sweating for his salary, like the French peasant crying out against the salt tax, like the Indians who followed Gandhi on the salt march to the sea, they could not live without it. They needed it to season their often-bland foods, and they needed it to preserve fish for the times when the sea was too rough to venture out.

In some areas, Kaena Point on Oahu or Kalaupapa on Molokai, the Hawaiians could simply collect salt from the rocky shoreline. High seas leave pools of salt water and when the steady sun evaporated these, the encrusted layers of salt could be scooped up. Once the salt was placed in gourds or baskets; now it is placed in grocery bags or burlap sacks and dried over discarded inner-spring coils.[3]

In other areas, such as Salt Pond Beach, the Hawaiians excavated salt ponds. Captain George Vancouver admired those on the barren lands of Kawaihae on the northern end of the Big Island when he visited the Islands in 1793.[4]

But Hawaii's most exotic source of salt was nothing less than a whole briny lake in an old volcanic crater between what is now downtown Honolulu and Pearl Harbor.[5] This became quite a tourist attraction, described as containing fathomless depths and as rising and falling with the tide. These mysteries were dispelled by Lieutenant Charles Wilkes. He surveyed it when he touched in at Hawaii on the Great Exploring Expedition of 1839–1842 and briskly dismissed local lore about its unplumbed depths and changing levels. The salt vanished when the crater was planted to cane, and artesian wells freshened the water. Now the neighborhood called Salt Lake is covered with high-rise apartment buildings.

For a number of years, salt provided a steady source of revenue for the Hawaiians. The four hundred or so vessels a year, most of them whalers, that anchored in the Islands in the mid-nineteenth century demanded salt meats for reprovisioning. Traders and shippers also bought salt to sell in the North Pacific. In 1842, for example, the Hudson Bay Company ordered several shipments, ranging in size from 500 to 1,000 barrels for their settlements on the Columbia River.

Adopted from seamen soon after European contact, salt meat and fish remain favorites of the Hawaiian diet. When R. H. Dana sailed to the Pacific he was appalled by all the salt junk he had to eat. He was still bemoaning it in 1840 in his memoirs, *Two Years before the Mast*.[6] The term "salt junk" apparently came from the seamen's word for old or inferior rope or cables. They applied it derisively to the tough and chewy salt beef that, together with salt pork, was the

RED SALT?

Yes, Hawaii has red salt. It is called *alaea* salt and it has been mixed with ferruginous red earth. The Hawaiians reserved it for important feasts; today it can be bought in any grocery store and is popular for the flavor it adds to grilled meat and fish.

A small traditional salt pan, Kohala Coast of the Big Island

only meat seamen (or, come to that, the urban poor or until quite recently even the well-to-do in winter) ever got to eat. It was not a new word. In the eighteenth century, the novelist Tobias Smollet had one of his characters insult another's mistress by saying that he valued her no more than "old junk, pork-slush, or stinking stock-fish."[7] Junk or not, salt beef was in great demand in Hawaii, both for reprovisioning the passing ships and for preservation in the tropical climate. As soon as there were cattle to be had in the Islands, salt beef became a part of the Hawaiian diet.

With the rising standard of living and the advent of refrigeration, well-made salt (or corned) beef ceased to be a mainstay in a monotonous diet, and became a welcome change from fresh meat. Tamar Luke Pane'e, when writing about Hawaiian food, described it as ranch food, no longer associating it with seafaring.[8] She suggested salting 25 pounds of rump, brisket, or plate for 4 to 6 weeks in 2 pounds of salt with the addition of 1 pound sugar and 1 quart water. The meat was then simmered until tender and served with boiled vegetables.

Many Hawaiians went to the Northwest, perhaps on the very vessels that carried the barrels of salt, signing on as crew members on vessels plying the fur trade. There they acquired a taste for salmon and brought it back to Hawaii preserved in salt.[9] A keg of salt salmon became a standard provision for a well-to-do Hawaiian household. Ironically now, people who move from Hawaii to the Northwest complain that it is difficult to find salt salmon or salt butterfish there. Presumably it is now made solely for shipping to Hawaii—one more way in which food customs long defunct elsewhere have survived in Hawaii. The tougher tail portion of salt salmon was cooked with greens. The tender bellies were lomied, from the Hawaiian word for massage or knead.[10]

LOMILOMI SALMON

(Salt Salmon and Tomatoes)

Whatever its origins, lomilomi salmon remains a local favorite, found in every grocery store and at every luau. (Those without the patience to deal with salt salmon eat canned salmon with sour poi and onions or with rice and soy sauce.)[11]

1 pound salt salmon, preferably fat belly
1 pound ripe tomatoes
Bunch of green onions, chopped

Skin the salmon and soak for several hours, changing the water frequently. Drain and flake. Skin the tomatoes and squeeze out the seeds and juice. Add to the salmon and lomi (rub between the fingers) until the flakes of salmon are suspended in a chunky tomato sauce. Serve chilled mixed with a handful of crushed ice cubes and, perhaps, a dash of hot sauce. Add the green onions at the last minute because they tend to sour the dish.

Yield: Four servings

ALOHA FARMER'S MARKET: HAWAIIAN FOODS

"Even in Hawaii it is not always possible to cook a pig."[1] Such was the laconic remark in *Trader Vic's Pacific Island Cookbook*, one of the books that introduced Hawaiian food to the rest of the world after World War II. Too true. If visitors have heard anything about Hawaii they have heard about luaus: those feasts of tender roast pig pulled from a pit dug in the ground accompanied by purple poi and coconut pudding. Buses take hundreds out to beaches to drink watery rum punch and watch the hip-twirling Tahitian hula.

Hawaiian plate lunch menu

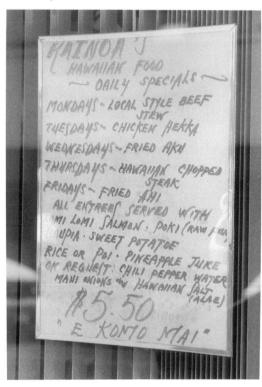

But in truth, cooking a pig in the traditional earth oven (the imu) is quite impossible for most people in Hawaii.[2] Luaus do still go on, planned well in advance and involving huge amounts of preparation. Buying a whole pig (assuming you buy it and don't raise and slaughter it yourself), keeping it refrigerated, finding a place to dig an imu, preparing laulaus, and collecting the varieties of raw seafood is a formidable task. Tamar Luke Pane'e described how these events are planned a year in advance, and gave explicit instructions on how to shoot the pig between the eyes, on how to build and fire the imu, and on how to feed the horde of workers during the day or two when you are preparing this feast.[3] For them, she suggested offering coffee and doughnuts for lunch, and adobo, teriyaki, beef hekka, jook, bean soup, pig's-feet soup, and stews of the pig's innards for lunch and dinner.

Many Hawaii residents, though, settle for alternatives: a church luau—Kawaiahao Church has a particularly popular one—or a catered baby luau, a festival for a baby's first birthday, enthusiastically celebrated by most ethnic groups, or a trip to Aloha Farmer's Market, less than a mile from Waikiki, to stock up on traditional Hawaiian foods. There, stalls such as

Haili's Hawaiian Market, established in 1867, or Bob's Fishmarket offer Hawaiian delicacies. Red dried tuna (aku), cut into wedge-shaped strips about 12 inches long, is piled up selling for the substantial price of over $10 a pound in the early 1990s (that is, unless you want the "nice kind dried aku," which is free of traces of dark flesh and which costs a dollar extra). Next to the dried aku are split and dried akule, a fish of the mackerel family, each a little larger than a man's palm, the bones showing white and bleached through the light brown flesh. Pink slabs of salt salmon butt up against white slabs of salt butterfish, and plastic bags of dull pink dried shrimp. The dried beef (pipikaula) comes in big brownish purple chunks with salt and spices still sticking to the outside. Equally craggy pieces of fat salt meat lie in a nearby tray.

Tiny plastic cups of ground inamona (roasted, ground kukui nut kernels) are lined up alongside the seaweed: walnut-sized balls of limu kohu rolled up like shaggy pinkish beige knitting wool and individual dishes of ogo. Then there are the precious opihi (limpets) picked off the rocks in the intertidal zone —an enterprise that claims a life every year.[4] Raw black crabs are arranged three to a saucer, their bodies no bigger than a quarter; they look larger than that, skittering over the black lava rocks that run out across the beaches of the Islands. Containers of pink lomilomi salt salmon with flecks of green onion, little dishes of the semisolid beige paste lomi oio (mashed bonefish), baked sweet potatoes, big round chunks of purple boiled taro, diced taro in coconut milk, paper containers with poi, chunks of snowy white haupia, and ready-prepared laulau complete the offerings.

The fish market has some unusual specialties: poke of dried fish, for example, as well as whole boiled tako (octopus), brownish red with white suckers, artistically arranged above the counter, or aku or ahi (tuna) eyes the size of golf balls. At Mayamasu's the sausages range from char siu sausage— "so ono" (so delicious)—to Italian, Jawaiian longaniza, sliced mild Maui

Portuguese sausage—"Maui no ka best" (Maui is the best)—and Uncle Toney's Portuguese sausage—"Ono-ono-licious. Nobody beats Toney's"). Or you can purchase ribs, belly or plate, unbleached tripe, honeycomb tripe, small leaf book tripe, fresh chitterlings flown over from Maui, and fresh pig's blood by the quart for $2.79.

KALUA PIG

(Pit-Cooked Pig)

Most people prepare kalua pig in the oven, using liquid smoke. For a long time I scoffed at this as a meretricious substitute for pit- or imu-cooked pig. But no longer. It really does taste good. Although at first the smell of liquid smoke is off-putting, as time passes this changes to an aroma reminiscent of pit-smoked barbecue. Indeed kalua pig is first cousin to mainland barbecue.

Best results are obtained with large pieces of meat; you can always shred leftovers and freeze in plastic bags. Some fat is important for flavor, so butt makes better-tasting kalua pig than does leg of pork. Much of the fat then drains off during cooking and can be discarded—it smells too strongly of smoke to be used for cooking. Ti leaves can be ordered from florists and do add to the taste. Dried banana leaves, which are better than nothing, can be found in Southeast Asian groceries.

4 pounds pork butt
2 tablespoons salt
2 tablespoons liquid smoke
1 banana leaf, preferably fresh
4–6 ti leaves

Score the roast on all sides and rub in the salt and liquid smoke. Wrap in the banana leaf. Remove the ribs from the ti leaves and wrap them over the banana leaf. Tie securely. Wrap the whole parcel in foil and refrigerate overnight. Next day roast at 350 degrees for 4 hours in a pan with water in the bottom. Remove fat from the pan and open the package. Shred the pork with your fingers into long pieces. Add any accumulated juices and salt if necessary. Besides eating with poi and laulaus and sweet potatoes as a luau meal, kalua pig is good piled on a bun. Not surprisingly, it is also excellent, though scarcely traditional, with barbecue sauce.

CHILI PEPPER WATER

Chili peppers were among the plants that Don Marin introduced to Hawaii and, like so many other peoples, the Hawaiians took to them with enthusiasm. A popular way of serving them was (and is) as chili pepper water: a bottle of chili pepper water sits alongside the soy sauce bottle and the salt and pepper in many households. Any bottle will do to hold the water—old ketchup bottles or beer bottles with corks are popular.

- **1 teaspoon salt**
- **1 teaspoon vinegar**
- **1 clove garlic, crushed**
- **6 small hot red chili peppers**

Sterilize a 16-ounce bottle by boiling in water for a few minutes and allow to cool a little. Bring 2 cups water to a boil. Place salt, vinegar, garlic, and chilies in the bottle. Pour the water into the bottle, stir with a chopstick, and leave for a couple of days to mature. Shake over food to season it, as you would soy sauce or salt and pepper.

Yield: 2 cups

• • •

DRIED AKU AND DRIED HEE (OCTOPUS)

Hawaiian households traditionally dried octopus, tuna, and other fish, usually by placing the salted fish in the hot sun for 2 or 3 days. Now they are also produced commercially to make use of a particularly large catch. Intensely flavored, they are eaten in small pieces as a relish along with onion, salt, and chili pepper.

AKE AND LIMU HULUHULUWAENA

(Raw Beef Liver with Seaweed)

This poke uses meat, not fish.[5]

5 pounds ake (raw beef liver)
Flour
Hawaiian salt
½ cup limu huluhuluwaena, a fine-stranded seaweed, salted and chopped
1 tablespoon inamona
3 finely chopped hot red peppers, optional

Cut membranes and veins out of liver and chop into bite-sized pieces. Roll in flour and lomi (massage thoroughly) with the fingers to remove the blood. Rinse. Repeat three times until the flour stays almost white. Add salt and allow to mellow for a day in the refrigerator. Rinse and drain. Add the inamona and the limu to taste and mix well. Serve chilled as an appetizer.

• • •

DRIED SHRIMP SOUP

Bags of dried shrimp are common in fish markets and in Chinatown for eating as a snack or for adding to Asian dishes. This is scarcely a traditional recipe, but it makes a tasty light lunch using an ingredient widely available in Hawaii.

10 ounces dried shrimp
4–5 cups water
1 clove garlic
Tabasco sauce
Chopped Chinese parsley and lime wedges to garnish

Put the shrimp in 2 cups of the water with the garlic clove, bring to a boil, simmer for 5 minutes, and then allow to sit for 5 minutes. Remove the garlic clove and shrimp. Set half the shrimp aside and blend the remaining shrimp and the garlic clove with the water. It will not make a smooth puree but a rather fibrous one. Add the remaining water. Bring to a boil again, simmer for 5 minutes, add the whole shrimp and tabasco to taste and simmer for another 3 minutes. Garnish with Chinese parsley leaves and lime wedges and serve in small bowls.

Yield: Serves six

PURE, SWEET, COOL, CLEAR AS CRYSTAL: HAWAII'S WATER

Flying to Hawaii from California the pilot jokes, "Sit back and enjoy the scenery," and for 4½ hours every time you open the shade and peek out, all you see is the wrinkled empty sea far below you, stretching into the burnished aluminum distance where it meets the sky. The wrinkles are cast and permanent, the visible sign of the ocean-wide swells. The chaos at ocean level is evened out here into this relentless series of crisscrossing wrinkles. No wonder the Hawaiian sailors of old navigated by these crosshatched swell patterns.

Superimposed on the wrinkles, rank upon rank of puffy white clouds cast passing dark gray shadows on the light gray ocean. You think you can distinguish an individual whitecap. But apart from that, nothing. There must be containerships plowing out from Seattle and San Francisco or an occasional fishing vessel or transpacific sailor, but only when you get close to the Islands do their passages converge with the plane's. Then you can detect them, crawling across the surface leaving faint marks, snail traces gleaming on the water far below. In the last few minutes of the flight, the Islands appear. The 13,000-foot peaks of Mauna Kea and Mauna Loa on the Big Island are dwarfed by the scale of the ocean. And if you come in high over Oahu, as sometimes happens, your eye can sweep the tiny island at a glance, green, fragile, and almost evanescent in the vastness that surrounds it. This is said to be the most isolated land on earth, 2,500 miles from the nearest landmass of the same size. How improbable that thousands of feet below you is a park, a park in the middle of the vast ocean, a park with a concert stand where the symphony plays.

That is now, on a plane that flies at 500 miles an hour. It makes the drama of the Polynesian exploration of the Pacific manifest. What drove the migrants can only be a matter for speculation. But it can have been no easy decision even for the Polynesian peoples who were skilled navigators, who had traveled much of the South Pacific, and who knew all those signs of the sea that most moderns no longer recognize: the seabirds and their distances from land, the changing

**Water for the taking at the
end of the road on the north
shore of the Big Island**

patterns of the ocean swells, the clouds that gather over the "high" islands, the
shadows cast by these clouds that can be seen yet farther out.

Yet even so, recent research suggests that the Hawaiian Islands were so far
from the usual routes that currents and winds carried travelers, indeed were
in absolute terms so far from any land, that their discovery has to have been
largely accidental. How many parties set out from the Marquesas, only to per-
ish at sea? What were the feelings of that first party that landed on Hawaii so
many hundreds and thousands of miles from the next nearest landfall? They
must have felt they had found a miracle.

In the middle of those thousands of square miles of salt water, they found
freshwater. They would have carried freshwater with them, stored in sealed
gourds, a necessity for any long sea voyage or even a short one when paddling
in the tropical heat. The success of their voyage depended not on finding land,
but on finding land with good, sweet freshwater. As they came closer to the
Islands, glancing up at the clouds hanging over the high mountain ranges,
the hearts of the paddlers must have lifted at the thought of the falling rain,
drenching the soil, soaking down to the roots of the plants that covered the
mountains, and coursing down the mountainsides. After weeks on the ocean,
these voyagers cannot have failed to be jubilant at the sight of that freshwater.
Then, over 1,500 years ago, freshwater was the difference between life and
death: freshwater for drinking; freshwater running through the terraces thick
with taro, the Hawaiian staple; freshwater ponds full of fish. Freshwater is no
less essential today.

To understand Hawaii is to understand water. Victoria Nelson, in a fine memoir, asked:

> What did I find in Hawaii? *Wai* and *kai*—that is freshwater and salt water.
>
> I found many ways of being wet: *howai, kakale, kalekale, kele wai, ho'okakale, ukalekale, okalekale, hokale, kele, kelekele, halahalawai, kewai, wawai, ohulu, palake.* I found cool water (*wai hu'ihu'i*), sprinkling water (*wai kapipi*), tingling water (*wai konikoni*), misty water (*wai noenoe*), the brackish water where stream mouths hit the ocean, quite correctly called *wai kai.*
>
> I found the mountain pool (*kio kawa*) and stream (*kahawai*). I found the waterfall, *wailele*, and the upside-down waterfall, *wai puhia* (these are common; the wind blows them back up).
>
> Most of all I found the ocean, *moana*, in all its shapes: the calm quiet sea (*kai malie, kai malino, kai malolo, kai ho'olulu, kai pu, kai wahine, kai kalamania, kaiolohia*), the strong sea (*kai ko'o, kai kane, kai nui, kai nu'u, 'okaikai*), the rough or raging sea (*kai pupule, kai pu'eone, kai akua*), the deep sea (*kai hononu, kai 'au, kai ho'e'e, kai lu he'e*), the place where sea and land meet (*'ae kai*), the sea almost surrounded by land (*kai haloko*), the eight seas around the Hawaiian islands (*na kai 'ewalu*). Swimming underwater in the salt sea, *kai pa'akai*, I found the miracle of the offshore freshwater springs, unexpected eye-sweetening uprushings from the sea floor.[1]

For all that, freshwater was (and is) not always easily come by in Hawaii. Rain falls only on certain parts of the Islands, and Hawaii's rainfall gradients are some of the steepest in the world. No more than a few inches fall each year over famous Waikiki Beach, for example, but just 10 miles away, at the top of Manoa Valley, 200 inches are recorded. Rain comes from the constant trade winds blowing from the northeast. After crossing thousands of miles of ocean these winds are laden with moisture. When they reach the Islands, they are forced up over the windward side of the mountains, they cool, and they drop their moisture as torrential rain. But already by the time they reach the leeward side, that moisture is exhausted, the clouds dissipate, the ground below is dry and dusty, a veritable desert. Smaller islands, such as Lanai and Kahoolawe, in the lee of the larger ones, or islands such as Nihoa, too low to force up the air currents, are also deserts.

To survive, the Hawaiians became masters of the art of surface water, cutting, and carving, and building, and shaping the Islands to suit their needs.[2] They built aqueducts, flumes, and ditches to carry water from streams and springs to their crops and to their fishponds. In the small town of Waimea on

Working the flume system to irrigate Waimea Plantation in the 1950s (HSA)

DITCHES?

The Waiahole Ditch System on Oahu was built by the Oahu Sugar Company between 1913 and 1916. Twenty-seven miles of ditches collect water on the windward side of the island and carry it to a tunnel through the Koolau Mountains that is 2.7 miles long. This delivers 30–60 million gallons of water a day to central and leeward Oahu.[3]

The East Maui System was begun in 1876 to supply the sugar plantation of Samuel Alexander and Henry Perrine Baldwin. Hamakua Ditch, which was 17 miles long, carried up to 60 million gallons of water a day. Today, a total of 74 miles of ditches and tunnels deliver 400 million gallons of water a day to central Maui.

Kauai, for example, you can still see the remains of the Kiki a Ola (the watercourse of Chief Ola, often called the Menehune Ditch). The ditch is made of cut and dressed stone brought from a site 7 miles away; it rose 24 feet above the level of the Waimea River on a base 20 feet thick, and the top of the wall was large enough to be used as a path into the interior of the island. No less than in ancient Egypt, or Mesopotamia, or China, or the Indus Valley, in Hawaii water was managed carefully. And no less than in those distant lands, control of water meant power. *Waiwai* (the word for water, *wai*, repeated for emphasis) came to mean things of great value: prosperity, wealth, ownership.[4] Rules for the distribution of water were called *kanawai* (pertaining to water), and from this comes the Hawaiian term for law. According to that law, water rights were more basic than land or property rights.

The law may have changed, but not the power of water. In the nineteenth century, the sugar planters scrabbled for water rights, because sugar is a plant greedy for water. The Hawaiian ethnobotanist Isabella Abbott reported that, in the late nineteenth century, her great-uncle found that water was no longer flowing in the ditch that his ancestors had been using since time immemorial.[5] Investigating, he found that it had been walled off on the order of the plantation: a series of confrontations occurred until he was arrested for taking water from the plantation. Unlike many such cases, when he went to court he was able to reach a compromise, 12 hours for him each day, 12 hours for the plantation. But when his niece inherited the land, the plantation put an end to the matter by offering an exchange of land for sole water rights.

The planters found that the wet windward sides of the Islands were too steep for large-scale sugar cultivation. To get the water to the flatter, but drier, central and leeward areas they built "ditches." These were no ordinary ditches, but huge irrigation systems.[6]

Often the planters began by following the courses that the Hawaiians had laid out so skillfully centuries earlier. In her torrid novel, *Hula*, Armine von Temski, who grew up on a ranch on the slopes of Mount Haleakala on Maui, described one such ditch being excavated:

Cleanly cut, deep, it went determinedly forward. There it bent around a bluff to vanish and reappear, diminished by distance, girdling a green ridge. It plunged into mountain spurs and emerged, its sides slathered with earth and uprooted trees. Ferns and bamboo lay crushed under the dirt thrown upon them; gnome-like workmen swarmed in and out of it with plying shovels. Hideous, mushroom-like camps thrust up out of the chaos of uprooted spots in the forest, the uncouth growth of a day or night of work. And still the ditch nosed forward like a vast red earthworm, uprooting everything that came in its path, burrowing through the portions of the mountain which it could not go around . . . Red *iwiwis* . . . green *amakihis*, . . . *apapanas* and parrakeets. . . . Gone, all of them, to their last fastness, the mountain top.[7]

Mark Twain, by contrast, saw only the benefits when in the 1860s he visited the Lewers plantation on the same island. "At a cost of less than $7,000," he reported, the owner had constructed "a broad and deep ditch, four miles long, which carries an abundant stream of clear water along the base of the rear hills and full length of his plantation. It can be used to irrigate not only the 530 acres now in cane, but will add 210 more that were never susceptible of cultivation before."[8]

Others exploited Hawaii's artesian water. The porous lava rocks of the major islands act as a sponge for the rain that falls on them. Over time, lenses of freshwater developed. Mark Twain enthused that: "the water is pure, sweet, cool, clear as crystal, and comes from a spring in the mountains, and is distributed all over the town through leaden pipes. You can find a hydrant spurting away at the bases of three or four trees in a single yard sometimes, so . . . cheap is this excellent water."[9]

Today the abundant blossoms and lush green lawns that visitors luxuriate in on the dry leeward sides of the Islands are kept alive by irrigation from the ditches and the artesian wells. Not so long ago they were dusty red deserts on the older islands, and raw black lava fields on the younger ones. Wrangling over the control of Hawaii's sweet water continues between town planners, hotel owners, golf club developers, and the large land owners.

From beginning to end, freshwater in the middle of the salty Pacific moat has been what has made Hawaii. The Hawaiians recognized it in their chant to Kane, the god of water:

> A query, a question
> I put to you:
> Where is the water of Kane?
> At the Easter Gate where the sun comes in at Haehae;
> There is the water of Kane.
>
> A question I ask of you:
> Where is the water of Kane?
> Out there with the floating Sun,
> Where cloud-forms rest on Ocean's breast,
> Uplifting their forms on Nihoa,
> This side the base of Lehua;
> There is the water of Kane.

DOWN MALIKO GULCH

In 1876, King Kalakaua gave Henry Baldwin and Samuel Alexander permission to build a ditch to water their plantation in central Maui. The snag was that the permission would be rescinded if the work were not completed in 2 years. Alexander had left for Europe, and there was no engineer for the project, but Baldwin forged ahead anyway. All went well until the excavations reached the Maliko Gulch, a 450-foot chasm on the slopes of Haleakala. Not a single worker would go down the rope to begin building the inverted siphon that Baldwin assured them would carry water to the other side. Determined to beat the deadline, Baldwin himself went over the cliff on a rope. Six months earlier, while checking the rollers in the crushing mill, he had lost his right arm.[10]

One question I put to you:
Where is the water of Kane?
Yonder on mountain peak,
On the ridges steep,
In the valleys deep,
Where the rivers sweep,
There is the water of Kane.

This question I ask of you:
Where, pray, is the water of Kane?
Yonder, at sea, on the ocean,
In the driving rain,
In the heavenly bow,
In the piled up mist-wraith,
In the blood-red rainfall,
In the ghost pale cloud form;
There is the water of Kane.

One question I put to you:
Where, where is the water of Kane?
Up on high is the water of Kane,
In the heavenly blue,
In the black piled cloud,
In the black, black cloud,
In the black-mottled scared cloud of the gods;
There is the water of Kane.

One question I ask of you:
Where flows the water of Kane?
Deep in the ground, in the gushing spring,
In the ducts of Kane and Loa,
A well-spring of water to quaff,
A water of magic power—
The water of life!
Life! O give us this life![11]

Epilogue
TREASURING HAWAII'S FOOD

As a child, I read and reread stories about tropical islands: Daniel Defoe's *Robinson Crusoe*, Robert Louis Stevenson's *Treasure Island*, and R. M. Ballantyne's *Coral Island*. But my favorite by far was *The Swiss Family Robinson*. I still have the copy that was given to me by my paternal grandmother. It must have impressed her too, because apart from a Bible and her gold and turquoise engagement bracelet, it was the only gift she ever gave me. It was written in the early nineteenth century by a Swiss pastor, who based it on the memory of tales his father, a professor of philosophy in Berne, had told him and his brothers when they were children. Father must have consumed the scientific travel literature so popular at the time: every detail of his tale was supported by references to scientific works. The book was a runaway success.

When I moved to the island of Oahu in the Hawaiian chain, my first tropical island, I went back to the Swiss Family Robinson. The tale of a family shipwrecked on a deserted island still had the power to grip me. How clever the family was to rescue from the wreck their cow, their donkey, their dog, their chickens and ducks, along with all manner of useful objects ranging from portable soup and ship's biscuits through tools to the indispensable guns and gunpowder. How lucky they were to find lobsters and oysters in the ocean the very first night while one boy trapped what he thought was a suckling pig. How clever of the father to realize, drawing on his memory of Monsieur de Courtils' voyage to San Domingo (Haiti), that this was no pig, but an agouti. How fortunate that the next day the family came across coconuts (even though this meant they had to listen to another dissertation from Father, this time on the principles of vegetable fermentation), a tree bearing gourds, a stand of sugarcane, and a group of monkeys. How resourceful the family was to capture one of the monkeys, tame it, and train it to gather fruit. True, as every Eden must, this one had its serpent, a boa constrictor, that caught the faithful family donkey, crushed it in its coils and swallowed it whole. I cannot have been the only child gripped with horror at the donkey's agony and morbidly fascinated by the bulge that passed slowly through the snake's body.

Tropical islands were paradise, that was the message. The author had superimposed his own vision of a primeval Eden on the more modest accounts of the travelers. The wonders of the animal, vegetable, and mineral kingdoms seemed endless, as the family went on to find penguins (as described by another naturalist, Monsieur Val de Bomaré) and jackals and turtles and porcupines and flamingos and bustards; figs and cacti and plantains and pineapples; not to mention salt mines and corals and pearls. When a ship arrived, much of the family opted to stay just where they were in their peaceful island kingdom far from the troubled European continent they had left behind.

This dreamy paradise was not what confronted the first peoples who moved to Hawaii. They could not simply trap pigs and tame monkeys and pluck the figs and plantains from the trees. Their reality was toiling by the sweat of their brows to plant the seeds they had imported, to dig irrigation ditches, to harvest the crops, and to cope with strange foods and unfamiliar ways of cooking and eating them. Nor did successive waves of migrants find the land any easier. They, too, set about transforming what they encountered into something that more closely resembled their idea of paradise.

This meant changing the natural environment. There are those who regret this, who lament what has happened to the Islands' environment since Statehood, or before that in the days of the plantations, or even since human habitation. There has been much concern over Hawaii's environmental fragility and much handwringing over what Hawaii's peoples have done to that environment. Efforts are under way to protect the Islands' endangered species, to make Locals and visitors alike aware of the treasures of the indigenous flora and fauna. What for the early settlers was a land largely barren of food, in the late twentieth century is an evolutionary treasure worthy of great care. Where once waves of immigrants saw a land that, if transformed, could provide food for themselves or for others elsewhere, now concerned citizens see a land to be protected from further incursions.

One would have to be mad to live in Hawaii and not despair over the greedy and thoughtless decisions that have been made about the land. Hawaii's natural environment is one of its treasures. But the balance should not be tipped too far. The human hard work and ingenuity—summed up in the irrigation ditches and the fishponds and the watercress farms and the plate lunch places and the mochi makers and all the other efforts that have created Hawaii's food—are also worthy of our pride and our admiration. Paradise, after all, historically has been considered a garden, not pristine nature. Only in fiction do Swiss Family Robinsons stumble on lands where everything necessary to survive is in place for those canny enough to use it. In real life, it is humans who create paradises by hard work and ingenuity. However imperfectly realized the dream of paradise may be in Hawaii, Hawaii's peoples, out across that vast ocean in the middle of the Pacific, have created something to treasure: their culinary heritage drawn from the far ends of the earth.

NOTES

INTRODUCTION

1. Pat Sasaki, Douglas Simonson, and Ken Sakata, *Pupus to da Max*.

PART 1
Local Food

Local Food as Creole Food

1. Hawaiian pidgin and creole have spawned a considerable scholarly literature; see, for example, John E. Reinecke, *Language and Dialect in Hawaii*; Elizabeth Ball Carr, *Da Kine Talk*; and Charlene Sato, "Linguistic Inequality in Hawaii."

2. Milton Murayama, *All I Asking For Is My Body*, 5.

3. Polly Lou Caple et al., *Pidgin Pie and Poi*; Judith Midgely Kirkendall, "Hawaiian Ethnogastronomy"; Pat Sasaki, Douglas Simonson, and Ken Sakata, *Pupus to da Max*; John Heckathorn, "Pidgin Cuisine."

4. *Honolulu Advertiser*, 30 June 1994 and 29 June 1994. Continental means mainland United States, not European. As early as 1938, Caroline W. Edwards (*Guidebook for Homemaking in Hawaii*) regularly used terms such as local ingredients, local fruits, and so forth.

5. See, for example, "Hold the Spam, Bacon, Sausage, Egg, Burger, Please," *Honolulu Advertiser*, 9 May 1991.

6. "Take Along a Taste of Home," *Honolulu Advertiser*, 27 August 1991.

The Plate Lunch, or What Counts as a Meal in Hawaii

1. *Frank De Lima's Joke Book*, 92. Roughly translated from Local pidgin, this means: I'm Local, I'm as brown as the shell of the limpet to be eaten raw, I'm as local as the pickle in the middle of the rice ball you eat for a snack, or as a lunch of spaghetti and sauce all mixed up, with rice and spicy Korean pickled cabbage on the side, I'm as local as the gravy over the rice on the lunch, as the different colored syrups poured over the jolly old shaved ice in a paper cone that I eat at the beach, I'm as local as a typical B-1-bomber-sized Hawaii cockroach coming at you from the direction of the Ewa plain to the northwest of Honolulu. (Quoted by permission of Frank De Lima and Patrick Downes.)

2. Judith Midgely Kirkendall, "Hawaiian Ethnogastronomy," 344–346.

3. Caroline W. Edwards, *Guidebook for Homemaking in Hawaii*, 99–100.

4. James Kelly, "Loco Moco." But see also "Finding Loco Moco Origin Isn't Gravy," *Honolulu Advertiser*, 21 November 1994.

5. "Isle McChief Calls It Quits after 19 Years," *Honolulu Advertiser*, 1 July 1994.

6. John Maybury, "The Lunch Wagons."

7. For example, in the 1990s the Chinese-style plate lunch at the Bon-Bon Cafe in downtown Honolulu included hamburger, omelette with SPAM, Portuguese sausage, or Vienna sausages, fried rice with SPAM, beef broccoli with steamed rice, roast chicken and fried noodles, sweet and sour spareribs and steamed rice, oxtail soup Chinese style, char siu omelette with chow fun, kau yuk (pot roast pork) with fried rice and wonton. A Korean plate lunch place included teri beef, hamburger, barbecue chicken, beef stew, shoyu chicken, chili frank, chicken katsu, loco moco, meat jun, kal bi ribs, mandoo, barbecue pork, and barbecue beef.

8. Elizabeth Andoh, *An American Taste of Japan*, 40.

9. This is according to Elaine Tanaka Beatson, who was raised in Hawaii and works for Kikkoman International, the company that manufactures the widely distributed soy sauce. Kikkoman information sheet, undated.

10. See, for example, *Hawaiian Cuisine*, put together by the proud new Hawaii State Society of Washington, D.C.

11. Mary Sia (*Chinese Cookbook*, 75) calls this "soy sauce chicken."

Our Daily Rice: Hawaii's Staple

1. "The New Price of Rice May Bowl You Over," *Honolulu Advertiser*, 5 January 1994; Judith Midgely Kirkendall, "Ha-waiian Ethnogastronomy," 139. A survey in the 1980s (Kirkendall, 185, 236, 265) showed that Hawaii Chinese ate rice at least twice a day, Japanese and Filipinos at least once.

2. See Bob Krauss with W. P. Alexander (*Grove Farm Plantation*, 167–168) for a fictional account (though one based on fact) of Chinese workers' rejection of poi on arrival at Grove Farm Plantation. See also Kirkendall, "Hawaiian Ethnogastronomy," 167.

3. Cristine Mackie, *Life and Food in the Caribbean*, 143.

4. Karol Haraguchi (*Rice in Hawaii*) lists printed materials, maps, photographs, oral histories, and historic sites and includes a brief history of rice in Hawaii, the source of most of the information about Hawaii's rice in this essay. See also David Livingstone Crawford, *Hawaii's Crop Parade*, 210–217 and the standard histories of the Chinese in Hawaii (pp. 258–259 nn. 4, 6).

5. Lum Chew Chang Ho, "Fun-filled days at a rice plantation," in Associated Chinese University Women, *Traditions for Living*, 95–97. The fried sparrows, frog legs, and snails described here were all typical Cantonese specialties that the Hawaii Chinese were able to duplicate in the Islands (Kenneth Lo, *Chinese Regional Cooking*, 74). The purple-green herb used to cook the snails was *Perilla nankinensis* (shiso in Japanese).

6. "War Shortage Fears Create a Run on Rice," *Honolulu Advertiser*, 16 January 1991; "Persian Gulf War Spurs Rice Hoarding and Panic Buying," 17 January 1991; "Despite Warnings on Panic Buying, Run on Rice Continues," 18 January 1991.

7. "Safeway Sales Put Rice Rush on a Roll," *Honolulu Advertiser*, 14 January 1994; "Rice: There's No Substitute," 14 January 1994.

8. Haraguchi (*Rice in Hawaii*). Hurricane Iniki did a great deal of damage; see "Haraguchi Family Tries to Preserve Kauai Rice Mill," *Honolulu Star-Bulletin*, 8 November 1994.

9. Roger Owen ("A rice landscape," in Sri Owen, *The Rice Book*, 3–90) gives an accessible overview of rices and their history and cultivation. I am grateful to Roger Owen for responding to questions about how the rice I encountered in Hawaii conformed to his descriptions. Also useful is *Bruce Cost's Asian Ingredients*, 269–284.

Poke: Or Hawaii's Ways with Fish

1. Honolulu Maritime Museum exhibit.

2. "The Dying Breed of Sampans," *Honolulu Advertiser*, 12 September 1993.

3. Margaret Titcomb, senior librarian of the Bishop Museum in Honolulu, with the assistance of Mary Kawena Pukui, translator of Hawaiian manuscripts and records for the museum, wrote *Native Use of Fish in Hawaii* in 1952, a treasure of Hawaiian fish lore. For sport fishing in Hawaii, see Jean Scott MacKellar, *Hawaii Goes Fishing*; Shirley Rizzuto, *Fish Dishes of the Pacific*; and Mike Sakamoto, *How to Hook and Cookbook*.

4. For family outings and the method of killing octopus (which is not unique to Hawaii), see "The Exciting Adventure of the Goat Island Tako," *Honolulu Advertiser*, 10 March 1992.

5. Mary Kawena Pukui and Samuel Elbert, *Hawaiian Dictionary*, 337.

6. For a lyrical evocation of the freshness of kinilaw, see Edilberto Alegre and Doreen Fernandez, *Kinilaw*.

7. Russell A. Apple, *Ancient Hawaii Shore Zone Fishponds*.

8. Carol Araki Wyban *(Tide and Current)* described how she and her husband put a Hawaiian fishpond back in working order and included a wealth of historical and practical detail.

9. Titcomb *(Native Use of Fish in Hawaii*, 20) used the term "poke" only for a crosswise cut of fish, not for a way of preparing it for eating. Katherine Bazore *(Hawaiian and Pacific Foods*, 149) described the Hawaiian dish of raw mashed fish as *ia maka* and made no mention of a dish of small blocks of fish. Pukui and Elbert *(Hawaiian Dictionary)* defined the word "poke" as to slice or cut crosswise; Elizabeth Ball Carr *(Da Kine Talk)* was totally silent on the subject of poke.

10. In 1982 *Hari Kojima's Favorite Seafood Recipes* gave recipes for raw lobster and raw sea cucumber but did not call them poke; by 1987 *Hari Kojima's Local-Style Favorites* listed four dishes labeled poke: aku, king clam, ginger, and tako.

11. Howard Deese of the Hawaii Department of Business, Economic Development and Tourism has been working with chefs and others to develop a description of the culinary properties of these various fish. I am grateful to him for information.

12. *Hari Kojima's Local-Style Favorites*, 18.

13. *Hari Kojima's Favorite Seafood Recipes*, 36.

Limu (Seaweed): Hawaii's Spice

1. The leading expert on the ethnobotany of Hawaiian limu, Professor Isabella Abbott, was kind enough to comment on this essay. I also learned much from Karla McDermid, in her classes at the Honolulu Aquarium, from Carol Hopper on reef walks, and from Heather Fortner's *The Limu Eater*.

2. Mary Kawena Pukui and Samuel Elbert, *Hawaiian Dictionary*, 207.

3. See Isabella Aiona Abbott *(La'au Hawai'i*, 19) for kapus on women's eating.

4. Compiled from Maui Home Demonstration Council (1959), Isabella Aiona Abbott and Eleanor Horswill Williamson *(Limu)*, and Fortner *(The Limu Eater)*.

5. From Fortner *(The Limu Eater)*.

Saimin, Manapua, and Musubi: Hawaii's Snacks

1. Shunzo Sakamaki, Hawaii-born Japanese-American University of Hawaii professor, quoted by Elizabeth Ball Carr *(Da Kine Talk*, 146). She continued: "the second element of the word, *min*, is easily identified as the Cantonese word for 'noodle,' but the first element, *sai*, is more difficult to identify. A plausible interpretation is that *sai* in this term may be a form of the Cantonese word for 'water.'"

2. *Bruce Cost's Asian Ingredients*, 295.

3. Hilo Woman's Club, *Hilo Woman's Club Cook Book*, 59.

4. The story goes that the very elderly Chinese used to peel off the thin stretchy skin that covers the doughy bun. To create this smooth shiny skin, the bakers apparently used to spray a mouthful of water over the dough. Friends of Waipahu Cultural Garden Park, *Plantation Village Cookbook*, 2–3.

5. Carr, *Da Kine Talk*, 87–88.

6. Friends of Waipahu Cultural Garden Park, *Plantation Village Cookbook*, 46–47.

7. Gaku Homma, *The Folk Art of Japanese Country Cooking*, 159–164.

8. "State Sees Risks in Bento Serving," "Meeting on Bento Rules Leaves Sides Still at Odds," "Of Spam and Rice: Tradition vs. Health Science," *Honolulu Advertiser*, 26 June, 20 July, 28 June 1994.

Sea Biscuits, Kanaka Pudding, and Saloon Pilots

1. Oswald A. Bushnell, *Molokai*, 85–87.

2. Ibid.

3. *Oxford English Dictionary*, Compact Edition, vol. 1.

4. Jacob's, for example, was founded in 1841. Information leaflet from Jacob's Company, Reading, England.

5. Caroline W. Edwards, *Guidebook for Homemaking in Hawaii*, 11.

6. Cream Crackers were first produced by Jacob's in 1885 and have been exported from Britain since before World War I. Information leaflet from Jacob's Company, Reading, England.

7. Tamar Luke Pane'e, *E Ho'olako Mau*, vol. 2, 220. She was given the method of making them by Eleanor Kalawai'akamali'iwahineli'ili'i Simeona Ahuna, a Hawaiian Homes Commissioner on the Big Island.

8. Peter Simmonds, *A Dictionary of Trade Products*.

9. Diamond Bakery promotional material. I am grateful to Paul Ishii, of the Diamond Bakery Company, for providing me with this.

10. Bushnell, *Molokai*, 85–87.

11. T. N. Harris, "Management and Preservation of Food," in Charles Singer et al., eds., *A History of Technology*, 35–37.

12. Pane'e, E Ho'olako Mau, vol. 2, 216.

13. Edwards, Guidebook for Homemaking in Hawaii, 203.

14. Maili Yardley, Hawaii Cooks, 150.

15. Dora Jane Isenberg Cole and Juliet Rice Wichman, The Kauai Museum Presents Early Kauai Hospitality, 68.

Coming to Terms with Spam (and Vienna Sausage and Corned Beef and Sardines)

1. SPAM® luncheon meat is a registered trademark for a pork product marketed only by Geo. A. Hormel & Co., Austin, MN 55912.

2. Ann Condo Corum, Hawaii's SPAM® Cookbook. My history of SPAM in Hawaii, as well as the ways of serving it, comes primarily from this source. See also "The United States of Spam," New York Times Magazine, 3 July 1994, in which Hawaii figured prominently.

3. "Some Facts to Go—with Fast Foods: Better Hold the Macaroni Salad, the Spam, and Shoyu," Honolulu Advertiser, 28 April 1991; "Carve Your SPAM," Honolulu Advertiser, 1 February 1995.

4. Isabella Beeton, The Book of Household Management, 399.

5. Arleen Lum, Sailing for the Sun, 182.

6. Hawaii Government Employees Association, HGEA/AFSCME Cooks II, 130.

Sorting Out Sushi

1. Nancy N. Sakamoto and Elaine Suzuki, Hawaii Style Sushi, i. I am grateful to Nancy Sakamoto for discussing this with me.

2. Adapted from Japanese Cultural Center of Hawaii, The Legacy of the Japanese in Hawaii.

Shave Ice: No Mere Snow Cone This

1. Mary Kawena Pukui and Samuel Elbert, Hawaiian Dictionary, 121. See also Elizabeth Ball Carr, Da Kine Talk, 147.

2. I am grateful to Donald Mizokawa for information about shave ice in the 1950s in the Islands and to Maureen Bartholemew for information about shave ice in Japan.

3. Friends of Waipahu Cultural Garden Park, Plantation Village Cookbook, 136.

4. Locals are quite insistent on this. See "Don't Be Snowed by an Imposter," Honolulu Advertiser, 13 October 1993.

5. Adapted from Japanese Cultural Center of Hawaii, The Legacy of the Japanese in Hawaii, 224.

6. I am grateful to Doreen Fernandez for unpublished notes on halo-halo. See also Gilda Cordero-Fernando, The Culinary Culture of the Philippines, 159.

Crack Seed: The Mei and the Ume

1. In 1994, the Honolulu Yellow Pages listed over 20 crack seed stores under the heading "Seeds—Chinese Preserved."

2. Judging by the labels on packets of crack seed, it is generally flavored with licorice today. But since licorice was not native to China, I suspect that originally the flavor came from star anise, which tastes very similar.

3. "Crack Seed Firm Well Preserved," Honolulu Star-Bulletin, 27 November 1992.

4. "Frederick Yee, of Yick Lung Crack Seed Fame, Dies at 74," Honolulu Star-Bulletin, 30 September 1991; "Yick Lung Company in Business 92 Years,"

Honolulu Star-Bulletin, 27 November 1992.

5. E. N. Anderson, The Food of China, 137; see also Frederick J. Simoons, Food in China, 221.

6. A Local Japanese friend told me that when he was growing up on Oahu, the tamarind was called the see mui tree. And the home economist for the Maui Electric Company, Bonnie Tuell, says that not only did the ripe pulp taste sour just like sour preserved seeds, but that the seeds could be cooked with brown sugar to make sweet-sour seeds. Tuell, Island Cooking, 62.

7. If mainlanders have not yet learned the joys of crack seed, Mexicans have. Pulling off the freeway to get gas at a small station between Phoenix and Tucson, I went into the convenience store to buy soft drinks. There on the ends of the aisles were the familiar little plastic packets of wrinkled fruits. But they were not labeled in English. These were described as saladitos (little salted things) and distributed from Taiwan. According to E. N. Anderson, they have been common in Mexico at least since the Chinese came in numbers to North America in the nineteenth century. But, he speculates, it is just possible that they have been there for centuries, from the days of the galleon that sailed annually from Manila to Acapulco.

The Matter of Mochi

1. I have tried making mochi flavored with sugar and orange or roseflower water and the result is indeed very similar to Turkish delight.

2. Ann Kondo Corum, Ethnic Foods of Hawai'i, 59.

3. Ibid., 113.

4. A "bibinca" of flour, egg yolks, coconut milk, and sugar (as well as one involving mashed potatoes) also cropped up in Jennifer Fernandes (*100 Easy-to-Make Goan Dishes*, 108) though the method of cooking is different: layer after layer of the batter built up by being successively browned under the grill. Nothing similar to the word "bibingka" is to be found in Portuguese dictionaries, at least that I have been able to discover. Thus there seems reason to believe that the Portuguese, in their voyaging across the Indian Ocean from the sixteenth century on, brought back this dish from the Philippines.

5. Similarly, Nancy N. Sakamoto and Elaine Suzuki (*Hawaii Style Sushi*, 153) offered recipes for pumpkin, sweet potato, and even poi mochi; all of these are fried mixtures of fruit or vegetable puree, sugar, and mochiko.

6. Koreans also make glutinous rice flour confections that can be found in Korean grocery stores but that have not entered the mainstream of Hawaii's cooking.

7. Adapted from a recipe submitted by Laurie La Madrid (Filipino Women's League, *Hawaii Filipina's Favorite Recipes*, 91).

Malasadas and Andagi: Doughnuts from Two Ends of the Earth

1. Gavan Daws, *Shoal of Time*, 161–162.

2. The spelling and indeed the very name of these doughnuts is in some dispute. In the Islands they are almost always spelled "malasadas." However, older recipes use a double "s"— "malassadas." Wanda Adams, Living Page editor of the *Honolulu Advertiser*, pointed out that malasadas is the correct spelling because the "s" sound is a soft one (*Honolulu Advertiser*, 2 Feb-

ruary 1995). Until the 1950s, they were often called "filoses," but that name now seems to have vanished. Katherine Bazore (*Hawaiian and Pacific Foods*, 261), for example, called Portuguese sweet doughnuts "filoses or malassadas."

3. Junior League of Hawaii, *A Taste of Aloha*, 121.

4. This recipe, although similar to the doughnut recipe that is common across Europe as a pre-Lent specialty, does not appear in most homeland Portuguese cookbooks, although this might just be an accident of selection. However, Marie de Lourdes Modesto, author of a careful survey of Portuguese regional cooking (*Traditional Portuguese Cooking*), identified malasadas as a specialty of São Miguel in the Azores, from whence large numbers of the Hawaiian Portuguese hail. E. Donald Asselin (*A Portuguese-American Cookbook*, 28) offered similar recipes from the Portuguese of the East Coast of the United States, many of them also from the Azores.

5. Hui o Laulima, *Of Andagi and Sanshin*, 1.

"Food Is Not a Racial Problem"

1. Leonard Lueras, *Kanyaku Imin*, 9.

2. Caroline W. Edwards, *Guidebook for Homemaking in Hawaii*, 212–220.

3. Dorothy Ochiai Hazama and Jane Okamoto Komeiji, *Okage Sama De*, 98.

4. Harvey Levenstein, *Paradox of Plenty*, 93.

5. Jane and Michael Stern (*Real American Food*) described the Southern plate lunch, the "meat and threes" (that is, meat and three vegetables). Unlike the Hawaii plate lunch, though, the Southern plate lunch makes the vegetables the serious part of the meal.

6. Sam Yamashita, personal communication about his father's memories. Judith Midgely Kirkendall ("Hawaiian Ethnogastronomy," 227) reported that the Japanese-American found octopus and freshwater eels in Italy and even succeeded in concocting soy sauce.

7. Caroline W. Edwards, "Community Feeding During an Emergency"; Kimie Kawahara and Yuriko Hatanaka, "The Impact of War"; Winifred Tom, "The Impact of War."

8. Edwards, "Community Feeding During an Emergency," 2.

9. Edwards, *Guidebook for Homemaking in Hawaii*, 75.

10. Gavan Daws, *Shoal of Time*, 308–311.

11. In fact, many immigrants may have had an impoverished diet for a variety of reasons, one being the desire to send money home regularly from a slim wage packet. See, for example, Carey Dunlap Miller and Helen Yonge Lind (*Food for Health in Hawaii*), who compared poor and improved diets for Chinese, haoles, Hawaiians, Filipinos, and Japanese.

12. Kirkendall, "Hawaiian Ethnogastronomy," 215–216.

13. Margaret Rossiter, *Women Scientists in America*, 200–202.

14. Carey Dunlap Miller, "From Stage Coach to Satellite."

15. Katherine Bazore, *Hawaiian and Pacific Foods*, xv.

16. Carey Dunlap Miller et al., *Vitamin Values of Foods Used in Hawaii*; Carey D. Miller and B. Branthoover, *Nutritive Values of Some Hawaiian Foods*; Carey D. Miller, *Japanese Foods Commonly Used in Hawaii*; Mary Murai, Carey D. Miller, and F. Pen, *Some Tropical South Pacific Island Foods*; Carey D. Miller, K. Bazore,

and Mary Bartow, *Fruits of Hawaii*; K. Bazore, *Hawaiian and Pacific Foods*.

17. See, for example, the list of acknowledgments in Edwards, *Guidebook for Homemaking in Hawaii*; Maui Extension Homemakers Council, *Our Favorite Recipes, More of Our Favorite Recipes, Still More of Our Favorite Recipes, Still Many More of Our Favorite Recipes*; Bonnie Tuell, *Island Cooking*; Muriel Kamada Miura, *Cook Japanese-Hawaiian Style, Hawaii's Favorite Maxi Meals*. Miura completed the cycle by going to Columbia for her master's degree after studying at the University of Hawaii. She became Home Economics Director for the Honolulu Gas Company.

18. Edwards, *Guidebook for Homemaking in Hawaii*, 1–3.

19. Masuoka, "Changing Food Habits."

20. Edwards, *Guidebook for Homemaking in Hawaii*, 68–69.

21. Ahmed, "Irritable-Bowel Syndrome."

22. Kirkendall, "Hawaiian Ethnogastronomy," 20.

PART TWO
Ethnic Food

The Immigrants

1. Ronald Takaki, *Pau Hana*, 180.

2. For overviews of the food of all immigrant groups, see Katherine Bazore, *Hawaiian and Pacific Foods*; Ann Kondo Corum, *Ethnic Foods of Hawaiʻi*; Friends of Waipahu Cultural Garden Park, *Plantation Village Cookbook*; Friends of Waipahu Cultural Garden Center, *The Second Plantation Village Cookbook*;

Judith Midgely Kirkendall, "Hawaii Ethnogastronomy."

3. For an overview of the immigrants, see Andrew Lind, *Hawaii's People*; Takaki, *Pau Hana*; and relevant portions of Lawrence Fuchs, *Hawaii Pono*; and Gavan Daws, *Shoal of Time*.

4. David Stannard, *Before the Horror*.

5. James Walter Girvin, *The Master Planter*, 28–29, 42.

6. Takaki, *Pau Hana*, 23.

7. *Mark Twain's Letters from Hawaii*, 16.

8. Franklin Odo, *A Pictorial History of the Japanese in Hawaii*, 165.

9. Odo, *A Pictorial History of the Japanese in Hawaii*, 75.

10. Karol Haraguchi, *Rice in Hawaii*.

11. Dorothy Ochiai Hazama and Jane Okamoto Komeiji, *Okage Sama De*, 234; Odo, *A Pictorial History of the Japanese in Hawaii*, 156–157; Kirkendall, "Hawaiian Ethnogastronomy," 215–216.

12. For Korean food in Hawaii, see Elizabeth Ahn Toupin (*Hawaii Cookbook*) and Mark and Kim Millom (*Flavors of Korea*). For Puerto Rican, Samoan, and Southeast Asian food, see Bazore (*Hawaiian and Pacific Foods*), Corum (*Ethnic Foods of Hawaiʻi*), and Kirkendall ("Hawaiian Ethnogastronomy").

13. Cristine Mackie (*Life and Food in the Caribbean*, 139–140) pointed out that the Chinese who went to the Caribbean similarly used watercress with enthusiasm.

14. "Farming Amidst the Concrete: Surrounded by Shopping Malls and Highways, the Sumida Family Continues Growing Watercress," *MidWeek*, 29 September 1993.

Roast Pig by the Grave: The Chinese and Ching Ming

1. "Cemetery Panel Plans Spirited Centennial," *Honolulu Star-Bulletin*, 2 April 1989. For a description of traditional customs, see Beatrice Liu Ching, "Ching Ming in Hawaii."

2. Celebrating the memory of the dead with food in this way is a custom practiced around the world; the Mexican Day of the Dead is a particularly famous example. In Hawaii, the Japanese also take food to their cemeteries. All year long, but particularly around Memorial Day and between Christmas and New Year, cars bring young married couples, old retired people, and whole families to tend to the graves in the Japanese cemetery on Nuuanu Avenue just north of downtown. The black granite headstones gleam in contrast to the reds of the bunches of red ginger and pots of scarlet poinsettia and ginger. On some tombs, families place tiny Christmas trees; on others mochi (glutinous rice cakes), oranges, and a favorite candy or drink, a Snickers Bar, a SevenUp, a Budweiser, or a little liquor in a glass.

3. Compiled from Associated Chinese University Women, *Traditions for Living*, vol. 1, 79–82. Kirkendall ("Hawaiian Ethnogastronomy," 167) reported that Captain John Cass, who brought the first group of laborers in 1852, also introduced mandarins, kumquats, lychees, longans, and pomelos.

4. Clarence Glick, *Sojourners and Settlers*, 71.

5. Glick, *Sojourners and Settlers*; Arlene Lum, *Sailing for the Sun*.

6. See footnote 2 on p. 254.

7. Chinese food traditions in Hawaii are described in Katherine Bazore, *Hawaiian and Pacific Foods*; Ann Kondo Corum, *Ethnic Foods of Hawai'i*; Associated Chinese University Women, *Traditions for Living*, vols. I and II, 1979 and 1989; Judith Midgely Kirkendall, "Hawaiian Ethnogastronomy"; and Lum, *Sailing for the Sun*.

8. Kirkendall, "Hawaiian Ethnogastronomy," 170.

9. Ibid., 185.

10. Ibid., 191.

11. These include Mary Sia, *Chinese Cookbook*; Clara Tom, *Old Fashioned Method*; Alyce and Theodore Char, *The Gourmet's Encyclopedia*; Patti Loo, *The Chinese Hawaiian Cookbook*; June Kam Tong, *Popo's Kitchen*.

12. Hawaii Government Employees Association, *HGEA/AFSCME Cooks II*, 20.

13. E. N. and Marja Anderson (in K. C. Chang, ed., 350) pointed out that the southern Chinese had a number of root crops that have declined in importance because of the importation of potatoes and carrots. The only one remaining of much importance is taro. "It is perhaps most familiar from its use in one of the very few Chinese dishes we really dislike: slices of taro bedded between fat bacon slices and then steamed, thus producing a starchy, greasy, bland, drippy dish worthy of a stereotypical British boardinghouse."

14. According to Soo Youn Huang, "Eating in Chinese."

Celebrating Japanese New Year in Hawaii

1. Okahata, *A History of Japanese in Hawaii*, 149.

2. I am grateful to Susan Harada for programs on Japanese New Year in Hawaii at Kapiolani Community College and to Shigeyuki Yoshitake for his presentation. See also Dorothy Ochiai Hazama and Jane Okamoto Komeiji, *Okage Sama De*, 263–265. Reiko Mochinaga Brandon and Barbara Stephan (Spirit and Symbol) give a visually exquisite account of Japanese New Year in Japan but say nothing about Hawaii.

3. For general histories of the Japanese in Hawaii, see James H. Okahata, *A History of Japanese in Hawaii*; Leonard Lueras, *Kanyaku Imin*; Franklin Odo, *A Pictorial History*; Hazama and Komeiji, *Okage Sama De*. Japanese food customs are discussed in Katherine Bazore, *Hawaiian and Pacific Foods*; Ann Kondo Corum, *Ethnic Foods of Hawaii*; and Judith Midgely Kirkendall, "Hawaiian Ethnogastronomy."

4. Hazama and Komeiji, *Okage Sama De*, 35.

5. J. Masuoka, "Changing Food Habits."

6. Okahata, *A History of Japanese in Hawaii*, 95 and 208–209. Odo, *A Pictorial History of the Japanese in Hawai'i*, 40 and 158. "Isle Sake Brewery Is One of a Kind," *Honolulu Star-Bulletin*, 17 January 1971. Kirkendall ("Hawaiian Ethnogastronomy," 218) reported that before World War II there were six sake breweries in Hawaii, two on Maui, two on Oahu, and two on the Big Island.

7. See Young Women's Christian Association, *Japanese Foods*; Muriel Kamada Miura, *Cook Japanese-Hawaiian Style*; the series of books called *Favorite Island Cookery* by the Honpa Hongwanji Hawaii Betsuin; the two books called *Simply Delicious Recipes* by the Koganji Temple; and Japanese Cul-tural Center of Hawaii, *The Legacy of the Japanese in Hawaii*.

8. Friends of Waipahu Cultural Garden Park, *Plantation Village Cookbook*, 58–59.

Sweet Potatoes and Okinawan Samurai

1. Hui o Laulima, *Okinawan Cookery and Culture*, 126–127.

2. Quoted in Hui o Laulima, *Okinawan Cookery and Culture*, 18.

3. Dorothy Ochiai Hazama and Jane Okamoto Komeiji, *Okage Sama De*, 217–218.

4. Ibid., 64. See also Hui o Laulima, "Pork for All Occasions," in *Of Andagi and Sanshin*, 22.

5. "Okinawan Cooking Show a Rare Treat," *Honolulu Advertiser*, 19 May 1993.

Pidgin, Pork, and the Portuguese

1. Luis Vaz de Camoes, *Os Lusiadas* (Lisbon, 1572), quoted on back cover of John Henry Felix, *The Portuguese Bicentennial Celebration*.

2. For the history of the Portuguese in Hawaii, see John Henry Felix and Peter F. Senecal, *The Portuguese in Hawaii*. Food customs are discussed in Katherine Bazore, *Hawaiian and Pacific Foods*; Ann Kondo Corum, *Ethnic Foods of Hawai'i*; and Judith Midgely Kirkendall, "Hawaiian Ethnogastronomy."

3. Stephan Ternstrom, *Harvard Encyclopedia of American Ethnic Groups*, 813–820.

4. Cristine Mackie, *Life and Food in the Caribbean*, 108.

5. Jean Anderson, *The Food of Portugal*, 139.

6. See, for example, Thirty-five Years' Resident, *The Indian Cookery Book*, 99.

7. Rafi Fernandez, *Malaysian Cookery*, 216.

8. Mackie, *Life and Food in the Caribbean*, 126.

9. Ibid., 83–88.

10. Felix and Senecal, *The Portuguese in Hawaii*, 128–130.

11. Portuguese Pioneer Civic Association, *Portuguese Cooking in Hawaii* and *The Pleasures of Portuguese Cooking*; John Peru, *Portuguese Cuisine Hawaii*.

Tracking Down the Kamias: Filipino Vegetables in Hawaii

1. *Honolulu Magazine*, March 1992.

2. Friends of Waipahu Cultural Garden Park, *Plantation Village Cookbook*. 18–19.

3. *Gertrude Stewart's Manila Cook Book*, Doreen Fernandez, a leading expert on the food and culture of the Philippines, told me that the best Filipino recipe book is Eniquela David Perez, *Recipes of the Philippines*, but it is hard to find in the United States.

4. Alan Davidson, *Fruit*, 98–99.

5. Particularly useful for vegetables in People's Open Markets are I. H. Burkill (*Dictionary of the Economic Products of the Malay Peninsula*) and Peter Johnson Wester (*The Food Plants of the Philippines*).

6. For discussions of Filipino food in Hawaii, see Katherine Bazore, *Hawaiian and Pacific Foods*; Ann Kondo Corum, *Ethnic Foods of Hawaiʻi*; and Judith Midgely Kirkendall, "Hawaiian Ethnogastronomy."

7. Kirkendall, "Hawaiian Ethnogastronomy," 260.

8. Filipino Women's League, *Hawaii Filipina's Favorite Recipes*.

9. Non-Filipinos make jokes about Filipino silverware (the fingers) and about eating dog, in spite of the facts that to this day poi is eaten with the fingers by Hawaiians and kamaainas alike and that Chinese, Koreans, and Hawaiians all eat dog as well (Pat Sasaki, Douglas Simonson, and Ken Sakata, *Pupus to da Max*, 47 and 143).

10. Doreen Fernandez and Edilberto Alegre (*Sarap*) and Gilda Cordero-Fernando (*The Culinary Culture of the Philippines*) celebrate the richness and variety of Filipino food.

PART THREE
Kamaaina Food

Hawaii's Crop Parade: The Vegetable Resources of the Tropics

1. Gast and Conrad, *Don Francisco de Paula Marin*, 1–45.

2. David Livingstone Crawford, *Hawaii's Crop Parade*, 33–47.

3. For a good summary of nineteenth-century economic botany and tropical plantations, see Daniel Headrick, *The Tentacles of Progress*, chap. 7.

4. For Vancouver, see Ralph S. Kuykendall, *The Hawaiian Kingdom*, vol. 1, 41; for Marin, see Ross H. Gast and Agnes C. Conrad, *Don Francisco de Paula Marin*, chap. 3.

5. The Islands were known as the Sandwich Islands in the nineteenth century.

Beefing Up Hawaii

1. George Vancouver, *Voyage of Discovery*, vol. 1, chap. 5; Joseph Brennan, *The Parker Ranch of Hawaii*, 23–31.

2. Gavan Daws, *Shoal of Time*, 24–28.

3. Brennan, *The Parker Ranch of Hawaii*, chaps. 4–7.

4. For this and more about beef, see David Livingstone Crawford, *Hawaii's Crop Parade*, 60–64.

5. Mary Kawena Pukui and Samuel Elbert, *Hawaiian Dictionary*, 315.

6. Adapted from Margaret Kapeka Stone, *Best-Tested Recipes of Hawaii*, 4.

7. Brennan, *The Parker Ranch of Hawaii*, 144–148.

8. Pukui and Elbert, *Hawaiian Dictionary*, 332.

9. Tamar Luke Pane'e (*E Hoʻolako Mau*, vol. 2) has an excellent section on ranch dishes.

10. It crops up, for example, in Hilo Woman's Club, *Hilo Woman's Club Cook Book*, 58.

Christian Food and Christian Living: The Impact of the Missionaries

1. Patricia Grimshaw (*Paths of Duty*, especially pages 102–112) described the diet of the missionaries; Mary Zwiep (*Pilgrim Path*) concentrated on a sympathetic analysis of the women's frame of mind.

2. Over the years they managed to have the prefabricated parts of frame houses shipped out from New England, and some of these are still standing in Honolulu.

The Want of Fruit: Still Felt in Hawaii

1. A city ordinance strictly limiting the use of fireworks in the mid-1990s changed this New Year's scene.

2. March 1866, *Mark Twain's Letters from Hawaii*, 38.

3. James Walter Girvin, *The Master Planter*, 17. This book deserves reprint-

ing for its picture of plantation life in the late nineteenth century. It is a fictional tale of a man and his family who arrive in Hawaii by way of California in the 1860s. After working a year as a "shipped man," the husband by humility, thrift, and diligence becomes one of the largest planters in the Islands and is revealed to be of old Boston stock.

4. Apart from Girvin (*The Master Planter*) and David Livingstone Crawford (*Hawaii's Crop Parade*, 129) who discussed the commercial future of sixty-eight different fruits, see Agnes B. Alexander (*How to Use Hawaiian Fruit*), who gave recipes for 21 fruits; Carey Dunlap Miller, Katherine Bazore, and Mary Bartow (*Fruits of Hawaii*), who gave recipes for 37; and the Hilo Woman's Club (*Hilo Woman's Club Cook Book*), with recipes for 16.

5. The two fruits that were native were akala and ohelo. The Hawaiians added bananas and mountain apples.

6. Marilyn Rittenhouse Harris' *Tropical Fruit Cookbook* suggested numerous recipes for Hawaii's fruits, both the common and the rarer varieties.

7. Girvin, *The Master Planter*, 117.

8. This recipe is from the fifth edition (1909) of the *Hawaiian Cook Book* compiled by the Woman's Society of Central Union Church in Honolulu. It was sufficiently popular to crop up in the American-Filipino cookbook, Mrs. Samuel Francis Gaches, *Good Cooking and Health in the Tropics*, 49.

9. Crawford, *Hawaii's Crop Parade*, 221.

10. For example, A. B. Alexander, *How to Use Hawaiian Fruit*, 63.

King Sugar

1. Quoted by Gavan Daws, *Shoal of Time*, 174.

2. Ibid., chaps. 5–8 give an overview of the history of the sugar industry. See also David Livingstone Crawford, *Hawaii's Crop Parade*, 246–256 and Jacob Adler, *Claus Spreckels*.

3. *Mark Twain's Letters from Hawaii*, 257–275.

4. Ronald Takaki, *Pau Hana*, 19.

5. Bonnie Tuell, *Island Cooking*, 21.

Juicy Pineapple from the Fair Hawaiian Isles

1. Richard B. Dole and Elizabeth Dole Porteus, *The Story of James Dole*, 60. Most of the information in this essay is taken from that book.

2. Ibid., chaps. 12 and 26. See also David Livingstone Crawford, *Hawaii's Crop Parade*, 197–206.

3. See, for example, the promotional cookbook, *The Thatched Kitchen*, put together by the Hawaii company Castle and Cooke in 1972 to promote canned pineapple with recipes such as color passion curry, tuna Polynesian, and Tahitian chicken.

4. Ross H. Gast and Agnes C. Conrad, *Don Francisco de Paula Marin*, 52.

5. Dole and Porteus, *The Story of James Dole*, 57.

6. *Jane Grigson's Fruit Book*, 338.

7. Hawaiian Electric Company, *Health for Victory Club*, 3–5. See also Hilo Woman's Club, *Hilo Woman's Club Cook Book*, which features Ham Hawaiian and Chicken Hawaiian, each with canned pineapple, in the meat and poultry sections, respectively; of the 17 recipes for pineapple as a fruit, only one specifies fresh, six specify canned, and the remaining recipes are ambiguous though the frequent mention of juice suggests cans be-

cause it is hard to juice a pineapple without an electric juicer.

8. Central Union Church, Honolulu, Woman's Society, *Hawaiian Cook Book*, 114.

9. Agnes B. Alexander, *How to Use Hawaiian Fruit*, 53.

10. Elizabeth Andoh, *An American Taste of Japan*, 241–242.

The Gracious Poi Supper

1. Maili Yardley, *Hawaii Cooks*, 18.

2. John F. McDermott, Wen-shing Tseng, and Thomas Maretzki, *Peoples and Cultures of Hawaii*, 28–31. See also Niklaus Schwizer, *Hawai'i and the German Speaking Peoples*.

3. The kapus (taboos) that constrained many aspects of women's eating, and particularly prohibited them from eating with men, had been successively broken in the decade between 1810 and 1820, thus making adaptation to haole ways possible. See Gavan Daws, *Shoal of Time*, 56–60.

4. Schwizer, *Hawai'i and the German Speaking Peoples*, 93–97.

5. Yardley, *Hawaii Cooks*, 14–17.

6. The classic kamaaina cookbooks, apart from Yardley (*Hawaii Cooks, Hawaii Cooks: The Island Way*; and *Hawaii Cooks Throughout the Year*), are *The Helen Alexander Hawaiian Cook Book*; Central Union Church, *Hawaiian Cook Book*; Dora Jane Isenberg Cole and Juliet Rice Wichman, *The Kauai Museum Presents Early Kauai Hospitality*; Hilo Woman's Club, *Hilo Woman's Club Cook Book* (frequently reprinted); and *The Epicure in Hawaii*.

7. Judith Midgely Kirkendall, "Hawaiian Ethnogastronomy," 121–122.

8. *The Helen Alexander Hawaiian Cook Book*, 199.

9. James Walter Girvin, *The Master Planter*, 119.

10. Carey Dunlap Miller, *Food Values of Poi, Taro, and Limu*; Martha Potgieter, "Taro as a Food."

Food for Visitors

1. The Chinese restaurant that advertises regularly in the *Mexico News*, for example, is called the Luau. In Montreal there is a "Hawaiian" restaurant that offers a drink called a "yellow bird," identified as the drink of Waikiki Island. Not only have I never come across such a drink in Hawaii, but Waikiki is not an island. But what does that matter to the freezing Montrealian? And there is a certain poetic justice: Waikiki is cut off from the rest of Oahu by a drainage canal.

2. For a classic account, see *Trader Vic's Pacific Island Cookbook*.

3. Because these are designed mainly for an audience of visitors and mainlanders, I have not attempted to list anything like all of them in the bibliography. But examples are *Trader Vic's Pacific Island Cookbook*; Don FitzGerald, *The Pacifica House Hawaii Cook Book*; Elizabeth Ahn Toupin, *Hawaii Cookbook*; and Hawaii State Society of Washington, D.C., *Hawaiian Cuisine*. The blurb on the back of *Hawaiian Cuisine* quoted the *Plain Dealer* of Cleveland, Ohio, as opining that "Luaus are so far in these days that they will probably be out before too long. We've had our first call of the season and expect many more as graduation and patio parties come full-blown."

4. *Sam Choy's Cuisine Hawaii*, 143.

5. Mary Kawena Pukui and Samuel Elbert, *Hawaiian Dictionary*, 282.

6. Maili Yardley, *Hawaii Cooks*, 32–33.

PART FOUR
In the Beginning: Hawaiian Food

What the First Immigrants Found

1. Isabella Aiona Abbott (*La'au Hawai'i*) and Beatrice H. Krauss (*Plants in Hawaiian Culture*) are the standard sources on Hawaiian ethnobotany. E. S. Craighill Handy and Elizabeth Green Handy (*Native Planters in Old Hawaii*) remains indispensable for Hawaiian horticulture, and Margaret Titcomb (*Native Use of Fish in Hawaii, Dog and Man in the Ancient Pacific*) for Hawaiian use of fish and dogs, respectively. The case of the sweet potato presents a fine whodunit. Generally supposed to be a plant of the New World, it was already in Hawaii when Cook arrived. Douglas Yen (*The Sweet Potato and Oceania*) suggested that it must have reached East Polynesia relatively early after initial settlement and been taken from there to Hawaii. How it reached East Polynesia remains a mystery.

2. Patrick Vinton Kirch (*Feathered Gods and Fishhooks*) summarized recent work on Hawaiian prehistory. Storrs L. Olson and Helen F. James (*Descriptions*) described the discovery of thirty-two previously unknown species of extinct birds and stated that "had not *Homo sapiens* arrived in these islands some 16 centuries ago, these birds would still be alive today—skin, feathers, songs, enzymes and all," 1.

A Taste for Taro

1. Samuel Manaiakalani Kamakau, *The Works of the People of Old*, 35.

2. E. S. Craighill Handy and Elizabeth Green Handy, *Native Planters in Old Hawaii*, 19; Isabella Aiona Abbott, *La'au Hawai'i*, 23–28; Beatrice H.

Krauss, *Plants in Hawaiian Culture*, 5–8. It should be noted that sweet potato served as a second staple, particularly in those areas that were too dry for taro.

3. Abbott, *La'au Hawai'i*, 25.

4. Patrick Vinton Kirch, *Feathered Gods and Fishhooks*, chap. 4.

5. David Stannard, *Before the Horror*.

6. Abbott, *La'au Hawai'i*, 27.

7. Tamar Luke Pane'e, *E Ho'olako Mau*, vol. 2, 4–5.

8. Abbott, *La'au Hawai'i*, 28.

9. In Waianae, a largely Hawaiian community on Oahu, Hawaiians with weight problems were put on a traditional diet of poi, fish, and fruits and vegetables and told they could eat unlimited quantities. Without the high fat of fast-food chains and plate lunches, they lost considerable amounts of weight. "Food for Thought: Dr. Terry Shintani Discovered the Benefits of a Healthy Diet When He Was in Law School," *Midweek*, 29 April 1992. See also Terry Shintani, *The Waianae Book of Hawaiian Health*.

10. Kirch, *Feathered Gods and Fishhooks*, 215–223; Kirch and Dana Lepofsky, "Polynesian Irrigation."

11. "Poi Shortage Most Severe in Forty Years," *Honolulu Star-Bulletin*, 30 May 1990; "Poi Prices Rise After Iniki," *Honolulu Star-Bulletin*, 5 April 1993; "Poi Shortage Has Roots in History," *Honolulu Star-Bulletin*, 28 July 1993; *Taro Tattler* 6.

12. Other products include taro flour, developed by the 1930s and heralded as a great advance for poi cocktails and for mixing with hot cereal; dehydrated poi; and taro pancake mix.

13. George Vancouver, *Voyage of Discovery*, vol. 1, 164–65.

14. Handy and Handy, *Native Planters in Old Hawaii*, 83.

15. Cristine Mackie (*Life and Food in the Caribbean*, 104) for a dish of lobster and salt beef steamed with taro leaves.

The Coconut and the Arrowroot

1. *Mark Twain's Letters from Hawaii*, 52.

2. Isabella Aiona Abbott, *La'au Hawai'i*, 34.

3. Gwen Skinner, *The Cuisine of the South Pacific*, 12–13.

4. Dora Jane Isenberg Cole and Juliet Rice Wichman, *The Kauai Museum Presents Early Kauai Hospitality*, 51.

5. Abbott, *La'au Hawai'i*, 41.

6. Layinka M. Swinburne ("Nothing But the Best") traced the botanical, historical, pharmaceutical, and culinary aspects of arrowroot in a fine piece of detective work.

Inamona: A Condiment to Please an Epicure

1. James Walter Girvin, *The Master Planter*, 118.

2. Isabella Aiona Abbott, *La'au Hawai'i*, and Beatrice H. Krauss, *Plants in Hawaiian Culture*.

3. "Hawaiian Kukui Nut Company Wins Appeals Court Suit to Stem Importation of Foreign Kukui Nuts," *Honolulu Advertiser*, 31 March 1990.

4. So much so that Sri Owen (*Indonesian Food and Cookery*, 68) admitted that for many years she confused the two, and Hiang Marahimin and Roos Djalil (*Indonesian Dishes and Desserts*, 6) gave candlenuts and macadamia nuts as alternative translations for *kemiri*.

Alan Davidson (*Fruit*) distinguished the two. The recipes in this section are adapted from these books.

Salt, Like the Sea, Like the Earth, Like Human Sweat and Tears

1. Maxine Hong Kingston, *China Men*, 96.

2. Helen Chu, who inherited rights from her husband's grandmother, described the process to Maili Yardley (*Hawaii Cooks: The Island Way*, 128–129).

3. Tamar Luke Pane'e, *E Ho'olako Mau*, vol. 2, 39–41.

4. George Vancouver, *Voyage of Discovery*, vol. 2, 117.

5. Thomas Thrum, "Hawaiian Salt Making."

6. Richard Henry Dana, *Two Years before the Mast*, 99.

7. *Oxford English Dictionary*, Compact edition.

8. Pane'e, *E Ho'olako Mau*, vol. 2, 194–195.

9. Almost as popular as salt salmon is salt butterfish (or black cod as it is also called in the Islands or sablefish, its name in the Northwest), which was soaked and fried or used in laulaus.

10. Judith Midgely Kirkendall ("Hawaiian Ethnogastronomy," 98) suggested that lomilomi salmon is derived from a Portuguese dish made with salt cod. Portuguese from New England sailed with whalers to the Pacific, so that is quite possible, though I have not found a specific Portuguese recipe that resembles lomilomi salmon.

11. Maile Yardley, *Hawaii Cooks*, 64.

Aloha Farmer's Market: Hawaiian Foods

1. *Trader Vic's Pacific Island Cookbook*, 35.

2. Indeed, ordinary Hawaiian families did not cook pork in an imu either. Instead, they salted the pigs and placed hot stones in the cavity to cook them (Judith Midgely Kirkendall, "Hawaiian Ethnogastronomy," 65, 90).

3. Tamar Luke Pane'e, *E Ho'olako Mau*, vol. 1, 195–213.

4. In the mid-1990s, opihi meat was selling for $88 a half gallon around graduation time. For the danger, see "Opihi: Hawaii's Most Dangerous Animal," *Honolulu Star-Bulletin*, 26 May 1991.

5. Heather Fortner, *The Limu Eater*, 46.

Pure, Sweet, Cool, Clear as Crystal: Hawaii's Water

1. Victoria Nelson, *My Time in Hawaii*, 4–5. I am grateful for permission to use this quotation.

2. Russell A. Apple, *Ancient Hawaii Shore Zone Fishponds*; Patrick Vinton Kirch and Dana Lepofsky, "Polynesian Irrigation"; Carol Araki Wyban, *Tide and Current*.

3. "Koolaus to Quench Central Oahu," *Honolulu Star-Bulletin*, 29 March 1992; "Windward Water Is as Crucial as Ever," *Honolulu Advertiser*, 22 March 1994; Seabury Hall Parents' Organization, *The Hele Mai, Ai Cookbook*, 63–64.

4. Mary Kawena Pukui and Samuel Elbert (*Hawaiian Dictionary*, 380) suggested that this might be related to another meaning of "wai," "to retain."

5. Isabella Aiona Abbott, *La'au Hawai'i*, 141.

6. Each pound of purified sugar required a ton of water to produce,
much of it in the growing cycle.
The sugar planters had a problem,
though. The windward sides of the
islands had plentiful water, but the
deeply eroded valleys made the shipping of sugar almost impossible and
cultivation itself difficult. The gentler
slopes of the leeward sides, with their
ripe, rich soil, were ideal for cultivation, but too dry. The answer was to
bring water from the windward sides
to the leeward sides, and this was un-
dertaken in epic proportions.

7. Armine von Tempski, *Hula*, 304–
305.

8. *Mark Twain's Letters from Hawaii*, 268.

9. Seabury Hall Parents' Organization,
The Hele Mai, Ai Cookbook, 63–64.

10. *Mark Twain's Letters from Hawaii*, 37.

11. Nathaniel B. Emerson, *Unwritten
Literature of Hawaii*, 259.

GLOSSARY

The cook in Hawaii faces a bewildering variety of culinary terms in markets, stores, restaurants, and cookbooks. I have paid special attention to terms peculiar to the Islands (Local and Hawaiian) and to terms for which there are few readily available glossaries (Filipino, as opposed to Chinese or Japanese, which are more familiar to cooks around the world). This glossary should enable the reader to cope with the more common items in restaurants and grocery stores, with Hawaiian fish and limu sold in the larger fish markets, and with Filipino vegetables sold in Open Markets. In such locales standard spelling is often ignored, so that kalamungay might also appear as calamungay. To avoid a hopelessly unwieldy glossary, I have not listed every variant but trust the reader to think phonetically. Where possible, Filipino names are specified as Ilocano or Tagalog. Diacriticals appear in Hawaiian terms here for the reader's information, but not in the text.

`A`awa. [Hawaiian]. Fish (*Lepidaplois bilunulatus or L. modestus*). Wrasse or sandfish. A common reef fish, available year round. Usually grilled or dried by Hawaiians.

Aburage. [Japanese]. Fried tofu (bean curd). Commonly available in plastic packets in Hawaii supermarkets. Rinsed to remove traces of oil, aburage is used by Japanese (and now by many others) to make cone sushi and a variety of other dishes.

Achiote. [Puerto Rican]. Coloring. A coloring made from seeds of the lipstick or annatto plant (*Bixa orellana*), a shrub that can be seen in yards in older sections of Honolulu. Used by Puerto Ricans and Filipinos to tint rice and other foods yellow.

Adobo. [Filipino]. Chicken or pork simmered in vinegar, garlic, and soy sauce. Similar to Portuguese vinha d'alhos, but usually moist rather than crispy.

Agar. Jelling agent. Known also as agar-agar and kanten.

`Ahi. [Hawaiian]. Fish (*Thunnus albacares*). Yellowfin tuna. Also used for big-eye tuna (*Thunnus obesus*). Shibi [Japanese]. Popular and widely available, with a meaty texture and flavor whether raw or cooked. The red flesh cooks to a light tan color. Ahi is good grilled or sauteed, but is particularly favored for sashimi and poke. Because it keeps well when salted and dried, it was used by Hawaiians of old on long voyages. Dried ahi can be purchased in most fish markets to be eaten as is or grilled.

Āholehole. [Hawaiian]. Fish *(Kuhlia sansvicensis)*. Sea bass. Common shore fish found in fresh and salt water. The Hawaiians traditionally ate it raw, grilled, or dried.

Ajinomoto. [Japanese]. Seasoning. The name of a popular brand of monosodium glutamate, now almost synonymous with the product itself. Originally Japanese, ajinomoto is used extensively in Island cooking. Often shortened to "aji" in recipes.

**`Ākala.** [Hawaiian]. Fruit *(Rubus sp.)*. This Hawaiian raspberry is one of the two fruits endemic to Hawaii, the other being the `ōhelo. It grows only above the 4,000-foot level.

Ake. [Hawaiian]. Liver. Beef liver is eaten raw by Hawaiians as one form of poke.

Aku. [Hawaiian]. Fish *(Katsuwonus pelamis)*. Skipjack tuna, ocean bonito. Also sometimes used for kawakawa (wavy-back skipjack tuna). Common in the summer months, this fish weighs between 15 and 30 pounds. Very popular with all groups, either raw in sashimi and poke or grilled. Hawaiians in particular enjoy strips of the dried flesh. Hawaiian legend has it that when early migrants from the South Pacific were threatened with high seas, a school of aku appeared and calmed the waters, preventing the overturning of their canoes.

Akule. [Hawaiian]. Fish *(Selar crumenophthalmus)*. Big-eyed scad or mackerel (a jack); this small fish is in season from February through September. Grilled or fried by most groups, also appreciated dried by Hawaiians. It is excellent dried and smoked.

`Alaea salt. [Hawaiian and English]. Sea salt colored red with a water-soluble ferruginous earth. Widely available in grocery stores and favored by many for grilling.

Albacore. Fish. See tombo.

Alokon, alocon. [Filipino]. Vegetable. Not given in Wester *(The Food Plants of the Philippines)*, but possibly *Garcinia dulcis*. Young leaves and stringy flowers of large tree. Ilocanos use these in soups and stews.

`Ama`ama. [Hawaiian]. Fish *(Mugil cephalus)*. Mullet. There are several species of mullet in Hawaii (and over a thousand species worldwide). Mullet were a favorite of the Hawaiians, who raised them in fishponds. Today they are popular with most other ethnic groups, frequently steamed Chinese-style with ginger and green onions.

Ampalaya. [Filipino/Tagalog]. Vegetable. See bitter melon.

An. [Japanese]. A sweetened paste made from red azuki beans. Commonly used in confectionery, shave ice, mochi, and doughnuts, with variants known as koshian and tsubushian (chunky an). Can be purchased ready-prepared in cans in supermarkets in Hawaii and in Asian stores elsewhere.

Andagi. [Okinawan]. A doughnut raised with baking powder.

Araimo

Araimo. [Japanese]. Vegetable. Known also as taro and dasheen.

Arare. [Japanese]. Thin cracker made of sweet (glutinous) rice flour, often flavored with additional ingredients such as dried seaweed. Locally known as mochi crunch.

**A`u.** [Hawaiian]. Fish *(Xiphias gladius)*. All billfish tend to be labeled a`u in Hawaii, although as their popularity for eating as well as for sport grows, finer distinctions are being made and a`u narrowed to broadbill swordfish. Shutome [Japanese]. A game fish, with fine, white, tasty flesh.

Avocado. Fruit and vegetable *(Persea americana)*. Large, handsome trees grow in gardens in older neighborhoods, overshadowing the houses. In the summer, the fruits join piles of mangoes placed on garden walls and fences to be had for the asking. Also available commercially. The flesh of avocados grown in Hawaii tends to be watery and sweetish rather than rich and oily. There are few special recipes, but it is often eaten between slices of bread as butter might be.

`Awa. [Hawaiian]. Plant *(Piper methysticum)*. An infusion of the roots of this mildly narcotic plant furnished the sacred drink of the Hawaiians, and of many other Pacific Islanders.

Awa. [Hawaiian]. Fish *(Chanos chanos)*. Ladyfish or milkfish. Bangus or bagos [Filipino]. Fish about a foot long, prized by Hawaiians and Filipinos.

Awamori. [Okinawan]. Hard liquor made from rice and black malt.

Azoni greens. [Japanese]. Vegetable. See mizoni.

Azuki beans. [Japanese]. Red beans *(Vigna angularis)*. Cooked by themselves, with rice, or sweetened; mashed to make a filling for mochi, doughnuts, and other confections. See an.

Bacalhao. [Portuguese]. Fish. Salt cod used by the Portuguese in a wide variety of dishes though now quite expensive.

Bagoong. [Filipino]. Sauce of salted and fermented fish, usually *dilis* (long-jawed anchovies, *Stolephorus commersoni*); extensively used to flavor Filipino dishes.

Bagos. [Filipino]. Fish. See awa.

Banana. Fruit. (*Musa paradisiaca*). Several varieties are available in Hawaii, including the common Williams banana, the tastier apple banana, and cooking bananas (plantains). The leaves are used by Filipinos and others to wrap foods; Filipinos also eat the tender parts of the banana flower, *puso* in Tagalog.

Bangus. [Filipino]. Fish. See awa.

Barbecue. Korean barbecue or *bulgogi*, beef marinated in soy sauce, sugar, sesame oil, garlic, and green onions and grilled. It has nothing to do with slow-cooked mainland pit barbecue of pork or beef in a red tomato-based or yellow mustard-based sauce.

Beefsteak plant. Herb. See shiso.

Beni shoga. [Japanese]. Pickled young ginger, usually in the form of delicate pink slivers. Served as a garnish with many Japanese dishes.

Bento. [Japanese]. Box lunch. The kind commonly available at lunch wagons, drug stores, and groceries consists of a black plastic box about 6 inches square with compartments for rice, some kind of meat, and a couple of pickles, all decorated with a little strip of green plastic bamboo leaf and covered with a transparent plastic lid to show the neatly arranged contents.

Bibingka. [Filipino]. Pudding of coconut and rice flour, traditionally steamed in banana leaves.

Bitsu-bitsu. [Filipino]. Fritters of grated sweet potatoes.

Bitter melon

Bitter melon. Vegetable (*Momordica charantia*). Ampalaya [Filipino/Tagalog] or paria [Filipino]. Karela [Indian]. A warty skinned squash ranging in size from a couple of inches long to a foot or so. Altogether there are forty-two species in the genus. Chinese, Filipinos, and Southeast Asians stuff bitter melon and also add them to soups and stews. Filipinos also eat the leaves.

Black cod. See butterfish.

Bok choy. [Chinese]. Vegetable (*Brassica campestris var. sinensis*). One of the cabbage family with thick, white stems and tasty, green leaves. Bunches of baby bok choy are tender and delicious sliced into soups and stir-fries.

Bottle gourd, loofah, a large and a small bitter melon, and daikon seeds

Bottle gourd. Vegetable (*Lagenaria siceraria*). A summer squash used by Filipinos, Southeast Asians, and Chinese.

Breadfruit. Fruit and vegetable (*Artocarpus altilis*). 'Ulu [Hawaiian]. Large, handsome trees with big green fruits, introduced by the Hawaiians, who, however, never depended on them as heavily as the Marquesans did. Used by Hawaiians and haoles in the nineteenth century and still to be seen in the Islands though not commercially available on a regular basis.

Broke da mout. Local expression meaning delicious.

Bulgogi. [Korean]. See barbecue.

Burdock. Vegetable. See gobo.

Butterbur. Vegetable (*Petasites japonica*). Introduced by Japanese.

Butterfish. Fish. Salted butterfish, or black cod, or sablefish as it is known in the Northwest, is particularly popular with Hawaiians for frying or seasoning laulaus. Desalted by soaking in water for a couple of days, changing the water every day, it is then served lomied, or boiled with gravy from a beef stew, or in a soup with watercress and chopped green onions and ginger (served in a saimin bowl), or fried. I suspect it is *Anoplopoma fimbria*, a pomfretlike fish (Davidson, *Seafood*, 96).

Butter mochi. [Local]. Cake made of mochiko (sweet rice flour), sugar, eggs, butter, and coconut milk.

Calabash. A vessel of wood or gourd for food, water, or other valuables. Metaphor for family circle (that is, those who eat out of the same pot, as in "calabash cousins").

Calamondin. Fruit (*Citrus mitis*). Kalamansi, calamansi [Filipino].

Marble-sized lime with an excellent flavor sold in Open Markets and in Filipino stores in Chinatown. Used by Filipinos to sour dishes.

Caldo verde. [Portuguese]. Soup named for the abundant shredded greens, usually kale, that it contains.

Chanpuru. [Okinawan]. A stir-fry or stew of vegetables and crumbled tofu.

Char siu. [Chinese]. Roast pork, reddish and slightly sweet, used in many Chinese dishes and by all groups for topping saimin.

Chinese date. [Chinese]. *(Zizyphus jujuba).* Seasoning. The dried, wrinkled fruit, which bears some slight exterior resemblance to a date, is used in a variety of Chinese dishes. Also known as jujube.

Chop suey yam

Chop suey yam. [Local]. Vegetable *(Pachyrrhizus erosus).* Jicama [Mexican]. Root vegetable about the size of a potato with crisp flesh that can be eaten raw or used as a substitute for water chestnuts in Chinese dishes, hence the Local name.

Chow fun. [Chinese]. Wide noodles.

Chun. [Korean]. See jun.

Cone sushi. Sushi in pockets of fried bean curd (aburage).

Crack seed. [Local]. Preserved salted and sweetened fruits, often with an anise flavor. Of Chinese origin, but much modified by Local innovation,

these are sold loose in crack seed stores and in cellophane packets in all convenience and grocery stores.

Daikon. [Japanese]. Vegetable *(Raphanus sativus longipinnatus).* Asian radish or turnip, depending on translation. Absolutely essential for local Japanese cooking, steamed or pickled or in other versions. Filipinos eat the seeds.

Dango. [Japanese]. Small dumplings of mochiko (mochi rice flour).

Chop suey yam (jicama), poi taro, and dasheen (araimo)

Dasheen. [Japanese]. Vegetable. Known also as taro and araimo.

Dashi. [Japanese]. Seasoned broth for soup traditionally made from sea vegetables *(kombu)* and dried, shaved bonito. Also called hondashi.

Dashi-no-moto. [Japanese]. The instant variety of dashi available in small foil packages in supermarkets in Hawaii and Asian stores elsewhere.

Delicatessen. A plate lunch place; no Jewish food nor even sandwiches.

Dim sum. [Chinese]. Small nibbles, often of stuffed pasta steamed or fried, eaten with tea for breakfast or lunch.

Dinuguan. [Filipino]. Pork sauteed and simmered in vinegar sauce and then thickened with blood.

Dragon's eye. Fruit. See longan.

Dried shrimp. Packets of pink dried shrimp are used by many ethnic groups, eaten out of hand as a snack or soaked and used as a soup base or to enhance dim sum stuffings. Shredded and colored dried shrimp are used by the Japanese to top sushi and other foods.

Drive-in. A plate lunch place, usually with little or no parking, and almost certainly no traditional drive-in.

Dun-kwa. [Chinese]. See winter melon.

Filoses. [Portuguese]. See malasadas.

Fishcake. There are a variety of items known as fishcake in Hawaii, including the paste of fresh fish of Chinese origin and the processed fishcake of the Japanese (kamaboko).

Five-spice powder. [Chinese]. Seasoning. A mixture of ground star anise, anise, fennel, cloves, and cinnamon; used in many Chinese dishes.

Furikake. [Japanese]. Seasoning. A mixture usually composed of salt, flaked dried seaweed, sesame seeds, and (sometimes) dried bonito flakes, ready-prepared for shaking over rice.

Gau. [Chinese]. Cake or pudding of steamed sweet rice flour, traditionally eaten at Chinese New Year.

Gaugee. [Local]. Deep-fried, pork-filled (or SPAM-filled) Chinese wontons, but larger and rectangular. An Island specialty.

Gobo. [Japanese]. Vegetable *(Arctium lappa).* Burdock root. A root vegetable about a foot in length, tapering from ¾ inch to ¼ inch in thickness. The Japanese peel and blanch it before using in soups, stews, and sushi.

Goma. [Japanese]. Seasoning. Sesame seed. Used as a garnish on many Local foods as well as in Chinese, Japanese, and Korean dishes.

Grinds. [Pidgin]. Local expression for food. To grind = to eat.

Guava. Fruit (*Psidium guajava*). Guava trees grow wild and are regarded as a weed. The commercial crop is used for juice or for jam and jelly, and guava jam and jelly and sweetened guava juice (often mixed with other tropical fruit juices) are readily available in grocery stores. Fragrant fresh guavas can often be picked up while hiking or found in Chinatown.

Halo-halo. [Filipino]. Dessert drink of shaved ice, mixed fruits (many of them preserved), and condensed milk or syrup.

Haole. [Hawaiian/Local]. Foreigner, literally, "outsider"; white person. Now used to denote a European-American or European.

Hapa-haole. [Hawaiian/Local]. Half haole.

Hapu`u. [Hawaiian]. Fish (*Epinephelus quernus*). Sea bass. Ala [Japanese]. The only commercially important grouper, most plentiful in fall and winter. When cooked it has firm, white flesh.

Hasu. [Japanese]. See lotus root.

Haupia. [Hawaiian]. Traditional sweet of coconut milk thickened with pia (Polynesian arrowroot). At the time of writing, cornstarch is almost invariably substituted.

Hawaiian salt. Coarse local sea salt, sometimes colored red by clay (`alaea salt). Sea salt or rock salt can be substituted.

Hawaiian sweet bread. Actually Portuguese sweet bread. See pão doce.

Heavy pupus. [Local]. Snacks of sufficient quantity and substance to make a meal.

Hebi. [Japanese]. Fish (*Tetrapaturus angustirostris*). Shortbill swordfish or spearfish, also known as *au*. (*Hebi* is also the Japanese word for snake.) One of the billfishes, with firm-textured flesh that turns from pink to white when cooked.

He`e. [Hawaiian]. Octopus. See tako.

Hīnālea. [Hawaiian]. Fish. Several different species and varieties seem to come under this category. Gizame [Japanese]. Green wrasse. Well-known, popular, and abundant reef fish.

Honu. [Hawaiian]. Turtle. Now endangered and no longer legally eaten.

Ika. [Japanese]. Octopus or squid.

Imu. [Hawaiian]. Traditional Hawaiian underground oven. A hole was dug and lined with porous stones, a fire was lit and allowed to die down, and then pig, fish, dog, taro, and sweet potatoes were placed in the cavity, covered, and allowed to cook in the residual heat. Still used for special occasions, though the problem of finding a site and the labor and skill required to dig the pit mean that it is not that common.

`Inamona. [Hawaiian]. Seasoning. Roasted kukui nut kernels (candlenuts), pounded and salted; used by Hawaiians as a relish for raw fish.

Jook. [Chinese]. Rice gruel traditionally served for breakfast. In Hawaii, it is often made into a major production with many additions to the basic gruel, and as such is served by ethnic groups other than Chinese and on occasions other than breakfast.

Jujube. Fruit. See Chinese date.

Jun. [Korean]. Thin slices of fried meat or fish in a crisp egg batter; a popular plate lunch item. Known also as chun.

Kajiki. [Japanese]. Fish (*Makaira nigricans*). Pacific blue marlin, one of the billfish.

Kākū. [Hawaiian]. Fish (*Sphyraena barracuda*). Great barracuda. Kamasu [Japanese].

Kalabasa. [Filipino/Tagalog]. Vegetable (*Curcubita maxima*). A squash; Filipinos eat the flowers and the tender shoots as well as the squash itself.

Kalamungay/calamungay. [Filipino]. Vegetable. See marungay.

Kal bi. [Korean]. Thin slices of grilled beef, previously marinated in soy sauce, ginger, and sugar.

Kale. Vegetable. A member of the cabbage family with dark green, crinkly leaves, sometimes referred to as Portuguese cabbage because of their liking for it, particularly in their soup, caldo verde.

Kalekale. [Hawaiian]. Fish. The young stage of opakapaka, the pink snapper.

Kalo. [Hawaiian]. Vegetable. See taro.

Kālua pig. [Hawaiian]. Pork cooked in an underground earth oven (imu) until very tender. It is eaten shredded. Other meats and turkey can be cooked the same way. Ready-prepared kālua pork is sold in grocery stores.

Kama`āina. [Hawaiian]. A term that originally meant native-born, it is now used by Locals to identify well-to-do haole Locals who have been in the Islands for several generations. Hotels and tour guides use it to allocate discounts to anyone living in the Islands: the "kamaaina rate."

Kamaboko. [Japanese]. Fishcake.

Kamias, kamyas, camias, pias, pyas. [Filipino]. Fruit *(Averrhoa bilimbi)*. A sour fruit the size, shape, and roughly the color of a gherkin, used by Filipinos for souring soups and salads. Available in Open Markets. Lemon juice can be substituted.

Kamote, camote. [Filipino]. Vegetable. See sweet potato.

Kampyo. [Japanese]. Strips of dried gourd used for tying bundles of food.

Kanaka. [Hawaiian]. The Hawaiians' name for themselves, commonly used by Hawaiians and others in the nineteenth century but now largely dropped.

Kanten. [Japanese]. Jelling agent; agar. A clear, colorless, tasteless gel produced from red algae; used in Asian cooking. It has the advantage over gelatin of remaining firm at room temperature and of jelling substances such as pineapple. It is most commonly bought in plastic packets with long, crinkly sheets of gel, which are then softened in water.

Katsu. [Japanese]. Breaded cutlet usually of pork (tonkatsu) or chicken (chicken katsu). Reputedly the term derives from the Japanese pronunciation of cutlet. A popular plate lunch item.

Katuday, catuday. [Filipino]. Vegetable *(Sesbania grandiflora)*. The large, white, fleshy flowers and the long, slender pods of this small tree, about 15–30 feet high, a native of India and Southeast Asia, are added to soups and stews.

Kau-kau. [Pidgin]. This widely used word for food is often thought to be Hawaiian, but it is apparently pidgin and possibly related to the Cantonese chow-chow.

Kau yuk. [Chinese]. Belly of pork, slow-cooked with red bean curd, popular in traditional Local Chinese restaurants.

Kelp. See kombu.

Kim chee. [Korean]. Hot pickle, made with salt, garlic, ginger, and chili pepper as a seasoning for a vegetable (usually cabbage, but also cucumber, daikon, certain seaweeds, etc.).

Kochu jang. [Korean]. Seasoning. Paste of chili pepper, soy beans, and glutinous (sweet) rice paste. Popular outside as well as within the Korean community.

Kombu/konbu. [Japanese]. Sea vegetable *(Laminaria* spp.). Kelp. Sold dried in long, brown, leathery strips, perhaps 3 to 6 inches wide and several feet long. Used by Japanese, Okinawans, and Koreans as a seasoning for soup and for wrapping meats and chicken.

Konnyaku. [Japanese]. A chewy transparent paste made from yams.

Koshian. [Japanese]. See an.

Kukui nut. [Hawaiian/Local]. Tree *(Aleurites moluccana)*. Candlenut. The trees on which these nuts grow—apparently introduced by the early Polynesians—are easily picked out on hillsides because of the pale yellowish green color of their leaves. The meat, which is sufficiently oily that the Hawaiians could use it for lighting, was and still is used as a relish (inamona). Very similar to macadamia nuts, which can be used as a substitute. Not available commercially except as the relish, or imported from Southeast Asia and sold as *kemiri* or candlenuts. The nuts can be picked up from many a sidewalk and mountain trail in Hawaii.

Kūmū. [Hawaiian]. Fish *(Parupeneus porphyreus)*. Goatfish. A red fish with a firm, white flesh that makes good eating raw, steamed, baked in ti leaves, or salted and cooked. Hawaiians used it as an offering to the gods.

Lānai. [Hawaiian/Local]. An outdoor living room, characteristic of dwellings in Hawaii, roofed against the frequent showers but open on one side.

Laulau. [Hawaiian]. A Hawaiian dish of pork, beef, or chicken (or all three) with salted butterfish, all swathed in taro tops and cooked in ti leaves.

Lemon grass. *(Cymbopogon citratus)*. Seasoning. A plant about the size of a spring onion but much tougher, with a lemony, acidy flavor in the leaves. Widely used in Southeast Asian cooking.

Li hing mui. [Chinese]. The dried, salted seed of the flowering apricot, the original crack seed.

Lilikoi. [Hawaiian]. Fruit *(Passiflora edulis)*. Passion fruit. Like guava, regarded as a weed in the wild and used for juice when commercially grown. It is most popular in Hawaii in a mixed fruit punch and as jelly.

Limu. [Hawaiian]. A term originally applied to plants growing in wet places but now reserved almost exclusively for edible seaweeds (sea vegetables). For a discussion of selected kinds, see the section on limu.

Linguiça. [Portuguese]. See Portuguese sausage.

Local. A person, custom, or object that has been in the Islands for a considerable time.

Loco moco. [Local]. A favorite fast food consisting of a hamburger patty on two scoops of rice, topped by a fried egg, and covered with brown gravy.

Lomi. [Hawaiian]. A word meaning to rub or press or massage, it is also used for food, particularly fish, that has been kneaded with the fingers.

Lomilomi salmon. [Hawaiian/Local]. Salt salmon massaged between the fingers and served chilled with tomatoes and onion as an appetizer or side dish.

Long bean. Vegetable (*Vigna sinensis/Dolichos sesquipedalis*). Sitaw [Tagalog]. A relation of black-eyed peas, widely used by Asian communities.

Long rice. [Local]. Thin rice or mung bean noodles. These are soaked and cooked briefly in boiling water. Chicken long rice is a familiar Local dish, often supposed to be Hawaiian but in fact originally Chinese.

Long squash. Vegetable (*Trichosanthesa cucumerina*). One of the many squashes available in Open Markets.

Longan. Fruit (*Euphoria longana*). Also known as dragon's eye. Similar to but smaller than a lychee.

Longaniza sausage. [Filipino]. A spicy sausage seasoned with vinegar, chili pepper, and garlic.

Loofah

Loofah. Vegetable (*Luffa cylindrica/acutangula*). Patola [Filipino]. Sponge gourd. A member of the squash family with sharp ridges down the sides. It is eaten when it is about 1 foot long. If it is allowed to grow larger, the flesh can be stripped away from the fibers to form the familiar bathtub scrubber.

Lotus. Vegetable (*Nelubium nuciferum*). Renkon [Japanese]. Much appreciated by the Chinese and Japanese. The root is sliced to use with a dip or stuffed with a meat, fish, or vegetable mixture and deep-fried.

Lū'au. [Hawaiian]. Traditional Hawaiian feast and now in a vastly modified form a major tourist attraction. The term is also used for the large green leaves of the taro plant and for the dish consisting of chopped taro leaves with coconut milk and chicken or octopus.

Lumpia. [Filipino]. A thin crepelike wrapper, usually bought ready-prepared. In the Philippines the wrapper is usually stuffed with a vegetable filling and can be eaten as is or deep-fried. In Hawaii, it is often deep-fried, and the stuffing usually contains meat.

Lunch wagon. A Local institution; an ancient truck packed with plate lunches to be found in parking lots in business districts, construction sites, parks, and beach areas.

Lychee. Fruit (*Litchi chinensis*). In midsummer, sprays of lychees fresh from the trees can be bought in Chinatown, to be peeled with the fingers to expose succulent white flesh. Not produced commercially in any quantity.

Macadamia nuts. (*Macadamia ternifolia*). Widely associated with Hawaii, these nuts originally came from Australia. The commercial crop is grown mainly for export. Insofar as they are used in home cooking in Hawaii, it is mainly for cookies, cakes, and pies. A macadamia nut oil is now being produced.

Mahimahi. [Hawaiian]. Fish (*Coryphaena hippurus*). Mansaku [Japanese]. Dolphinfish or dorado. Not a dolphin but a large blunt-nosed fish with a tapered body found in the open ocean. When fried, grilled, or sauteed, the flesh is firm and delicate, making it a favorite both in plate lunches and with visitors.

Mai tai. Drink of rum, pineapple, and citrus juices.

Malasadas. [Portuguese]. Deep-fried yeast-raised doughnuts with a high proportion of egg; originally Portuguese but now enjoyed by all ethnic groups. A variant spelling is mallasadas; also known as filoses.

Manapua. [Hawaiian/Local]. Apparently telescoped from the Hawaiian *mea* (thing) + 'ono (delicious) + pua'a (pig). A steamed Chinese bun, usually stuffed with sweetened pork (char siu); a ubiquitous Island snack available in every grocery store.

Mandoo. [Korean]. Dumplings (similar to potstickers) filled with chopped meat and vegetables; a common offering on a Korean plate lunch.

Mango. Fruit (*Mangifera indica*). Pirie and Hayden varieties are widely available in Hawaii, and gardens in older neighborhoods are often shaded by the attractive trees. They are eaten ripe in desserts or out of hand. During the summer mango season, their owners give grocery sacks of mangoes to anyone who will take them. The common variety of mangoes is used green for pickles, salads, and chutney or for eating out of hand with a dash of soy sauce or salt.

Manini. [Hawaiian]. Fish (*Acanthurus triostegus*). Surgeonfish or tang. This small, attractive, striped fish is one of the most popular reef fishes with

Hawaiians despite its tough skin and numerous bones. In pidgin, the term "manini" indicates small, stingy, or skimpy—a manini problem is a small problem.

Manju. [Japanese]. Wheat flour confections widely available in grocery stores in Hawaii.

Marungay. [Filipino]. Vegetable (*Moringa oleifera*). Horseradish tree. This has nothing to do with European horseradish. It was apparently so named because the grated root tastes somewhat like horseradish. Not only the roots but also the leaves, handsome sprays of rather rounded leaves, and the fruit, foot-long, pencil-thin, ridged green cylinders, are eaten, particularly by Filipinos. Also known as calamungay/kalamungay.

Melon pan. [Japanese]. Slightly sweet yeast pastry with currants.

Mirin. [Japanese]. Sweet rice wine used for cooking.

Miru. [Japanese]. See rat's-foot limu.

Miso. [Japanese]. Fermented soy bean paste. Ranges from a mild white version to a stronger red version. Used in many Japanese dishes. Miso soup is popular, particularly for breakfast.

Mizoni. [Japanese]. Vegetable. Also known as azoni, mizuna, and other names. Particularly important for Japanese New Year celebrations. Good in salads.

Moana. [Hawaiian]. Fish (*Parupeneus multifasciatus* and maybe other species). Goatfish. Six inches to 1 foot in length, with whiskers under the chin that perhaps explain the English name.

Mochi. [Japanese]. A "cake" made of cooked, pounded mochi rice or of steamed sweet rice flour (mochiko).

For New Year, mochi without filling is used in a traditional soup, ozoni. For other occasions, mochi, sometimes flavored or filled with *an*, is eaten as a sweet. There are a number of establishments in Hawaii that specialize in making mochi, and attractive packages of mochi, (or mixed mochi and manju) are available in grocery stores.

Mochiko. [Japanese]. Flour made from sweet or mochi rice, widely used in Asian desserts. Blue Star, produced in California, is a popular variety.

Moi. [Hawaiian]. Fish (*Polydactylus sexfilis*). Threadfin. Twelve to 18 inches long with color varying according to the bottom over which it swims. In the past, only the chiefs were allowed to eat this fish.

Moonfish. Fish. See opah.

Mountain apple. Fruit (*Syzygium malaccense*). Originally introduced by the Hawaiians, this fruit vaguely resembles an apple in taste and texture. Trees still grow wild in the forests. Also known as ʻōhiʻa ʻai.

Mūheʻe. [Hawaiian]. Ika [Japanese]. Squid.

Musubi. [Japanese/Local]. Rice cooked and shaped into a ball, triangle, or block, sometimes wrapped in nori, and eaten as a snack. It is one of Hawaii's most popular fast bites, found in grocery stores, drug stores, and convenience stores.

Nairagi. [Japanese]. Fish (*Tetrapturus audax*). Striped marlin, a fish with a rich, mild, moist flavor.

Namasu. [Japanese]. Cucumber, carrot, daikon, sea vegetables, or ginger, or a combination in a slightly sweet rice vinegar dressing, eaten as a side dish.

Nantu. [Okinawan]. Okinawan mochi; a soft confection of cooked and pounded sweet rice or sweet rice flour.

Nenue. [Hawaiian]. Fish (*Kyphosus fuscus*). Sea chub. This fish, about a foot long, is of medium popularity.

Nishime. [Japanese]. A stew of vegetables with perhaps a little tofu or pork added.

Nori. [Japanese]. Blackish/purplish/greenish sheets of dried *Porphyra* seaweed (limu paheʻe in Hawaii, laver in English) used to wrap sushi or musubi, eaten cut into squares as a snack or appetizer, or crushed as a garnish for other Japanese dishes. It is available in cellophane packets or jars, packed with a dehydrating agent to keep it crisp. It should be toasted over a flame gently to bring out the flavor or bought pretoasted. Paste nori is the same kind of seaweed cooked to a paste and sold bottled.

ʻOama. [Hawaiian]. Fish. Young weke, slender silver white fish about 3–4 inches long, plentiful in late summer and early fall.

Ogo. [Japanese]. Sea vegetable. Also known as limu manauea. See the section on limu.

ʻŌhiʻa ʻai. Fruit. See mountain apple.

ʻŌhelo. [Hawaiian]. Fruit (*Vaccinium reticulatum*). One of Hawaii's two native fruits, this shrub related to cranberry grows in the mountains. It is occasionally available in markets.

ʻŌʻio. [Hawaiian]. Fish (*Albula vulpes*). Bonefish or ladyfish. A fish about 2 feet long that is a delicacy in Hawaii despite its many bones, which are sufficiently fine that if eaten raw they slip down the throat. The flesh is scraped away from the bones with a spoon to make fish paste.

Okara. [Japanese]. The residue left behind after tofu making; often added to dishes as tofu might be.

Okazuya. [Japanese]. Japanese plate lunch place.

Okinawan sweet potato. Vegetable *(Ipomoea batatas)*. Botanically this is simply sweet potato. A wide variety of sweet potatoes are grown in Okinawa, the oldest variety being a golden yellow. But in Hawaii, an Okinawan sweet potato means a sweet potato that has the usual rough tan skin outside but inside cooks to a gorgeous deep purple. See also sweet potato.

`Ōkolehao. [Hawaiian]. Liquor. Originally this was made from ti root. Since the Depression, the term has been used for all kinds of liquor, especially illicit liquor.

Okra. Vegetable *(Hibiscus esculentus)*. Grown by Filipino truck farmers for the Open Markets.

`Ōmilu. [Hawaiian]. Fish. Blue crevally. See ulua, of which it is a close relative.

Onaga. [Japanese]. Fish *(Etelis coruscans)*. Ruby red snapper, most common in midwinter. A popular fish, especially at New Year when its red color, which signifies good luck, is much appreciated.

Ong choy. [Chinese]. Vegetable *(Ipomoea aquatica)*. Swamp cabbage. A deservedly popular vegetable in Hawaii especially among Chinese and Filipinos, somewhat like a cross between spinach and watercress.

`Ono. [Hawaiian/Local]. A term meaning "delicious," sometimes used to create the neologism "onolicious."

Ono. [Hawaiian]. Fish *(Acanthocybium solandri)*. Wahoo or king mackerel. Long (5 to 6 feet), skinny fish with pink-tan flesh that turns white when grilled or sauteed.

`O`opu. [Hawaiian]. Fish. Formerly abundant in Hawaii's streams, this was a popular eating fish.

`Ōpae. [Hawaiian]. Shrimp. Ebi [Japanese].

Opah. Fish *(Lampris regius)*. Moonfish. A beautiful silvery fish with a round body and red fins that grows to a hundred pounds or more. Pinkish red flesh turns white when grilled or sauteed to provide tender, sweet meat.

**`Ōpakapaka.** [Hawaiian]. Fish *(Pristipomoides filamentosus and other species)*. Pink snapper, most common in midwinter. Like the other snappers, `ōpakapaka is particularly popular at Christmas and New Year because its red color signifies good luck.

`Ōpelu. [Hawaiian]. Fish *(Decapterus sanctae-helenae)*. Saba [Japanese]. A small jack or mackerel about 1 foot long, with a moist, oily flesh that makes excellent eating.

`Opihi. [Hawaiian]. A Hawaiian limpet that lives in the surf zone; so popular eaten raw that one or two people get killed every year gathering it.

Otaheite apple. See wi.

Ozoni. [Japanese]. First meal of the New Year, consisting of a broth containing mochi and vegetables, usually mizoni greens.

Pako. [Filipino]. Vegetable *(Athyrium esculentum)*. Warabi [Japanese]. Fern shoots. Popular with Filipinos, Japanese, and Hawaiians.

Palani. [Hawaiian]. Fish *(Acanthurus dussumieri)*. Surgeonfish. A small reef fish with strong odor said to be reminiscent of perspiration; if the odor can be eliminated, it apparently makes good eating.

Paltat. [Filipino]. Catfish. Usually imported from the Philippines for the Filipino community.

Pan. [Japanese]. Bread, the term presumably derived from various European cognates.

Pan de sal. [Filipino]. Soft bread rolls often served for breakfast.

Pão doce. [Portuguese]. Hawaiian sweet bread. Slightly sweet Portuguese festival bread.

Papa`i. [Hawaiian]. Crab. Kani [Japanese].

Papaya. Fruit *(Carica papaya)*. A commercially grown fruit; the small Solo variety specially developed for Hawaii is widely used for breakfast with a squeeze of lime juice. Also used green as a vegetable by Filipinos and Southeast Asians.

Pāpio. [Hawaiian]. Fish. Pompano. See ulua.

Paria. [Filipino]. Vegetable. See bitter melon.

Passion fruit. Fruit. See lilikoi.

Patis. [Filipino]. Clear fish sauce extensively used for seasoning Filipino dishes. Thai fish sauce can be substituted or, in a pinch, a little Worcestershire sauce, though this is not recommended.

Pia. [Hawaiian]. Starch *(Tacca leontopetaloides)*. Polynesian arrowroot, botanically distinct from but with similar culinary properties to West Indian arrowroot. Now no longer available. Cornstarch is usually substituted for dishes such as haupia that were originally thickened by pia.

Pias. [Filipino]. Fruit. See kamias.

Pidgin. Local name for the creole that many Locals speak as their first language.

Pilot crackers. Also known as saloon pilots.

Pineapple. Fruit *(Ananas comusus).* A major plantation crop through most of the twentieth century, and the fruit most widely associated with Hawaii because of the advertising skills of James Dole.

Pipi. [Pidgin]. Hawaiian form of the word "beef"—pipi stew, for example.

Pipi. [Hawaiian]. Hawaiian pearl oyster, popular eaten raw, particularly by Hawaiians.

Pipikaula. [Hawaiian/Local]. Beef jerky made Hawaiian-style.

Plate lunch. Standard Island lunch of some kind of meat plus two scoop [sic] sticky rice and some potato or macaroni salad.

Pohā. [Hawaiian]. Fruit *(Physalis peruviana).* Cape gooseberry, an imported fruit. Popular in ice cream.

Poi taro and luau leaf

Poi. [Hawaiian]. The traditional Hawaiian staple of taro root steamed or boiled and then pounded to a paste. It is often allowed to ferment slightly to a sour taste.

Poke. [Hawaiian]. To cut in blocks or slice crosswise. Now used to refer to fresh raw fish usually seasoned with

soy sauce, salt, inamona, sesame seed paste, chili peppers, or seaweed.

Pokpoklo. [Filipino]. Sea vegetable. Also known as limu wāwae'iole. See section on limu.

Portuguese sausage. A spicy pork sausage introduced, as the name suggests, by the Portuguese. Eaten with rice, this is one of the most popular Island breakfasts. Also known as linguica.

Pot stickers. Chinese dumplings, steamed and fried.

Pumpkin flower. Vegetable. Also known as kalabasa [Filipino].

Pūpū. [Hawaiian/Local]. Hawaiian word used to refer to cocktail snacks or hors d'oeuvres. Heavy pupus constitute a meal.

Rafute. [Okinawan]. Pork cooked with sugar and liquor to preserve it.

Rat's-foot limu. Sea vegetable, also known as limu wāwae'iole and miru [Japanese]. See section on limu.

Saimin. [Local]. Noodles in a Japanese dashi or chicken broth with a variety of toppings such as green onions, strips of omelette, char siu, fishcake, or SPAM. Bamboo skewers of barbecued chicken or pork are often served on the side.

Salmon, salt. Very popular with Hawaiians since it was first imported from the Northwest in the nineteenth century, particularly kneaded between the fingers (lomied).

Sashimi. [Japanese]. Raw saltwater fish, most often one of the tunas, thinly sliced, always popular but essential at New Year.

Sayote. [Filipino]. Vegetable *(Sechium edule).* Also known as chayote, choko, or mirliton. In the Tropics it grows

easily and produces fruit that can be as embarrassingly plentiful as zucchini in the mainland United States. A pleasant but scarcely spectacular squashlike fruit. The seed is the best part.

Senbei. [Japanese]. Thin rice crackers. The sweetened variety are similar to the familiar American Chinese fortune cookie.

Shave ice/ice shave. [Local]. Ice thinly shaved off a large block, mounded into a paper cone, and doused in sweet fruit-flavored syrup; sometimes it tops bean paste or ice cream. Of Japanese origin, this is now enjoyed by all ethnic groups.

Shiso. [Japanese]. Herb *(Perilla frutescens).* A plant with handsome, purple-green, heart-shaped leaves used by Japanese and Chinese.

Shoyu. [Japanese/Local]. Seasoning. Better known elsewhere as soy sauce.

Shrimp flakes. [Japanese]. Dried shavings of shrimp, often colored red or green, used to decorate sushi, and other foods.

Shutome. [Japanese]. Fish. See au.

Sinigang. [Filipino]. Sour fish soup.

Soba. [Japanese]. Buckwheat noodles, often eaten cold in the summer. In some parts of Japan where rice was difficult to grow, soba was the staple.

Somen. [Japanese]. Fine wheat noodles.

Soursop. (Genus *Annona*). There are many different species in the custard-apple family, the two most common in Hawaii being the soursop proper with its prickly spines and the now commercially produced cherimoya. Both have a creamy interior that lends itself to frozen soufflés and sherbets.

Spearfish. Also known as hebi.

Star apple. Fruit *(Chrysophyllum cainito)*. About the size of an apple with a smooth, inedible green skin, the ripe star apple unexpectedly feels like a plastic bag filled with water when you pick it up. Inside is a delicately flavored, white slippery pulp with a star-shaped arrangement of edible black seeds in the center. Good eaten out of the skin. A few drops of lime juice bring out the flavor. Can be found in Chinatown in spring.

Star fruit. Fruit *(Averrhoa carambola)*. Carambola. A handsome fruit, star-shaped in cross section, with an acid flavor. A native of Malaysia that can be used like so many tropical fruits either ripe for eating out of hand and in desserts or unripe for tanginess.

Sudare. [Japanese]. Split bamboo mat used for rolling certain kinds of sushi.

Sugarcane. *(Saccharum officinarum)*. Kō [Hawaiian]. Sugar, "King cane" until recently in Hawaii. Where older recipes specify mill sugar, a brown sugar such as the raw sugar now marketed commercially in Hawaii or demerara can be used.

Sushi. [Japanese]. Rice flavored with a sweet vinegar sauce and dressed in a variety of ways.

Sweet potato. Vegetable *(Ipomoea batatas)*. Kamote or camote [Filipino]. 'Uala [Hawaiian]. Okinawan sweet potato. Familiar to Americans from Thanksgiving dinner, sweet potatoes were first brought to the Islands by the Hawaiians (an unsolved culinary mystery as to how they could get here before Columbus discovered the Americas) and now have a prominent place in the diet of many of the ethnic groups. Filipinos also eat the leaves.

Taape. A recently introduced snapper, less popular than the other species.

Taegu. [Korean]. Seasoned dried cuttlefish or codfish; sometimes also used for raw seafood dishes.

Tako. [Japanese]. He'e (Hawaiian). Octopus.

Takuwan. [Japanese]. Pickled daikon (Asian radish or turnip), often colored bright yellow.

Tamarind. Fruit *(Tamarindus indica)*. This tree, introduced in the late eighteenth century, is common in Hawaii. It produces a brittle, brown pod about 5 inches long. Inside is an acid pulp surrounding the seeds. The pulp is chewed by children and used to sour foods, to make an acid drink, and as a substitute for crack seed.

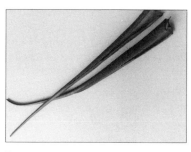

Taro stems

Taro. [Tahitian]. Vegetable *(Colocasia esculenta var. antiquorum)*. Kalo [Hawaiian]. Tuber with heart-shaped leaves rising from underground corms. Widely used in Southeast Asia and the South Pacific. Chinese (bun long) and Japanese (araimo or dasheen) taros are also available in Hawaii.

Tempura. [Japanese]. A fritter, believed to have been introduced to Japan by the Portuguese. Very popular in Hawaii.

Teri. [Japanese]. See teriyaki.

Teriyaki. [Japanese]. Sweetened soy sauce with a little ginger. Widely used in the Islands for grilling beef, pork, chicken, hamburgers, and fish. Often shortened to teri.

Ti. [Hawaiian]. Leaves for wrapping. *(Cordyline terminalis)*. Ti plants were planted close to Hawaiian underground ovens (imus). They have a thin stem topped by a tuft of green or reddish leaves. The smooth, spear-shaped leaves are used to wrap food and add a fine flavor. Every garden in Hawaii has a few ti plants, straggly stems about 5 feet tall, topped with the smooth blade-shaped leaves. It is strange that the leaves are not sold in grocery stores in Hawaii. The easiest way to get them—on the mainland too—is to buy them at a florist.

Tinola. [Filipino]. Vegetable *(Coccinia grandis)*.

Tofu. [Japanese]. Bean curd widely used by Chinese and Japanese. The Chinese variety is firmer than the Japanese.

Tombo. [Japanese]. Fish *(Thunnus alalunga)*. Albacore tuna.

Tongan. [Japanese]. See winter melon.

Tonkatsu. [Japanese]. Breaded pork cutlet. See katsu.

Tremoco. [Portuguese]. Dried lupine (fava) beans, soaked and salted and eaten as a snack. Not available commercially.

Tsubushi an. [Japanese]. A variety of an (sweetened red azuki bean paste). See an.

Udon. [Japanese]. Thick wheat noodles.

Uhu. [Hawaiian]. Fish *(Scarus species)*. Parrotfish. An iridescent reef fish with jaws adapted to chew on corals. It is a very popular eating fish, particularly with Hawaiians.

Uku. [Hawaiian]. Fish *(Aprion virescens)*. Gray snapper or jobfish. Tasty deep-water fish, ideal for grilling.

Ula. [Hawaiian]. Spiny lobster.

'Ulu. [Hawaiian]. Vegetable. See breadfruit.

Ulua. [Hawaiian]. Fish (species of Carangidae). Papio. Jack crevally. A prized gamefish that grows to over 5 feet and 100 pounds with dense, meaty, white flesh. Good dried and smoked.

Ume. [Japanese]. Pickled fruits of *Prunus mume*, often called a plum tree, the same "plums" that are used for crack seed. The Japanese often eat an ume for breakfast (much as others might take a glass of juice), and they are commonly placed in the middle of musubi.

Vinha d'alhos. [Portuguese]. Pork or fish marinated in vinegar, garlic, and chili pepper before being simmered until dry.

Wana. [Hawaiian]. Sea urchin. The roe is especially popular with Hawaiians and Japanese.

Warabi. [Japanese]. Vegetable. See pako.

Wasabi. [Japanese]. Hot green paste used to accompany sashimi or to form a base for the topping of sushi. It can be bought ready-mixed in a tube or as a powder in a small can to be mixed with water.

Water chestnut. Vegetable *(Eleocharis dulcis)*. Widely used in Chinese dishes, fresh water chestnuts can be found in Chinatown. Wash off the muddy exterior, peel, and eat raw or in stir-fries.

Weke. [Hawaiian]. Fish (species of Mullidae). Goatfish. About 8 inches long; a popular fish.

Wī. [Hawaiian]. Fruit *(Spondias dulcis)*. Also called Otaheite apple in Hawaii. A lemon-shaped, smooth-skinned fruit that grows on a tree in the same family as the mango. It is pleasantly sour when green, crisp and almost applelike when yellow. In January and February, it can sometimes be found in Open Markets and Chinatown.

Winter melon. Vegetable *(Benincasa hispida)*. Dun-kwa [Chinese]. Tongan [Japanese]. Large, handsome squash, much used for soup.

HAWAII'S COOKBOOKS: A SELECT BIBLIOGRAPHY

This bibliography concentrates on books written for an audience in the Islands rather than those written to introduce a version of Hawaii's food (usually "luau" food) to the wider world.

Alexander, Agnes B. *How to Use Hawaiian Fruit.* (Hilo, Hawaii: Petroglyph Press, 1974).

A fine book. The first edition (in 1910), by Jessie C. Turner and Agnes B. Alexander, was published by the Honolulu Gazette Company.

Alexander, Helen. *The Helen Alexander Hawaiian Cook Book.* (Honolulu: Advertiser Publishing Co., 1938).

Kamaaina food with brief sections on Oriental and Hawaiian recipes.

Bazore, Katherine. *Hawaiian and Pacific Foods: A Cook Book of Culinary Customs and Recipes Adapted for the American Hostess.* (New York: Barrows, 1940, reprint 1960).

A pioneering account of Hawaii's ethnic foods by a home economist at the University of Hawaii. Some adjustments to mainland tastes, but overall an invaluable resource for the foods of Hawaii in the 1940s.

Caple, Polly Lou, Mindy Lou Stephens, Dolly Loo, and Gilbert Loo. *Pidgin Pie and Poi (a Cook Book): A Small Taste of Contemporary Hawaii by the Lou-Loos.* (Kapaau, Hawaii: Kohala Krafts, 1978).

A pamphlet interesting chiefly for its pidgin introductions to Hawaiian, Samoan, Chinese, Japanese, Filipino, Portuguese, Puerto Rican, and haole recipes.

Centennial Celebration Cook Book Committee of Immaculate Conception Church. *A Book of Favorite Recipes.* (Shawnee Mission, Kansas: Circulation Service, 1984).

A high proportion of ethnic recipes in this collection from Lihue, Kauai, with Portuguese, Filipino, and Puerto Rican cuisines well represented.

Central Union Church, Honolulu, Woman's Society. *Hawaiian Cook Book.* (Honolulu: Hawaiian Gazette Co., 1909).

A collection from one of the kamaaina bastions of the Territory of Hawaii; originally published in 1882. Very popular; this is the fifth edition. Apart from a few recipes for taro, breadfruit, and luau, almost exclusively haole recipes, most of them deriving from New England.

Char, Alyce and Theodore. *The Gourmet's Encyclopedia of Chinese-Hawaiian Cooking.* (New York: Exposition, 1972).

A distinct Local flavor in this book by a couple active in business and philanthropy; many recipes show Hawaiian influence.

Choy, Sam. *Sam Choy's Cuisine Hawaii: Featuring the Premier Chefs of the Aloha State.* (Honolulu: Pleasant Hawaii, 1990).

Hawaii Regional Cuisine, enlivened with anecdotes by the Hawaiian-Chinese author, who grew up in Laie on the windward side of Oahu.

Cole, Dora Jane Isenberg, and Juliet Rice Wichman. *The Kauai Museum Presents Early Kauai Hospitality: A Family Cookbook of Receipts, 1820–1920.* (Lihue, Kauai: Kauai Museum Association, 1977).

Recipes, reminiscences, photographs, and letters from well-to-do Kauai kamaaina families.

Corum, Ann Kondo. *Ethnic Foods of Hawai'i.* (Honolulu: Bess Press, 1983).

A clear, practical guide to ethnic foods in Hawaii with details on food habits and festivals and a handy selection of recipes.

———. *Hawaii's SPAM® Cookbook.* (Honolulu: Bess Press, 1987).

Exhaustive.

Epicure in Hawaii, The. (San Francisco: Colt, 1938).

An elegant little book, with luau recipes, standard kamaaina food, and "tsukiyaki, sai men and Chinese fowl."

Filipino Women's League. *Hawaii Filipina's Favorite Recipes.* (Honolulu: self-published, 1975).

To my knowledge the only Filipino-Hawaiian cookbook, with lots of recipes and a glossary but little in the way of commentary.

FitzGerald, Don, ed. *The Pacifica House Hawaii Cook Book.* (Los Angeles: Pacifica House, 1965).

One of the many books primarily concerned to sell a mythologized luau food to the mainland.

Fortner, Heather. *The Limu Eater: A Cookbook of Hawaiian Seaweed.* (Honolulu: University of Hawaii Sea Grant College Program, 1978).

A fine introduction to limu, with historic photographs and recipes; one of the best seaweed recipe books in print.

Friends of Waipahu Cultural Garden Park. *Plantation Village Cookbook.* (Mililani, Hawaii: Wonder View Press, 1985).

The first of two particularly interesting community cookbooks with recipes arranged by ethnic group, historic photographs, and anecdotes about food on the plantations.

Friends of Waipahu Cultural Garden Center. *The Second Plantation Village Cookbook.* (Mililani, Hawaii: Wonder View Press, 1987).

Second in the series, this one includes notes by Margie Pang on the medicinal use of different plants.

Fumiko. *Sukiyaki: The Art of Japanese Cooking.* (Honolulu, n.d.).

Gray, Barbara, ed. *Oahu Market: Island Recipes and Shopper's Guide* (Honolulu: Oahu Market Associates, 1984).

A pleasant and informative little book produced in support of Oahu Market in Chinatown.

Harris, Marilyn Rittenhouse. *Tropical Fruit Cookbook.* (Honolulu: University of Hawai'i Press, 1993).

Recipes for Hawaii's fruit adapted to the tastes of the 1990s.

Hawaii Government Employees Association. *HGEA/AFSCME Cooks II.* (Honolulu: HGEA, 1991).

The government employees' branch of the AFL-CIO, founded in 1933 was part of the combined movement of unions and immigrant groups in the creation of modern Hawaii. This book includes photos of local celebrities and unknowns and a mix of Local recipes (oxtail soup and crispy roasted pig's head) with the new decreolized cuisine (U.S. House of Representatives member Patsy Mink on beef goulash, for example).

Hawaii State Society of Washington, D.C. *Hawaiian Cuisine.* (Rutland, Vermont: Charles E. Tuttle Co., 1963).

Recipes of different ethnic groups presented with the enthusiasm of early statehood.

HEI (Hawaiian Electric Industries) Family Favorites. (Honolulu, 1991).

The usual eclectic selection of recipes ranging from chicken divan to sesame taegu, but especially strong on Portuguese recipes.

Henderson, Janice Wald. *The New Cuisine of Hawaii: Recipes from the Twelve Celebrated Chefs of Hawaii Regional Cuisine.* (New York: Villard, 1994).

Introduces the Hawaii Regional Cuisine of the professional chefs, with biographies, recipes, and gorgeous color photos of carefully designed food.

Hilo Extension Homemaker's Council. *Favorite Recipes for Islanders.* (Hilo, 1953).

Hilo Woman's Club. *Hilo Woman's Club Cook Book.* (Hilo: Hilo Tribune Herald, 1937; revised, 1943, 1946, 1947, 1948, 1953, 1963, 1967, 1970, 1974).

Intelligently arranged by local ingredients, the changing recipes over the years track the history of kamaaina food in Hawaii and its gradual assimilation with the foods of other ethnic groups.

Honpa Hongwanji Hawaii Betsuin. *Favorite Island Cookery.* (Honolulu: Honpa Hongwanji Mission, 1973; subsequent cookbooks issued as follows: Book II, 1975; Book III, 1979; Book IV, 1985.

Interesting essays on Japanese food and customs and recipes with a Japanese slant.

Hui o Laulima. *Okinawan Cookery and Culture.* (Honolulu: Hui o Laulima, 1975).

Lots of good recipes, including their cultural background, which is fortunate because this is the only English-language Okinawan recipe book.

Japanese Cultural Center of Hawaii. *The Legacy of the Japanese in Hawaii: Cuisine.* (Honolulu, 1989).

Spiral-bound, but handsomely produced and edited by Muriel Miura-Kaminaka, who is a food professional. Interesting sidebars on the history of Japanese food and on its modifications in Hawaii.

Japanese Women's Society of Honolulu. *Hawaii's Aloha Recipes.* (Honolulu, 1982).

Broader than the title suggests, with American, Chinese, Filipino, Hawaiian, Japanese, and Korean recipes, each introduced with a photograph of that most Local of all phenomena, the ethnic beauty queen.

Josselin, Jean-Marie. *A Taste of Hawaii: New Cooking from the Crossroads of the Pacific.* (New York: Stewart, Tabori & Chang, 1992).

Hawaii Regional Cuisine, with elegant photographs.

Junior League of Hawaii. *A Taste of Aloha: A Collection from the Junior League of Hawaii.* (Honolulu: Junior League of Hawaii, 1983).

Almost exclusively haole recipes, with a very useful description of Island fish.

Kahikolu Congregational Church. *The Kahikolu Country Cookbook.* (Captain Cook, Hawaii: Kahikolu Congregational Church, 1982).

Put together for the restoration of one of Hawaii's oldest churches, this collection is particularly strong on Hawaiian recipes.

Koganji Temple. *Simply Delicious Recipes.* (Honolulu: Cookbook Committee of Koganji Temple, 1988).

The emphasis is on Japanese recipes, with a foreword on herbal remedies by the Abbess Jikyu Rose.

————. *Simply Delicious Recipes, Book II.* (Honolulu: Koganji Temple, 1991).

Kojima, Hari. *Hari Kojima's Favorite Seafood Recipes.* (Honolulu: Hari K., Inc., 1982).

Interesting recipes unpretentiously presented.

————. *Hari Kojima's Local-Style Favorites.* (Honolulu: Hari K., Inc., 1987).

Kona Outdoor Circle. *Kona Kitchens.* (Kailua-Kona, Hawaii: Kona Outdoor Circle, 1988).

Over 700 recipes, the more interesting because their contributors describe their background, occupation, and when they moved to the Kona Coast. A strong Hawaiian section, with an unusual recipe for a dish of raw squid and half-cooked lobster, for example.

Loo, Patti. *The Chinese Hawaiian Cookbook.* (Honolulu: W. W. Distributors, 1976).

Maui Home Demonstration Council. *Our Favorite Recipes.* (Wailuku, Hawaii: Maui Extension Homemakers Council, 1959).

The first in a series that set the standard for spiral-bound cookbooks in Hawaii.

————. *More of Our Favorite Recipes.* (Wailuku, Hawaii: Maui Extension Homemakers Council, 1964).

————. *Still More of Our Favorite Recipes.* (Wailuku, Hawaii: Maui Extension Homemakers Council, 1967).

————. *Still Many More of Our Favorite Recipes.* (Wailuku, Hawaii: Maui Extension Homemakers Council, 1972).

Miller, Carey Dunlap, Katherine Bazore, and Mary Bartow. *Fruits of Hawaii: Description, Nutritive Value, and Recipes.* (Honolulu: University Press of Hawai'i, 1936; 4th ed., 1965).

Reports on unsurpassed research on the nutritive value of tropical fruit, with photographs, and recipes typical of the 1940s.

Miura, Muriel Kamada. *Cook Japanese-Hawaiian Style.* (Honolulu: self-published, n.d.).

Japanese recipes by the University of Hawai'i and Columbia-trained home economist who became Home Economics Director of the Honolulu Gas Company.

————. *Hawaii's Favorite Maxi Meals For Mini Money.* (Honolulu: Associated Printers, 1975).

Simple versions of many Island favorites.

Molokai Lions Club Lionesses. *From the Hawaiian Kitchens of the Molokai Lions: A Book of Favorite Recipes Compiled by the Lionesses of the Molokai Lions Club.* (Shawnee Mission, Kansas: Circulation Service, 1968).

The only cookbook I know of from Molokai. Like many community cookbooks from the outer islands, this is less affected by mainland fashion than those from Oahu.

Pane'e, Tamar Luke. *E Ho'olako Mau: All Hawaiian Cook Book, Vol. 2.* (Honolulu: Pacific Printers, 1987).

Full of stories about growing up Hawaiian in Hawaii and about how food was gathered and prepared.

———. *E Ho'olako Mau: All Hawaiian Cook Book, Vol. 1.* (Honolulu: Pacific Printers, 1990).

Dedicated to what are now called luau foods, this is a mine of information on Hawaiian food.

Pereira, Anna Seabury. *Cooking With Taro and Poi.* (Honolulu: self-published, 1983).

Ways of incorporating taro and poi into (mainly) haole breads and desserts.

Peru, John. *Portuguese Cuisine Hawaii.* (Honolulu: self-published, n.d.).

Recipes by a Local Portuguese chef that appear to have been influenced by modern Portuguese cookbooks.

Portuguese Pioneer Civic Association. *Portuguese Cooking in Hawaii: 101 Recipes for 101 Years, 1878–1979.* (Honolulu: self-published, 1979).

The major cookbook to be produced by the Portuguese community in Hawaii.

———. *The Pleasures of Portuguese Cooking: 1937–1987.* (Honolulu: self-published, 1987).

Rizzuto, Shirley. *Fish Dishes of the Pacific.* (Honolulu: Hawaii Fishing News, 1986).

A wide variety of recipes, many of them Local, by the monthly food columnist for *Hawaii Fishing News.*

Sakamoto, Mike. *How to Hook and Cookbook.* (Honolulu: Bess Press, 1988).

Fishing stories, hints on how to fish, and recipes, many of them contributed by the author's friends.

Sakamoto, Nancy N., and Elaine Suzuki. *Hawaii Style Sushi and Other Local Favorites.* (Honolulu: self-published, 1986).

Designed to describe Hawaii-style sushi, "distinctly different from sushi served elsewhere." Includes a wide range of other Local recipes, especially Japanese.

Sananikone, Keo. *Keo's Thai Cuisine.* (Honolulu: self-published, 1985).

Thai recipes adapted to American taste by one of Hawaii's most successful restaurateurs.

Sasaki, Pat, Douglas Simonson, and Ken Sakata. *Pupus to da Max: The All-Purpose Illustrated Guide to the Food of Hawaii.* (Honolulu: Bess Press, 1986).

Invaluable and sometimes hilarious guide to Local food, even if the jokes are often in-jokes.

Seabury Hall Parents' Organization. *The Hele Mai, Ai (Come Eat) Cookbook; Flavors of Upcountry Maui, History and Hospitality.* (Makawao, Maui: Seabury Hall Parents' Organization, 1977).

Many local recipes, interesting essays, and drawings of historic spots; menus for hikers into Haleakala Crater.

Sia, Mary. *Chinese Cookbook.* (Honolulu: University of Hawai'i Press, 1956; reprinted 1984).

A book that has sold steadily for many years.

Steinberg, Rafael, and the Editors of Time-Life Books. *Pacific and Southeast Asian Cooking.* (New York: Time-Life, 1970).

This volume in a classic series includes a brief section on Hawaii, concentrating on luau food and tropical drinks.

Stone, Margaret Kapeka. *Best-Tested Recipes of Hawaii.* (Honolulu: Aloha Publishing, 1984).

A wry, intelligent book by a haole who married a Hawaiian-New Englander; good recipes and good photographs.

Tam, Rod, ed. *Ohana Recipe Book II.* (Honolulu: self-published, n.d.).

A campaign booklet by a state representative with some interesting Local recipes.

Tom, Clara. *Old Fashioned Method of Cantonese Chinese Cooking.* (Singapore: Hawaiian Service, 1965; 11th ed., 1993).

Cantonese recipes, with a distinct Local slant, from an experienced teacher of Chinese cooking, attested by her pupils' enthusiastic references bound at the back of the book.

Tong, June Kam. *Popo's Kitchen.* (Honolulu: self-published, 1988).

Designed to celebrate 200 years of the Chinese in Hawaii by preserving the homestyle recipes rarely seen in restaurants.

Toupin, Elizabeth Ahn. *Hawaii Cookbook and Backyard Luau.* (Norwalk, Connecticut: Silvermine, 1964; reprinted, 1967).

A knowledgeable account of Hawaii's food with a Korean emphasis.

Trader Vic's Pacific Island Cookbook. (New York: Doubleday, 1968).

An unexpectedly good section on Hawaii, by one of the popularizers of "luau food."

Tuell, Bonnie. *Island Cooking: Favorite Hawaiian Islands Recipes.* (Maui: Skipper Printing and Graphics, n.d.).

An invaluable guide to what to do with Local produce, including many unusual products, by the Maui Electric home economist.

Wadsworth, Frances. *Maui Cookery.* (Maui, Hawaii, 1953).

Wailua High and Intermediate School. *Proud Traditions: 50th Anniversary Cookbook.* (Mililani, Hawaii: Wonder View Press, 1986).

This school in a plantation town on the North Shore of Oahu includes reminiscences in this cookbook arranged by ethnic group.

Wailua Sugar Company. *What's Cooking at Wailua?* (Wailua, Hawaii: Wailua Sugar Co., 1973).

Put together to celebrate the 75th anniversary of the company, this slim volume includes many good recipes from management and workers alike.

Wright, Charlotte. *A Fish Feast.* (Seattle: Pacific Search Press, 1982).

Recipes by an accomplished cook who moved to Hawaii from the Northwest; it provides a useful introduction to Island fish, though the recipes owe more to mainland and international cooking than to Local ethnic traditions.

Yardley, Maili. *Hawaii Cooks.* (Rutland, Vermont: Charles E. Tuttle Co., 1970).

Recipes culled from the kamaaina kitchens of the author's friends. A period classic by a food columnist for a local newspaper.

———. *Hawaii Cooks: The Island Way.* (Honolulu: Topgallant, 1982).

Instructions for making salt duck eggs jostle against bovril butter, how to do a turkey imu against Hawaiian salt making.

———. *Hawaii Cooks Throughout the Year.* (Honolulu: Editions Limited, 1990).

Some seasonal recipes and evocative full-color paintings by the author's husband.

Young Women's Christian Association International Institute, Hui Manaloana. *Japanese Foods (Tested Recipes).* (Honolulu: self-published, 1951; reprinted, 1969).

Urged on by Catherine Cox, an education and volunteer advisor at the YWCA, this adult group put together "a compilation of written recipes to perpetuate the culinary art introduced by the first generation from their native country." The period advertisements from Local firms, many of them owned by Japanese, such as the Flamingo and Pagoda Restaurants, Honolulu Sake Brewery and Ice Co., and the Hawaiian Miso and Soy Co., add Local flavor.

OTHER REFERENCE WORKS

Abbott, Isabella Aiona. *La`au Hawai`i: Traditional Hawaiian Uses of Plants.* Honolulu: Bishop Museum Press, 1992).

Abbott, Isabella Aiona, and Eleanor Horswill Williamson. *Limu: An Ethnobotanical Study of Some Edible Hawaiian Seaweeds.* (Lawai, Hawaii: Pacific Tropical Botanical Garden, 1974).

Adler, Jacob. *Claus Spreckels: The Sugar King in Hawaii.* (Honolulu: Mutual, 1966).

Ahmed, H. F. "Irritable-Bowel Syndrome with Lactose Intolerance." *Lancet* 2:319–320 (1975).

Alegre, Edilberto, and Doreen Fernandez. *Kinilaw: A Philippine Cuisine of Freshness.* (Metro Manila: Bookmark, 1991).

Anderson, E. N. *The Food of China.* (New Haven, Connecticut: Yale University Press, 1988).

Anderson, Jean. *The Food of Portugal.* (New York: Morrow, 1986).

Andoh, Elizabeth. *An American Taste of Japan.* (New York: Morrow, 1985).

Apple, Russell A. *Ancient Hawaii Shore Zone Fishponds: An Evaluation of Survivors for Historic Preservation.* (Honolulu: National Park Service, 1975).

Asselin, E. Donald. *A Portuguese-American Cookbook.* (Rutland, Vermont: Charles E. Tuttle Co., 1966).

Associated Chinese University Women. *Traditions for Living: A Booklet of Chinese Customs and Folk Practices in Hawaii Volume 1.* (Honolulu: Associated Chinese University Women, 1979; 3rd edition 1989).

Associated Chinese University Women. *Traditions for Living: A Booklet of Chinese Customs and Folk Practices in Hawaii Volume 2.* (Honolulu: Associated Chinese University Women, 1989).

Beckwith, Martha. *Hawaiian Mythology.* (Honolulu: University of Hawai`i Press, 1942).

Beeton, Isabella. *The Book of Household Management.* (London: Ward, Lock & Co., 1861; reprinted, 1888).

Bird, Isabella. *Six Months in Hawaii.* (London: KPI, 1875; reprinted, 1986).

Brandon, Reiko Mochinaga, and Barbara Stephan. *Spirit and Symbol: The Japanese New Year.* (Honolulu: Honolulu Academy of Arts, 1994).

Brennan, Joseph. *The Parker Ranch of Hawaii: The Saga of a Ranch and a Dynasty.* (New York: Harper & Row, 1974).

Brissenden, Rosemary. *South East Asian Food.* (Harmondsworth, England: Penguin, 1969).

Burkill, I. H. *Dictionary of the Economic Products of the Malay Peninsula,* 2 vols. (Kuala Lumpur: Ministry of Agriculture and Cooperatives, 1935; reprinted, 1966).

Bushnell, Oswald A. *Molokai.* (Honolulu: University Press of Hawai'i, 1963).

Carlquist, Sherwin. *Hawaii: A Natural History: Geology, Climate, Native Flora and Fauna above the Shoreline,* 2nd ed. (Honolulu: Pacific Tropical Botanical Garden, 1980).

Carr, Elizabeth Ball. *Da Kine Talk: From Pidgin to Standard English in Hawaii.* (Honolulu: University of Hawai'i Press, 1972).

Castle and Cooke. *The Thatched Kitchen.* (Chicago: Tested Recipe Publishers, 1970).

Chang, K. C., ed. *Food in Chinese Culture: Anthropological and Historical Perspectives.* (New Haven, Connecticut: Yale University Press, 1977).

Ching, Beatrice Liu. "Ching Ming in Hawaii," in Associated Chinese Women of Hawaii, *Traditions for Living: A Booklet of Chinese Customs and Folk Practices in Hawaii,* vol. 1 (Honolulu: Associated Chinese Women of Hawaii, 1989), 96–99.

Cordero-Fernando, Gilda, ed. *The Culinary Culture of the Philippines.* (Manila: Bancom Audiovision Corp., 1976).

Cost, Bruce. *Ginger: East to West. A Cook's Tour with Recipes, Techniques and Lore.* (Berkeley, California: Aris, 1984).

———. *Bruce Cost's Asian Ingredients: Buying and Cooking the Staple Foods of China, Japan, and Southeast Asia.* (New York: Morrow, 1988).

Crawford, David Livingstone. *Hawaii's Crop Parade: A Review of Useful Products Derived from the Soil in the Hawaiian Islands, Past and Present.* (Honolulu: Advertiser Publishing Co., 1937).

Dana, Richard Henry. *Two Years before the Mast.* (Franklin Center, Pa.: Franklin Library, 1840; reissued, 1977).

Davidson, Alan. *Seafood: A Connoisseur's Guide and Cookbook.* Illustrated by Charlotte Knox. (London: Simon & Schuster, 1989).

———. *Fruit: A Connoisseur's Guide and Cookbook.* Illustrated by Charlotte Knox. (London: Simon & Schuster, 1991).

Daws, Gavan. *Shoal of Time: A History of the Hawaiian Islands.* (Honolulu: University of Hawai'i Press, 1976).

De Lima, Frank. *Frank De Lima's Joke Book.* (Honolulu: Bess Press, 1991).

Dole, Richard B., and Elizabeth Dole Porteus. *The Story of James Dole.* (Aiea, Hawaii: Island Heritage, 1990).

Egerton, March. *Adventures in Cheap Eating: Hawaii. The Comprehensive Guide to Righteous Deals and Authentic Meals on Oahu.* (Honolulu: Tsunami Press, 1993).

Edwards, Caroline W. *Guidebook for Homemaking in Hawaii.* (Honolulu: New Freedom Press, 1938).

———. "Community Feeding During an Emergency: A Manual for Volunteer Food Handlers." (Territory of Hawaii, Department of Public Instruction, Division of Vocational Education, 1942. Typescript).

Emerson, Nathaniel B. *Unwritten Literature of Hawaii: The Sacred Songs of the Hula.* (Rutland, Vermont: Charles E. Tuttle Co., 1965).

Facciola, Stephen. *Cornucopia: A Source Book of Edible Plants.* (Vista, California: Kampong, 1990).

Félix, Guy. *Genuine Cuisine of Mauritius.* (Mauritius: Editions de l'Océan Indien, 1988).

Felix, John Henry, comp. *The Portuguese Bicentennial Celebration in Hawaii.* (Honolulu, 1990).

Felix, John Henry, and Peter F. Senecal, eds. *The Portuguese in Hawaii.* (Honolulu: John Henry Felix, 1978).

Fernandes, Jennifer. *100 Easy-to-Make Goan Dishes.* (New Delhi: Vikas, 1977; reprinted, 1990).

Fernandez, Doreen, and Edilberto Alegre. *Sarap: Essays on Philippine Food.* (Manila: Mr. and Mrs., 1988).

Fernandez, Rafi. *Malaysian Cookery.* (Harmondsworth, England: Penguin, 1985).

Forbes, David. *Encounters with Paradise: Views of Hawaii and Its People, 1778–1941.* (Honolulu: Honolulu Academy of Arts, 1992).

Fuchs, Lawrence. *Hawaii Pono: A Social History.* (New York: Harcourt, Brace & World, 1961).

Gaches, Mrs. Samuel Francis. *Good Cooking and Health in the Tropics.* (Manila: Bureau of Printing, 1922).

Gast, Ross H., and Agnes C. Conrad. *Don Francisco de Paula Marin: A Biography,* by Ross H. Gast. *The Letters and Journal of Francisco de Paula Marin,* edited by Agnes C. Conrad. (Honolulu: University of Hawai'i Press for the Hawaiian Historical Society, 1973).

Girvin, James Walter. *The Master Planter, or, Life in the Cane Fields of Hawaii.* (Honolulu: Hawaiian Gazette Co., 1910).

Glick, Clarence. *Sojourners and Settlers: Chinese Migrants in Hawaii.* (Honolulu: University of Hawaiʻi Press, 1980).

Griffin, Stuart. *Japanese Food and Cooking.* (Rutland, Vermont: Charles E. Tuttle Co., 1956).

Grigson, Jane. *Jane Grigson's Vegetable Book.* (London: Penguin, 1978; paperback, 1980).

———. *Jane Grigson's Fruit Book.* (London: Penguin, 1982; paperback, 1983).

Grigson, Jane, and Charlotte Knox. *Exotic Fruits and Vegetables.* (New York: Holt, 1987).

Grimshaw, Patricia. *Paths of Duty: American Missionary Wives in Nineteenth-Century Hawaii.* (Honolulu: University of Hawaii Press, 1989).

Handy, E. S. Craighill, and Elizabeth Green Handy, with the collaboration of Mary Kawena Pukui. *Native Planters in Old Hawaii: Their Life, Lore, and Environment.* Bernice P. Bishop Museum Bulletin 233 (1972).

Haraguchi, Karol. *Rice in Hawaii: A Guide to Historical Resources.* Edited by Linda K. Menton. (Honolulu: Humanities Program of the State Foundation on Culture and the Arts in cooperation with the Hawaiian Historical Society, 1987).

Hawaiian Electric Company, Home Service Department. *Health for Victory Club: Meal-Planning Guide.* (Honolulu, 1944).

Hazama, Dorothy Ochiai, and Jane Okamoto Komeiji. *Okage Sama De: The Japanese in Hawaii 1885–1985.* (Honolulu: Bess Press, 1986).

Headrick, Daniel. *The Tentacles of Progress.* (New York: Oxford University Press, 1988).

Heckathorn, John. "Pidgin Cuisine." *Honolulu Magazine* (June 1994), 19–39.

Herklots, G. A. C. *Vegetables in Southeast Asia.* (London: George Allen & Unwin, 1972).

Homma, Gaku. *The Folk Art of Japanese Country Cooking: A Traditional Diet for Today's World.* (Berkeley, California: North Atlantic; Denver, Colorado: Domo, 1991).

Hong Kingston, Maxine. *China Men.* (New York: Ballantine, 1980).

Huang, Soo Youn. "Eating in Chinese." In Associated Chinese University Women, *Traditions for Living: A Booklet of Chinese Customs and Folk Practices in Hawaii,* vol. 1, 42–44 (Honolulu: Associated Chinese University Women, 1989).

Hui o Laulima. *Of Andagi and Sanshin: Okinawan Culture in Hawaiʻi.* (Honolulu: Hui o Laulima, 1988).

Hwan, Suh. *All Purpose Guide to Korean Food.* (Seoul, Korea: Seoul International Publishing House, 1987).

Jaffrey, Madhur. *World of the East: Vegetarian Cooking.* (New York: Knopf, 1981).

Kamakau, Samuel Manaiakalani. *The Works of the People of Old: Na Hana a ka Poʻe Kahiko.* Translated from the newspaper *Ke Au ʻOkoʻa* by Mary Kawena Pukui. Bernice P. Bishop Museum Special Publication 61 (1976).

Kawahara, Kimie, and Yuriko Hatanaka. "The Impact of War on an Immigrant Culture." In *Community Forces in Hawaii: Readings from Social Process in Hawaii,* edited by Bernhard L. Hormann, 190–198 (Honolulu: University of Hawaiʻi, 1956).

Kelly, James. "Loco Moco: A Folk Dish in the Making." *Social Process in Hawaii* 30:59–64 (1983).

Kirch, Patrick Vinton. *The Evolution of the Polynesian Chiefdoms.* (Cambridge: Cambridge University Press, 1984).

———. *Feathered Gods and Fishhooks: An Introduction to Hawaiian Archaeology and Prehistory.* (Honolulu: University of Hawaiʻi Press, 1985).

Kirch, Patrick Vinton, and Dana Lepofsky. "Polynesian Irrigation: Archaeological and Linguistic Evidence for Origins and Development." *Asian Perspectives* 32:183–204 (1993).

Kirkendall, Judith Midgely. "Hawaiian Ethnogastronomy: The Development of a Pidgin-Creole Cuisine." Ph.D. diss., University of Hawaiʻi, 1985.

Krauss, Beatrice H. *Ethnobotany of the Hawaiians.* (Honolulu: Harold L. Lyon Arboretum, University of Hawaiʻi, 1975).

———. *Plants in Hawaiian Culture.* (Honolulu: University of Hawaiʻi Press, 1993).

Krauss, Bob, with W. P. Alexander. *Grove Farm Plantation: The Biography of a Hawaiian Sugar Plantation.* (Palo Alto, California: Pacific Books, 1948; 1965).

Kuykendall, Ralph S. *The Hawaiian Kingdom, 1778–1854,* vol. 1 (Honolulu: University of Hawaiʻi Press, 1938).

Levenstein, Harvey. *Paradox of Plenty: A Social History of Eating in Modern America.* (Oxford: Oxford University Press, 1993).

Lin, Florence. *Florence Lin's Complete Book of Chinese Noodles, Dumplings and Breads.* (New York: Morrow, 1986).

Lin, Hsiang Ju and Tsuifeng. *Chinese Gastronomy.* (New York: Hastings, 1969).

Lind, Andrew. *Hawaii's People.* (Honolulu: University of Hawai'i Press, 1955).

Lo, Kenneth. *Chinese Regional Cooking.* (New York: Pantheon, 1979).

Lourdes Modesto, Maria de. *Traditional Portuguese Cooking.* (Lisbon: Verbo, 1990).

Lueras, Leonard, ed. *Kanyaku Imin: A Hundred Years of Japanese Life in Hawaii.* (Honolulu: International Savings and Loan Association, 1985).

Lum, Arlene, ed. *Sailing for the Sun: The Chinese in Hawaii.* (Honolulu: Three Heroes, 1988).

MacKellar, Jean Scott. *Hawaii Goes Fishing.* (Rutland, Vermont: Charles E. Tuttle Co., 1968).

Mackie, Cristine. *Life and Food in the Caribbean.* (London: Weidenfeld & Nicolson, 1991).

Madlener, Judith Cooper. *The Seavegetable Book.* (New York: Potter, 1977).

Marahimin, Hiang, and Roos Djalil. *Indonesian Dishes and Desserts.* Translated by Yanti Subiakto Spooner. (Jakarta: Gaya Favorit Press, 1988).

Masuoka, J. "Changing Food Habits of the Japanese in Hawaii." *American Sociological Review* 10: 759–65 (1945).

Maybury, John. "The Lunch Wagons." *Honolulu Magazine* (1980), 19–39.

McDermott, John F., Wen-Shing Tseng, and Thomas Maretzki. *Peoples and Cultures of Hawaii: A Psychocultural Profile.* (Honolulu: University of Hawai'i Press, 1980).

Menard, H. W. *Islands.* (New York: Freeman, 1986).

Miller, Carey Dunlap. *Food Values of Poi, Taro, and Limu.* Bernice P. Bishop Museum Bulletin 64 (1927).

———. *Japanese Foods Commonly Used in Hawaii.* (Hawaii Agricultural Experiment Station Bulletin 68 (1933).

———. "From Stage Coach to Satellite: The Life of Carey Dunlap Miller." In "Makers of Destiny—Hawaiian Style: The Stories of Pioneer Women Educators in Hawaii," edited by Mildred O. Gordon. (Honolulu, Hawaiian Collection, University of Hawai'i at Manoa Library, n.d.). Typescript.

Miller, Carey Dunlap, and B. Branthoover. *Nutritive Values of Some Hawaiian Foods in Household Units and Common Measures.* (Honolulu: Hawaii Agricultural Experiment Station, 1957).

Miller, Carey Dunlap, and Helen Yonge Lind. *Food for Health in Hawaii: Notes on Choosing Food and Planning Meals with Recipes and Menus.* Hawaii Agricultural Experiment Station Bulletin 88 (1942).

Miller, Carey Dunlap, B. Branthoover, N. Seguchi, H. Denning, and A. Bauer. *Vitamin Values of Foods Used in Hawaii.* (Honolulu: Hawaii Agricultural Experiment Station, 1956).

Millom, Mark and Kim. *Flavors of Korea.* (London: Deutsch, 1991).

Mintz, Sidney W. *Sweetness and Power: The Place of Sugar in Modern History.* (New York: Penguin, 1985; paperback, 1986).

Murai, Mary, Carey D. Miller, and F. Pen. *Some Tropical South Pacific Island Foods: Description, History, Use, Composition, and Nutritive Value.* (Honolulu: University of Hawai'i Press, 1958).

Murayama, Milton. *All I Asking For Is My Body.* San Francisco: Supa Press, 1959; Honolulu: University of Hawai'i Press, 1988).

Nagata, Kenneth. *The Story of Pineapple in Hawaii.* (Aiea, Hawaii: Island Heritage, 1990).

Neal, Marie C. *In Gardens of Hawaii,* rev. ed. (Honolulu: Bishop Museum Press, 1965).

Nelson, Victoria. *My Time in Hawaii.* (New York: St. Martin's, 1989).

Odo, Franklin. *A Pictorial History of the Japanese in Hawaii, 1885–1924.* (Honolulu: Bishop Museum, 1985).

Okahata, James H., ed. *A History of Japanese in Hawaii.* (Honolulu: United Japanese Society of Hawaii, 1971).

Olson, Storrs L., and Helen F. James. *Descriptions of Thirty-Two New Species of Birds from the Hawaiian Islands: Part I. Non-Passeriformes.* (Washington, D.C.: American Ornithologists' Union, 1991).

Owen, Sri. *Indonesian Food and Cookery,* 2nd ed. (London: Prospect Books, 1986).

———. *The Rice Book: The Definitive Book on the Magic of Rice, with Hundreds of Exotic Recipes from Around the World.* (New York: St. Martin's, 1994).

Pollock, Nancy. *These Roots Remain.* (Honolulu: University of Hawai'i Press, 1990).

Potgieter, Martha. "Taro (*Colocasia esculenta*) as a Food." *Journal of the American Dietetic Association* 16:536–540 (1940).

Pukui, Mary Kawena, and Samuel Elbert. *Hawaiian Dictionary.* (Honolulu: University of Hawai'i Press, 1986).

Punchbowl Holy Ghost. *Centennial Booklet*. (Honolulu, 1991).

Ramos, Teresita V., and Josie Clausen. *Filipino Word Book*. (Honolulu: Bess Press, 1993).

Reinecke, John E. *Language and Dialect in Hawaii: A Sociolinguistic History to 1935*. Edited by Stanley M. Tsuzuki. (Honolulu: Social Science Research Institute, University of Hawai'i and University of Hawai'i Press, 1969; paperback, 1988).

Rossiter, Margaret. *Women Scientists in America: Struggles and Strategies*. (Baltimore: Johns Hopkins University Press, 1982).

Sato, Charlene. "Linguistic Inequality in Hawaii: The Post-Creole Dilemma." In *Language of Inequality*, edited by N. Wolfson and J. Manes (Berlin: Mouton, 1985).

Schneider, Elizabeth. *Uncommon Fruits and Vegetables: A Commonsense Guide*. (New York: Harper & Row, 1986).

Schwabe, Calvin E. *Unmentionable Cuisine*. (Charlottesville, Virginia: University of Virginia Press, 1977).

Schwizer, Niklaus. *Hawai'i and the German Speaking Peoples*. (Honolulu: Topgallant, 1982).

Shintani, Terry. *The Waianae Book of Hawaiian Health*. (Honolulu: Self-published, 1991).

Simmonds, Peter. *A Dictionary of Trade Products*. (London: Harlan, 1858).

Simoons, Frederick J. *Food in China: A Cultural and Historical Inquiry*. (Boca Raton, Florida: CRC Press, 1991).

Singer, Charles, E. J. Holmyard, A. R. Hall, and Trevor I. Williams, eds. *A History of Technology: The Late Nineteenth Century*. (New York: Oxford University Press, 1958).

Skinner, Gwen. *The Cuisine of the South Pacific*. (Auckland: Hodder & Stoughton, 1983).

Sokolov, Raymond. *Why We Eat What We Eat: How the Encounter Between the New World and the Old Changed the Way Everyone on the Planet Eats*. (New York: Summit, 1991).

Stannard, David. *Before the Horror: The Population of Hawai'i on the Eve of Western Contact*. (Honolulu: Social Science Research Institute, University of Hawai'i, 1989).

Stern, Jane and Michael. *Real American Food: Jane and Michael Stern's Coast-to-Coast Cookbook: from Yankee Red Flannel Hash and the Ultimate Navajo Taco to Beautiful Swimmer Crab Cakes and General Store Fudge Pie*. (New York: Knopf, 1986).

Stewart, Gertrude. *Gertrude Stewart's Manila Cook Book*. (Manila: Evening News, 1958).

Swinburne, Layinka M. "Nothing But the Best: Arrowroot—Today and Yesterday." In *Here Today, Gone Tomorrow: Disappearing Foods*, edited by Harlan Walker. Oxford Food Symposium. (London: Prospect Books, 1994).

Takaki, Ronald. *Pau Hana: Plantation Life and Labor in Hawaii, 1835–1920*. (Honolulu: University of Hawai'i Press, 1983).

Taro Tattler: For Growers, Shippers, and Processors of Chinese, Poi, Dasheen and Pacific Islands Taros from Hawaii, vol. 6. Department of Agricultural and Resource Economics. University of Hawai'i (1993–1994).

Ternstrom, Stephan, ed. *Harvard Encyclopedia of American Ethnic Groups* (Cambridge, Massachusettes: Belknap Press/Harvard University Press, 1980).

Thirty-Five Years' Resident, A. *The Indian Cookery Book*. (Calcutta: Thacker, Spink & Co., [1869] reprinted 1901).

Thomas, Mifflin. *Schooner from Windward: Two Centuries of Hawaiian Interisland Shipping*. (Honolulu: University of Hawai'i Press, 1983).

Thrum, Thomas. 1923. "Hawaiian Salt Making." *Hawaiian Almanac and Annual for 1924*, 113–117, Honolulu.

Titcomb, Margaret, with the collaboration of Mary Kawena Pukui. *Native Use of Fish in Hawaii*. (Honolulu: University Press of Hawai'i, [1952] 1972).

———. *Dog and Man in the Ancient Pacific, with Special Attention to Hawaii*. Bishop Museum Special Publication 59 (1969).

Tom, Winifred. "The Impact of War on Chinese Culture." In *Community Forces in Hawaii: Readings from Social Process in Hawaii*, edited by Bernhard L. Hormann, 199–203 (Honolulu: University of Hawai'i, 1956).

Tsuji, Shizuo. *Japanese Cooking: A Simple Art*. (Tokyo: Kodansha International, 1980).

Twain, Mark [Samuel L. Clemens]. *Mark Twain's Letters from Hawaii*. Edited by A. Grove Day. (Honolulu: University Press of Hawai'i, 1975).

Uchinanchu: A Pictorial Tribute to Okinawans in Hawaii. (Honolulu: EastWest Magazine Co., 1990).

University of Hawai'i at Manoa, Ethnic Studies Program. Ethnic Studies Oral History Project. *Uchinanchu: A History of Okinawans in Hawaii*. (Honolulu: Ethnic Studies Program, University of Hawai'i at Manoa, 1981).

Vancouver, George. *Voyage of Discovery to the North Pacific Ocean and Round the World*, 3 vols. (New York: Da Capo. [1798] 1968).

Von Tempski, Armine. *Hula: A Romance of Hawaii*. (Woodbridge, Connecticut: Ox Bow Press, [1927] 1988).

Wester, Peter Johnson. *The Food Plants of the Philippines*, 3rd rev. ed. (Manila: Bureau of Printing, 1924).

Wilcox, Barbara Stevens. *The Kahuku Sugar Mill Story*. (Norfolk Island, Australia: Island Heritage, 1975).

Wyban, Carol Araki. *Tide and Current: Fishponds of Hawaii*. (Honolulu: University of Hawai'i Press, 1992).

Wyss, J. R. *The Swiss Family Robinson*. (London: Dent [1812–1813] 1949).

Yen, Douglas. *The Sweet Potato and Oceania*. (Honolulu: Bishop Museum Press, 1974).

Zwiep, Mary. *Pilgrim Path: The First Company of Women Missionaries to Hawaii*. (Madison, Wisconsin: University of Wisconsin Press, 1991).

RECIPE INDEX BY ETHNICITY

RECIPE INDEX BY CATEGORY

GENERAL INDEX

For recipes, please consult the recipe indexes.